BOTHAM'S CENTURY

BOTHAM'S
CENTURY

MY 100 GREAT CRICKETING CHARACTERS

IAN BOTHAM
with PETER HAYTER

CollinsWillow
An Imprint of HarperCollinsPublishers

Peter Hayter is the cricket correspondent of the *Mail on Sunday*, having also written for the *Observer* and the *Independent*. He is the author of a number of books on cricket, including a collaboration with Ian Botham on his bestselling autobiography, and the *Botham Report*. He lives with his wife and two children in Shropshire.

First published in hardback in 2001 by
CollinsWillow
an imprint of HarperCollins*Publishers*
London

First published in paperback in 2002

3 5 7 9 8 6 4 2

A CIP catalogue record for this book is
available from the British Library

ISBN 0 00 218958 5

Illustrations by Ken Taylor

Printed and bound in Great Britain
by Clays Ltd, St Ives plc

The HarperCollins website address is
www.fireandwater.com

Photographic acknowledgments
Allsport 1tl, 1b, 2tl, 2tr, 3t, 3bl, 4tl, 5t, 6tl, 8t, 9t, 9b, 10t, 10b,
11br, 13t, 14t, 14cr, 14cl, 15b, 16t, 16b;
Patrick Eagar 1tr, 2b, 3br, 4t, 4b, 5b, 6b, 12tl, 12tr, 12b, 13c, 13b;
Empics 6tr, 14b, 15t, 15c;
Graham Morris 7tl, 7tr, 7bl, 7br, 8b, 11t.

All statistics correct to 11/2/02

Contents

Acknowledgments

To Mary, Max and Sophie, thanks for sparing me.
To Linda Hurcombe, thanks for deciphering the often
indecipherable. Finally, thanks to John Etheridge,
David Norrie, Graham Otway and Mike Walters.

PETER HAYTER

Preface

Botham's Century is not a selection of my favourite hundred cricketers; nor are the players I have written about necessarily the best hundred I ever saw or played with or against. Indeed some of the characters in the book might only use a cricket bat for leaning on. In essence the book is a collection of my thoughts and impressions of one hundred people who have had an impact on my cricketing life, however tenuous. It has been my good fortune to know them all.

IAN BOTHAM

Curtly Ambrose

'Hey, Beefy, man.' The drawl could only have belonged to His Royal Highness King (later Sir) Vivian Richards.

'Yes, Smokes,' I replied.

'Beefy, you know Big Bird is retiring.'

The year was 1986 and I had indeed heard that Joel Garner, my buddy from Somerset and my enemy on the pitch in matches between the West Indies and England, had decided to call it a day, and it goes without saying I was gutted that I would never again have the pleasure of taking my life in my hands against him on a cricket field.

'Yes, Viv.' I said. 'Shame.'

'Well, Beef, don't fret. We got another. Only problem is he don't like cricket. Jeez, Beefy ... he wants to play baaasketbaall, man.'

If only. If only. All those hours of torment for England batsmen might never have happened. Then again, world cricket would have been immeasurably poorer for Curtly Ambrose's absence.

The good people of his tiny home village of Swetes in Antigua may have grown a mite tired of it, but the sight and sound of Curtly's mum ringing the bell outside her house every time the radio told her that her boy had struck again for the West Indies is one of the great romantic images of the modern game.

Over the years from his debut against Pakistan in 1987 to the moment at the end of the 2000 series against England at The Oval when he and his partner Courtney Walsh were afforded the rare honour of a standing ovation from opponents and spectators alike, the bell tolled for the best batsmen in world cricket, for some over and over again – in total more than 300 times – Curtly's partnership with the giant gentleman Jamaican, based as much on profound mutual respect as acute inter-island and personal rivalry, was one of the most penetrative of all time.

'Many bowlers have tried to put batsmen off their stroke by utilizing various forms of verbal and physical intimidation. Curtly intimidated you with hush.'

The abiding impression I had of Amby as a bowler and an opponent was that, for a cricketer who thrived on aggression and menace, he was one of the quietest I ever encountered. Sometimes, even in a moment of great triumph 'long bones' appeared the most reluctant and detached of heroes.

I can honestly say that in the Test arena I never saw him bowl badly. Of course, he was miserly accurate. Of course, he had the stamina of a horse. Of course, he never seemed to give you anything to hit, and of course, when the mood took him as it did when he obliterated Mike Atherton's England side for 46 at Port of Spain in 1994, he could be as unforgiving and as devastating as a hurricane. In certain conditions at his peak he was virtually unplayable. But maybe, of all these weapons, the most potent was his silence.

Curtly never said much on the field and off it, particularly to the press; practically nothing. The fact is that he never needed to. Many bowlers have tried to put batsmen off their stroke by utilizing various forms of verbal and physical intimidation. Curtly intimidated you with hush.

On the field, even the idea of sledging was just a waste of energy, time and breath to him. When a batsman played and missed, instead of blathering on about it as some did, the usual response was either a 'tut-tut', a flash of the widest, toothiest grin in the game, or a perplexed raise of the eyebrow as if to enquire: 'Can you really be as bad as you look?'

'The abiding impression I had of Amby as a bowler and an opponent was that, for a cricketer who thrived on aggression and menace, he was one of the quietest I ever encountered.'

As for King Curt's attitude to the media, and his mischievous sense of humour, it is best summed up for me by a story I heard concerning the attempts of one of Her Majesty's press to interview him during the West Indies' tour to England in 1991. The *News of the World* instructed their man David Norrie to find Amby and get him to bare his soul. Norrie, aware of the generally-held belief that it was almost impossible to persuade Curtly to open his mouth, let alone his heart, decided he had better try to enlist some help. Having had some dealings with Viv Richards over the years, the intrepid newshound approached the Masterblaster outside the dressing room in Swansea and asked if he would mind asking Curtly if he would spare him a few minutes of his valuable time for an interview. Viv said he would do his best and advised Norrie to wait. Soon afterwards, the huge figure of Curtly came to the dressing-room door and the reporter reached for his notebook, understandably elated that his ingenious approach had enabled him to crack the toughest nut in the game.

'You want to talk to me?' asked Curtly.

'Yes I do,' replied Norrie.

'OK. This is how it works. You want to talk to Viv, you ask Viv. You want to talk to Curtly, you ask Curtly.'

'Fine,' said Norrie, 'I follow you. Sorry about the misunderstanding. I thought it might be better if I went through Viv.'

'Fine,' said Curtly. 'No problem.'

'Fine,' said Norrie. 'So, can I talk to you?'

'No,' said Curtly, 'Curtly talks to no one.'

I can still hear the big man cackling now as he does every time he reminds me of the famous incident at the Oval in 1991, when Jonathan Agnew and Brian Johnston immortalized my failed attempt at getting my leg over the stumps against his bowling.

Interestingly, he saved some of his fiercest stuff for his fellow West Indians; either in Caribbean domestic cricket for the Leewards, or in the county championship for Northamptonshire, and I believe that was because, like Viv and Andy Roberts before him, he was immensely proud of being able to place the name of one of the smallest of those islands on the sporting map.

BEEFY ON AMBROSE

Born: 21 September 1963, Swetes Village, Antigua
Country: West Indies
Tests: 98
Wickets: 405
Average: 20.99
Beefy analysis: Devastating, often unplayable right-hand fast bowler with the toothiest grin in the game. 'Long Bones' didn't need to use verbal intimidation. Silence was enough.
Beefy moment: Failing to get my 'leg over' to King Curt's bowling, words immortalised by Brian Johnston.
Do mention: Port of Spain, 1994 (England all out for 46)
Don't mention: Media interviews.

John Arlott

Think of the sights and sounds of cricket in the twentieth century and the voice of John Arlott will come to you without prompting.

From the end of World War II to the time of his retirement in 1980, John's gravelly Hampshire burr and the thoughts and feelings it conveyed were more than just those of the professional commentator. For the millions in England and around the globe whose main, and sometimes only, contact with the game they loved was live reporting on BBC Radio, John represented the heart and soul of cricket.

In all that he did and all that he was, John was a gentleman and a gentle man. Imbued with a humility sadly too rare in those who make their living conveying their views on cricket through the broadcast media or in print, one of John's great qualities was that he never believed he knew it all.

In general, and for obvious reasons, professional cricketers have always enjoyed a healthy scepticism about the views of those who have not played the game to their standard. But John was the exception that proved the rule. He earned the respect of players because, while on occasion he could be highly critical when he felt the need, he never talked down to them. In discussion, however, up to the latter part of his life, by which time bad health and melancholy had taken their toll, his almost schoolboyish enthusiasm for the game and the way he felt it should be played left people in no doubt as to the depth of his passion. In that respect, a chat with John was invariably a tonic and always left you wanting more.

'In all that he did and all that he was, John was a gentleman and a gentle man. Imbued with a humility sadly too rare in those who make their living conveying their views on cricket through the broadcast media or in print, one of John's great qualities was that he never believed he knew it all.'

As for his broadcasting, his reputation as the master was well deserved. He knew the power of silence and had the priceless ability to say more worth listening to in a few words than most of his rivals could muster if they talked all day and all night.

My first recollection of listening to his commentary as a lad exemplified that skill. Charlie Griffith, the ferocious West Indies paceman who terrorized the best batsmen in the world in the late 1950s and through the 1960s, was past his best when he toured England in 1966. But he was still plenty quick enough. What is more, for years many had suspected, and others even gone on record to state that, from time to time, he chucked his bouncer. So, while John was on air, when Charlie unleashed one on tail-end batsman

Derek Underwood (breaking the unwritten rule of those pre-helmet days that bouncers were not bowled at guys down the order who were unable to defend themselves, let alone chucked at them) the sadness and anger in John's voice were impressively moving, even to the ears of an eleven-year-old.

'Oh, no, no, no, no, no, no, no,' John growled. Then he paused for what seemed an eternity, before adding: 'Griffith has thrown in his bouncer.'

'As for his broadcasting, his reputation as the master was well deserved. He knew the power of silence and had the priceless ability to say more worth listening to in a few words than most of his rivals could muster if they talked all day and all night.'

The double-meaning was quite deliberate and it left you in no doubt as to how far John believed Charlie had overstepped the line. Listening to him was almost scary. He sounded like a policeman issuing a final warning to an errant teenager in the days when that meant something. You could tell how good John must have been at his first job, a country copper on the beat.

My first encounter with John came when I was a sixteen-year-old on the Somerset groundstaff. I arrived at the county ground in Taunton one morning to perform the usual duties of looking after the first-team guys and fetching Brian Close his fags and a copy of *The Sporting Life*, when I was approached by the secretary, Jimmy James, who told me he had a job that needed doing.

I was to meet Mr Arlott of the BBC in the car park and help him take his equipment up the rickety stairs to the radio box. Until that moment I hadn't realized they made lip-mikes and earphones out of glass. Once there, John thanked me, sat himself down, opened up the basket, laid out his French bread, cheese and pâté, popped open one of the bottles of claret, offered me a glass and began the first of a thousand conversations we enjoyed over the next 20-odd years. I never forgot the gesture.

Like every other cricket-mad youngster I knew who John Arlott was, but he wouldn't have known this no-account young scruff from

Adam. Yet he took the time and the trouble for a convivial chat, and gave me the impression he was genuinely interested in what I had to say. The wine and cheese were delicious, too.

John was a man of strong opinions and he expressed them forcibly. If he felt someone deserved criticism he would not shirk from making it, as he proved when filling in the section entitled 'race' included in the immigration form for entry to South Africa just after the Second World War. 'Human,' he wrote. But his most enduring quality was a generosity of spirit that never ceased to amaze those who knew what sadness he'd had to endure in his personal life.

Until his dying day John wore a black tie in remembrance of the son who died in a car crash in the sports car John had given him for his 21st birthday. And towards the end of his life chronic emphysema meant that he needed constant medical care and the use of a nebulizer. For a man who was blessed with such wonderful powers of communication and conversation, the frustration of having to take minutes to say only a few words must have been unimaginable.

There is no doubt that by the time he decided to quit in 1980 he had fallen out of love with some aspects of the modern game. He never rammed the old days down your throat, but, although he understood the players' perspective over the Packer affair that split the game, he longed for gentler, less materialistic times. He loved the way I approached cricket, for instance, which was to try to win, while having fun as well, and he feared that as time progressed the fun simply would not survive.

He took his leave from his devoted listeners in typically undemonstrative fashion. Declining the offer from *Test Match Special* producer, Peter Baxter, to do the final stint of the Centenary Test between England and Australia at Lord's in 1980, he stuck to the rota he had adhered to for donkey's years and finished with: '...and after a few words from Trevor Bailey, it will be Christopher Martin-Jenkins.' And when the man on the public-address system announced to the crowd that John had made his final broadcast for *Test Match Special*, he missed the applause led by the players on the field because he was at the back of the commentary box being interviewed for the PM programme.

After I bought a place on his home Channel Island of Alderney, our chats were just as regular and, health permitting, sometimes just as animated.

'Come to the house, Ian,' he would telephone me, 'and bring your thirst with you.' We often disagreed violently on various issues – his politics were as far removed from mine as it is possible to be – but however harrowing the experience was of seeing him fighting to get his words out, they were always, always worth the wait.

It was during one of these conversations, many years later, that John told me the biggest regret of his career was that, by retiring when he did he missed the chance to describe the events of the 1981 Ashes series, Headingley and all. Come to think of it, that is probably one of the biggest regrets of my career too.

Robin Askwith

There is, of course, a perfectly innocent explanation for the moment I was stopped by police on Wimbledon Common with a six-foot blow-up doll of Mr Blobby and the star of soft-porn movie classic *Confessions of a Window Cleaner.*

I'd been invited by actor and bon viveur Robin Askwith to appear in pantomime with him during one of those winters when that other seasonal cabaret, the England cricket team, had set off on tour without me. 'Squiffy' – as he is known to his mates – has been a good friend for many years.

On the 1990–91 Ashes tour of Australia, when David Gower

and John Morris were fined by the England management for hiring a Tiger Moth and 'buzzing' the Carrara Oval, it was Squiffy who responded by chartering a plane that flew over the Adelaide Oval during the fourth Test a few days later, trailing a banner which read 'Gower and Morris are innocent.' Gower thought the stunt was hilarious; needless to say, tour manager Peter Lush was less amused.

'Actor and bon viveur, Robin Askwith – 'Squiffy' as he is known to his mates – has been a good friend for many years.'

Anyway, during this 10-week stint treading the boards at Wimbledon, I decided a life-size inflatable of Mr Blobby – a character enjoying popular appeal on a madcap Noel Edmonds TV show – would make a perfect Christmas present for my youngest daughter, Becky. After the performance one night, Squiffy and I took the short-cut back across Wimbledon Common as usual to our hotel at 1 am ... with this conspicuous, pink-and-yellow latex lunatic for company. Some of the looks we got from late-night revellers swaying home from the pub were priceless – and then came a flashing blue light.

I can't remember exactly how the conversation went, but once the police had established there was nothing sinister about our behaviour, they released all three of us – Squiffy, Botham and Blobby – without a caution and they accepted that the blow-up doll was all part of the pantomime buffoonery. Back at the hotel, Mr Blobby took up residence in the doorway between our adjoining rooms and he scared the life out of one night porter who brought us

'He's one of the funniest men I've ever met – a natural comedian. But he is also one of the vainest.'

sandwiches on room service, only to find this rubbery monster answering the door. Becky? She loved her Christmas present. She thought it was mind-blowing.

Panto with Squiffy was always a lark. He's one of the funniest men I've ever met – a natural comedian. But he is also one of the vainest. Every morning, from the room next door, I would hear him asking, 'Mirror, mirror, on the wall – who is the fairest of them all?' And after a couple of strokes of the comb, the same voice would reply, 'Why, Squiffy, of course!' He was also paranoid about catching colds or the 'flu, in case his speaking voice disintegrated into a croak, and he did more for the sales of Lemsip and Sudafed than anyone I've ever known. Just one sniffle, or one cough, and Robin was convinced he had contracted some weird, incurable disease.

For all the sachets in his medicine cabinet, however, Squiffy is a talented guy and great company, serious enough about his work to be a thorough professional, but also modest enough to laugh at himself. He is probably best-known for those *Confessions* films. One night, after appearing together in *Dick Whittington* at the Theatre Royal in Bath, we returned to our hotel, turned on the TV and there he was, helping a young lady out of her clothes in a re-run of *Confessions of a Window Cleaner.*

'For all the sachets in his medicine cabinet, however, Squiffy is a talented guy and great company, serious enough about his work to be a thorough professional, but also modest enough to laugh at himself.'

Keen student of the acting business that I am, I was only too glad to watch the master at work on the small screen – to see if I could pick up any tips for my own dramatic presence in pantomime, of course. But those films have aged so quickly, and the music sounds so tinny, that they just appear barmy now: within 10 minutes, Squiffy and I were laughing so much we could barely breathe.

Living these days on the tiny Mediterranean island of Gozo, next door to Malta, Squiffy has a private yacht which is his pride and joy. Whether I would set sail with him further than crossing the Serpentine in Hyde Park is another matter!

Mike Atherton

I've never met a man who cared less about his public image than Mike Atherton. Some cricketers can never get enough of being in the spotlight; whether it be in print, on radio or television, beaming out from advertising hoardings or at the front of the players' balcony whenever the champagne corks are popping. Others even love the glare of notoriety. Mike always gave the impression he would rather have his teeth pulled out with rusty pliers as his extraordinarily low-key farewell to English cricket at the end of the 2001 Ashes series underlined.

Athers made an art form of being his own man. From the moment he took over the captaincy of England from Graham

Gooch halfway through the 1993 Ashes series, to the emotional farewell to his defeated troops at the end of the 1997–98 series against West Indies in the dressing room at St John's in Antigua, the main feature of his leadership was that, in pursuit of his ambition to succeed, he didn't give a monkey's who he upset. When he gave the order that wives and girlfriends were not welcome on the England tour to Zimbabwe and New Zealand in 1996–97, his action proved conclusively that, if and when he felt it necessary, this approach even extended to his team-mates. I didn't agree with his decision to declare with Graeme Hick on 98 not out on the Ashes tour of 1994–95, but I admire his courage in making it.

'I've never met a man who cared less about his public image than Mike Atherton. Some cricketers can never get enough of being in the spotlight; Mike always gave the impression he would rather have his teeth pulled out with rusty pliers.'

As a senior player when Athers made his first steps in 1989, I couldn't help feeling that he didn't want us around much longer, and later, reading between the lines of his first utterances as skipper before he picked the squad for the following winter tour to West Indies, the message was clear: 'Bog off, you old gits.' I had retired by then, so that didn't matter to me personally. But I do remember thinking such an attitude was either extraordinarily brave or extraordinarily naïve.

Regarding that tour to the Caribbean, although Gooch had decided to make himself unavailable, at the time David Gower was still musing over the pros and cons of retirement. I'm sure a call to Gower to give the team the benefit of his class and experience out there might have persuaded the outstanding left-handed England batsman of his generation to delay his exit. And even when Athers was prevailed upon to recall Gooch, then later Mike Gatting, it was pretty clear it was against his better judgement.

I know Mike himself believes that had he been allowed to pursue a new-broom policy without interruption, England might have made more progress more quickly. Then again, he never counted on the dirt-in-the-pocket affair during the Lord's Test against South Africa in 1994 that effectively handed over the final say in selection to Raymond Illingworth, with whom he was subsequently to fight and lose too many battles over personnel.

I do think that one of the reasons the captaincy got to him in the end was that he didn't feel able to communicate with or confide in guys like myself from a slightly older generation who might have been able to offer advice in certain situations. But whether he was right or wrong, his attempt to put his own mark on things from the start, whatever the fall-out, offered an insight into the single-mindedness that is at the core of his character.

'Courage, stubbornness, obstinacy, bravery. They say that a cricketer's batting gives the clearest insight into his character; has there been a more transparent case of someone whose batting was so obviously what made them tick inside?'

In certain situations, of course, for single-mindedness read bull-headed obstinacy. First, consider events at Lord's in '94, when he was spotted on television seeming to apply dust to the ball in what could only be described as suspicious circumstances, then copped a fine after he admitted to not telling the match referee Peter Burge exactly what he was carrying in his pockets at the time. The cricketing public were split right down the middle over whether he should quit the job, and even some of his closest friends thought he would. It took a certain kind of dog-with-a-bone stubbornness to hold on to the captaincy and his sanity while the debate raged around him. In the end he felt that carrying on was the right thing to do for the good of the side. Understanding what kind of scrutiny he was bound to be under from then on, that was an extremely courageous call.

A little more than a year later, as we went head-to-head in the Cane rum & Coke challenge to celebrate his marathon 185 not out to save the Wanderers Test against South Africa, one of the things Athers revealed to me was how much he regretted bring economical with the truth when interviewed by Burge. He genuinely panicked, I believe, and no matter how hard he tried to rationalize his actions subsequently, I don't believe he will ever be able to rid himself of the feeling that he let himself down badly that day.

Courage, stubbornness, obstinacy, bravery. They say that a cricketer's batting gives the clearest insight into his character; has there been a more transparent case of someone whose batting was so obviously what made them tick? Athers loved a fight; the tougher the opponent, the more he relished the challenge and, no matter what personal differences might have arisen, the longer he carried on the more his players respected him for it.`

'He loved a fight; the tougher the opponent, the more he relished the challenge and, no matter what personal differences might have arisen, the longer he carried on the more his players respected him for it.'

Take a look through memories of some of his most defiant innings, such as the aforementioned epic at The Wanderers to snatch the most unlikely draw. And later, to his great delight, painstaking hundreds against West Indies at the Oval and Pakistan in Karachi in 2000 to secure historic wins for his side. The vision of the full face of the bat comes inexorably towards you time and again, only occasionally barged out of the way by a full-on glare at Allan Donald, Curtly Ambrose, Glenn McGrath or Wasim

BEEFY ON ATHERTON

Born: 23 March 1968, Failsworth, Lancs
Country: England
Tests: 115
Hundreds: 16
Average: 37.69
Beefy analysis: Courageous right-hand opening batsman, once a useful leggie, always the most prized wicket for the opposition.
Beefy moment: 'Bog off, you old gits' – Atherton's response to the old guard on his elevation to the England team.
Do mention: The Wanderers, Johannesburg, 1995 (his 185* against South Africa).
Don't mention: Illy, Dirt, Glenn McGrath.

Akram, or the exquisite execution of the off-side drives he unleashed with drop-dead timing when at the very top of his game.

As if the mere statistics of these and other achievements were not enough, remember this: for almost all of his career, Athers suffered from back pain that could only be kept at a tolerable level by a constant diet of painkillers which occasionally made him nauseous and cortisone injections that carried a significant health risk. He rarely mentioned his back, never made a fuss about it, and was rightly proud of the fact that he was fit enough to captain England in 52 successive Tests. A lesser character would never have come close.

Away from the fray, and for some reason I suspect we shall never fully understand, Athers put up barriers to people which he would only raise when he was absolutely sure he could trust someone. You could see why sometimes that would alienate, antagonize and offend people, and there is no doubt that at times he suffered because of it. I admit that at first I just didn't know how to take him. But, as I came to know him better later in his Test career, I realized that the stern-faced exterior that made many misread him as aloof was probably only the defence mechanism of a paralyzingly shy person.

What I do know is that, during the second half of the 1990s, no side in world cricket relied so much upon the efforts of one man as did England. The rule of thumb during that period was that once the captain got out it was 'man the lifeboats'. How richly deserved were the rewards that finally came the way of unquestionably the most complete England batsman of his generation.

Douglas Bader

O ne of the most enthralling evenings of my life was spent talking with, but mainly listening to, the amazing World War II fighter pilot, Douglas Bader.

Bader is remembered as the man who taught himself not just to walk again, but also to fly again during the Battle of Britain after losing both legs in a flying accident in 1931. His extraordinary courage and determination gained an international audience through Kenneth Moore's portrayal of him in the successful film, *Reach for the Sky*. What is not so well known is that Group Captain Sir Douglas Bader, CBE,

DSO, DFC – to give him his full title – was an outstanding sportsman. The accident – 'my own bloody stupid fault' – after attempting a low roll at 50ft in a British Bulldog biplane at the civilian airfield of Woodley, near Reading, came the week after he played fly-half for Harlequins against the Springboks, and just before his expected selection for the England debut against South Africa.

I was in my third summer as an England cricketer when Douglas Bader rang me out of the blue. I'd met him once before, very briefly. He'd been to the cricket, liked the way I played the game, heard that I was attempting to qualify for a pilot's licence, and wondered whether I'd like to pop round to his mews house in London for a drink. I was round like a shot. As when I met Nelson Mandela, I was immediately aware that I was in the presence of someone very special. I couldn't imagine what it must have been like to have lost both legs at the age of 20 with the sporting world his for the taking. He was a talented cricketer, and had captained the 1st XI at St Edward's School, Oxford as an attacking bat and fast-medium bowler. The summer before his accident, Douglas top-scored for the RAF with 65 against the Army, in what was then a first-class fixture. But there was no moaning about his bad luck, nor any hint of regret at what fate had dealt him, or any sense of his being 'disabled'.

'One of the most enthralling evenings of my life was spent talking with, but mainly listening to, the amazing World War II fighter pilot, Douglas Bader.'

The only problem was that he wanted to talk about sport – cricket, rugby and golf – while I wanted to know what it was like to fly a Spitfire and be in a dogfight. As ever, Douglas Bader's persistence won the day. I was astonished about his knowledge of sport, and fascinated at his fight to become a decent golfer after his accident. He was determined to compete at some sport, now that rugby and cricket was lost to him, and at first it was an unequal struggle. Every time he swung the club, he would end up in a heap. As with everything else he tried, his simple refusal to be beaten by his disability enabled him to succeed in the end. Indeed, when I told him of my own concern about missing out on a licence because of my colour-blindness, he let me in on a little secret. He also suffered.

Eventually, by way of discussing the film *Reach for the Sky*, I managed to coax some recollections of life in the air during World War II – being shot down, getting replacement legs flown out to the French Hospital where he was prisoner so he could attempt to escape, and his days in Colditz Castle. He felt that the movie had rather glamourized the Battle of Britain, suggesting there was not a lot of romance involved in the experience of fighting for your very existence. One of his abiding memories was just how tiring it all was. The RAF were running out of pilots and planes; every time the Germans attacked, the squadrons were 'scrambled' and up they went, again and again. The only respite came when the weather was bad, and the pilots would lie back on their beds, exhausted.

Douglas was much older than most of the pilots, who were in their teens or early twenties. His life in the services seemed to have ended in late 1931 with his accident, but after the outbreak of world war in 1939 a chronic shortage of experienced pilots, his desire to get back in the air and his persistence in trying to persuade the RAF that he could still do a job earned him another chance to fly. He told me to forget the war films in which the fighter pilots stayed in the air for hours with endless supplies of ammunition. The actual firing time available in the spitfire was about three and half seconds. If you weren't on the ball and your aim was off, you would run out of ammo before you had time to blink. The fuel gauges weren't always that accurate either, and pilots would end up having to bale out over the sea or find a field somewhere near home. It also surprised me when he told me he was not fighting an anonymous enemy; on many occasions he could almost see the eyes of German pilots that were trying to shoot him down.

Douglas Bader must have been an inspiration to the RAF Young Guns, as much as he was to the next generation in Britain when his story was told. Douglas was a guy who was determined to succeed in whatever he did. He was so enthusiastic and wholehearted and did not know any other way. But he also had a very practical view of life. That was evident even when he was awarded his knighthood. Buckingham Palace called to make sure that, with his tin legs, he would be able to kneel on the cushion when the Queen touched his shoulders with the sword. Douglas replied that he wasn't sure but would go away and have a go. 'No good,' he told the Palace, 'I've had two goes at it and fallen on my arse both times!'

I enjoyed my evening and it convinced me this was someone who would have been a lot of fun to be with, especially in his younger days. Those who think I'm not a fan of old ways and the older generation are way off the mark. It's the person who impresses or distresses me. Age has nothing to do with it.

I'm not sure today's youngsters appreciate the sacrifices made by Douglas' generation. I did, not only because of the films. My parents had been through the War. It's 60 years ago now and I suppose those days have passed from the memory into history. Not that Douglas was one for living in the past. I was rather saddened a few years ago when the television programme, *Secret Lives*, tried to slur his reputation. His widow Lady Joan Bader said at the time, 'People either say he was a super guy or an absolute bastard.' I'm firmly in the 'super guy' camp. I'm sure there was more of a touch of arrogance in his younger days, but so what? He lived life to the full. There are always people ready to try and bring down those who have made the most of their time and refuse to compromise or be beaten.

My evening with Douglas Bader was an experience I will always cherish.

Ken Barrington

Kenny Barrington and I shared a birthday, 24 November, and a whole lot more besides.

People often ask me who was my favourite cricketer when I was first getting interested in the game. Bearing in mind the way I played, most assumed that I took my lead from somebody like Sir Gary Sobers, the greatest all-rounder I ever saw, or a swashbuckling cavalier like Ted Dexter.

But when I told them Kenny Barrington was my favourite, almost all were nonplussed. Kenny could play. Make no mistake about that.

He scored 20 Test hundreds and nearly 7,000 runs in all, and if you look at the list of those batsmen with the highest Test averages of all time you'll find K. F. Barrington at number six, with an average of 58.67. To put that in its proper context, of the all-time greats he made his runs at an average higher than Wally Hammond, Sobers, Jack Hobbs, Len Hutton and Denis Compton, and of the modern giants, higher than Sachin Tendulkar, Steve Waugh, Brian Lara and Viv Richards. He could play all right.

The problem for those who assume that someone like me takes their lead from a similar player is the way Kenny generally batted. If you wanted to be kind, you'd call him obdurate. Others, less kind, said that on occasion, watching Kenny grind out the runs was like watching your fingernails grow.

But what I loved about The Colonel, as he was known and revered, was neither the number of runs he made nor the way he made them. It was simply the look of him. Had they made a film of his life, Jack Hawkins would have been perfect for the part. Kenny brushed his teeth like he was going to war. When he marched out to bat, he looked ready to take on an army single-handed. With his great, jutting jaw and hook nose almost touching in front of gritted teeth, the expression on his face said, 'You'll never take me alive,' and it made an impression on the young Botham that deepened as I grew to know him personally in his roles as England selector and later coach.

Before I met Kenny I was actually quite apprehensive about the kind of bloke he might turn out to be. Bearing in mind what he looked like in action, scary was the word that crossed my mind. But it didn't take me long to realize that although he was ice-cold on the outside, the guy had the warmest heart in cricket. What is more, he was held in exactly the same high regard wherever he went. There wasn't a dressing room in the world where Kenny wasn't welcome.

One of the reasons was the humour that went with him; some of it was even intentional. The rest, down to the fact that for years he waged a losing battle with a tongue that simply refused to say what he wanted. 'Carry on like that,' he told me once, 'and you'll be caught in two-man's land.' 'Bowl to him there,' he urged, 'and you'll have him between the devil and the deep blue, err ... sky.'

But he was far more than a figure of fun. In fact, I would go so far as to say that had untimely death not cut short his second career, I believe Kenny would have become a truly great coach. Confidant, technician, helper and motivator; these were his responsibilities as he saw them. And he was excellent at all of them.

'Before I met Kenny I was actually quite apprehensive about the kind of bloke he might turn out to be. Bearing in mind what he looked like in action, scary was the word that crossed my mind.'

The last thing a player wants to hear from a coach is the sentence that begins with the dreaded words: 'In my day.' I never once heard him utter them. He was happy enough to talk about the past and his career as a player – and I for one never tired of hearing him recount hitting the mighty Charlie Griffith back over his head for the six with which he reached a century against the West Indies in Trinidad on the 1967–68 tour, his last in Test cricket – but the crucial thing was that he only did so when asked.

The key to Kenny's success as a coach was that he never spoke down to his players. In later years it became the norm for the coach to adopt a much more authoritarian approach and believe they should 'run' the team. Kenny never told anyone to 'do this' or 'do that'; instead, he posed the question: 'What if you did this?' or 'How would you feel about doing that?', and we responded because we all felt our opinions were being considered.

As a technical coach he was brilliant at spotting little problems and addressing them before they took hold. On my second tour of Australia in 1979–80 he corrected something in my batting that altered the way I played for the rest of my career. I used to take guard on middle-and-leg stumps, then just before the bowler reached the moment of delivery I would move back and across to get right in line. Early in the tour I found I was getting out lbw on a regular basis and couldn't understand why. The incident that brought things to a head happened in Adelaide, when a South Australian quickie by the name of Wayne Prior won an lbw decision against me with a ball I was convinced was drifting down the leg side.

Kenny saw I was cross when I got back to the dressing room, but when I watched the replay on the television link-up I was amazed to see that I was in fact plumb. Kenny waited until I'd calmed down then quietly took me to one side and suggested we have ten minutes with the bowling machine in the nets. That was all it took. He spotted that I was moving too far across my stumps before the bowler let go, so that balls I thought were going to miss the leg stump were actually hitting about middle and leg.

'Try taking leg stump guard,' he said, and for the rest of my career, apart from when specific situations demanded otherwise, I did.

He became a massive influence on me personally. Which is why his sudden death during the Barbados Test on the 1980–81 tour of the West Indies hit so hard. When I took the phone call from A. C. Smith, our manager, I just didn't want to believe what he was telling me – that Kenny had suffered a heart attack in the night. My immediate reaction was that we shouldn't play the next day's cricket, but after a team meeting to discuss what we should do, it soon became clear that the only thing to do was to carry on, for Ken.

I have often wondered how my career and my life might have been different if Kenny had been around to guide me. Regrets, I've had a few, etc. But there were times, particularly

'The guy had the warmest heart in cricket. What is more, he was held in exactly the same high regard wherever he went. There wasn't a dressing room in the world where Kenny wasn't welcome.'

following the amazing triumphs of 1981, that I allowed success to go to my head and in what came to be known as the 'sex, drugs and rock'n'roll' days of the mid-80s. Would Kenny have been a sobering influence when I needed one? Many friends of mine believe Kenny was taken at the very time I needed someone like him to make me see sense. All I know is that I missed him terribly.

Bill Beaumont

I regard Bill Beaumont as the best ambassador for British sport there has ever been. After his distinguished rugby career as captain of England and the British Lions, Bill has continued to give of his time and considerable experience to rugby as it struggled with professionalism.

The name of Beaumont is linked with mine because we spent eight years in opposition as the team captains in *A Question of Sport* with David Coleman in the chair trying to keep order, but our first memorable evening was years earlier, on the night that Bill led England to their first Grand Slam for 23 years at Murrayfield.

I was in the company of my father-in-law, Gerry, a big rugby nut, and Tony Bond, the England centre who had broken his leg at the start of the Five Nations against Ireland. He was still on crutches. In the lobby of the team hotel, the North British, Bill saw us and invited us into the official reception for a drink. Standing around with some of the England players, chatting and enjoying a glass, we were pounced upon by some Scottish MacJobsworth and told that I had to leave. I explained I was not a gatecrasher; Bondie had been a member of the England squad until his injury, and we had been asked in by the victorious England captain and coach, Mike Davis, so I thought that would be the end of the matter. Not with this Rob Roy.

'We are paying for this function, and we'll decide who comes in. You are not wanted, out you go.'

'Well, if you paid for this gin and tonic, you'd better have it back,' I replied and I promptly tipped it over his head.

The trio of us were frog-marched out, closely followed by most of the England squad, who decided to join us. That's why the England captain spent most of the evening sitting on the stairs outside the Scottish Rugby Union reception. Every so often, one of the players would come out with a tray of drinks to keep us going. It was the start of a very memorable evening.

Bill was forced to retire from the game a couple of years later after being told that another kick on the head could have serious consequences. His England career finished at Murrayfield, but his last appearance at Twickenham saw that famous half-time streak from the well-endowed Erica Roe. Bill had his back to the action and couldn't understand why his emotional team-talk was not being received with the same intense concentration as usual, until his scrum-half, Steve Smith, explained: 'Sorry, Bill, but some bird has just run on wearing your bum on her chest!'

Bill and I enjoyed a tremendous rivalry during our time on *A Question of Sport*. Bill is as competitive as me, and his sporting knowledge is extensive. His three specialist subjects were cricket, rugby and motor racing – he loved showing up my weakness on the cricket questions. But on golf, or soccer, he didn't have a weakness. He was hard to beat. I'm glad that we both decided to call it a day together after eight years. I couldn't have imagined doing the show without him.

Despite his good nature, Bill was not beyond some skullduggery. I remember the night when Gazza (Paul Gascoigne) was on the show. He wasn't supposed to be drinking, but was getting fed up with the taste of bitter lemon and tonic water. As Gazza was going to be a member of Bill's team, when he asked if there was anything else non-alcoholic he could try, I suggested advocaat. I knew the taste would disguise the alcohol and its effects were slow-acting. Gazza promptly drank a bottle and half in about an hour and half before the show. Imagine my horror when I discovered that Bill had worked out what was going on and I found myself with Gazza on my team. We lost, and the show took twice as long as normal to record.

> 'I regard Bill Beaumont as the best ambassador for British sport there has ever been. After his distinguished rugby career as captain of England and the British Lions, Bill has continued to give of his time and considerable experience to rugby as it struggled professionalism.'

One of the funniest holidays Kath and I ever had was with Bill and his wife, Hilary, when we went to Courcheval in the Alps to learn to ski. Because of the insurance, I was never allowed to ski when I was playing. Can you imagine Beaumont and Botham on the nursery slopes? Even trying to get our skis on took half a morning and nearly caused an avalanche. We had these all-in-one ski suits and as we came down the nursery slopes rather sedately, all these little kids, some aged about three, were shooting past, weaving in and out, and cutting across us, regularly causing us to fall apex over tit. After a couple of days of this, Bill had had enough and was looking for an opportunity to spear someone with his ski stick. The trouble was that every time he made that sort of move, over he went. I've never spent so much time on my backside.

Lunch on the third day was the turning point. After a couple of bottles of Dutch courage, Bill and I decided to leave the nursery slopes and graduate to something a little more testing. We felt reasonably confident as we'd just about learnt to keep upright in a straight line. It hadn't occurred to us that stopping was another crucial skill that didn't come naturally. We both realized our predicament at about the same time ... I can tell you that Beaumont and Botham out of control on the pistes is not a pretty sight.

Franz Beckenbauer

Just one of the true giants of football to whom I was compared during my all-too-brief reign as the leading centre-half in the English game. Norman 'bites yer legs' Hunter, Ron 'Chopper' Harris, and Vlad 'on me 'ead son' the Impaler, were among the others. The debate rages on.

Actually, I might have been good enough to have made a professional career in soccer. When I was 15, Bert Head, the Crystal Palace manager and, clearly, one of the shrewdest judges around, thought enough of my potential to offer me a trial at Selhurst Park.

I'd been playing for Somerset Schools and training with Yeovil Town for a couple of years. At the time, the manager there was Ron Saunders, who went on to become one of the best in the league, and he recommended me to Bert.

In the end I chose cricket, and the decision to do so came about as a result of me listening to my father, Les, for once. He was a top all-round sportsman himself, who'd represented the navy at soccer – good enough for Bolton Wanderers to try and prise him away from a life on the ocean waves – and he was the one I turned to when the time came for me to pick which horse to ride.

'It comes down to this,' he said. 'You're a good footballer, but I think you're a much better cricketer.'

Although I never regretted the decision I made, because I had a marvellous life in cricket, met some wonderful people, enjoyed some amazing experiences, and am grateful for everything the game enabled me to do, the enormous difference in earning potential between the two sports these days means that if I had to make the same choice now my decision would be different.

When I put on my boots again ten years later I did so as an amateur with Scunthorpe United, and I enjoyed every kick. We were living about 15 miles from Scunthorpe at the time, in the village of Epworth; a mate of mine there called Steve Earle who was playing for the club invited me to do my off-season training with them, and within a year I'd progressed from the reserves to the first team. I very nearly had one of the greatest debuts in soccer history, by the way. Trailing 3–1 at Bournemouth when I came on as sub on 25 March 1980, we ended up drawing 3–3 with me having a shot blocked on the line in the dying seconds. If only. Sadly, I never got as close to the opposing goal again. We celebrated in an unusual fashion on the way home that evening, my great mate Joe Neenan and I sitting on the central reservation of the A1 scoffing daffodils for a bet. As you do.

My first manager, Ron Ashman, had a unique way of preparing us for big games. Once, the day before an FA Cup match, he called us into the directors' lounge. You never quite knew what Ron had up his sleeve, but this time we were expecting just the usual 'death-or-glory' speech. Ron had other ideas, though. He'd prepared a foul-smelling potion concocted from raw eggs and sherry, and encouraged us all to take a cup of it. Although you had to pinch your nose to avoid expelling the liquid as fast as you drank it, the stuff turned out to be quite palatable. What's more it had the kick of a mule. One or two of the lads enquired whether a second helping might be in order, Ron kept filling up the punch bowl, one thing led to another, and when the cleaners came in several hour later they walked into a scene of utter devastation. I believe we lost the match.

My greatest soccer memory – apart from Chelsea winning the FA Cup against Leeds in a replay at Old Trafford in 1970 – is of my penultimate match for the club, against deadly local rivals Hull City on Boxing Day 1983 in front of a capacity crowd of 17,500. My job for the day was simple – to make sure their centre-forward, Billy Whitehurst, didn't get a kick. I played out of my skin, even if I say so myself, and the mission was accomplished in my usual 'uncompromising' style. Some years later, and completely out of the blue, I read an article about Billy, who, for a brief period in the late 1980s was one of the top players in the old First Division. In the article he was asked who his toughest opponent had been. 'That bloody cricketer,' he said, 'The bugger kept coming back for more.'

My worst soccer memory involves the mad Neenan. A redhead, he was, as they say, 'fiery'. We were playing Altrincham in an FA Cup replay, with the knowledge that victory would give us a dream tie against Liverpool in the next round. Joe had been wound up and roughed up by their centre-forward in the first match, including a blind-side head-butt, and had vowed to gain revenge. Unfortunately, he chose about the worst possible moment to exact it. With time running out, another replay beckoning and the prospect of a trip to Anfield, their striker burst clear and found himself in a one-to-one with Joe. It wasn't even subtle. Joe ran out and booted him in the meat and two veg. Penalty. 1–0. Bye-bye Anfield. So long Wembley.

My brief but glorious career came to an end when the England management decided they did not want me risking my bones on the football field. It was fun while it lasted. Just call me 'Kaiser'.

Richie Benaud

Being in the same commentary box as Richie Benaud meant just as much to me as being on the same cricket field as Viv Richards. Richie is the doyen of cricket commentators, the television voice of cricket, just as John Arlott and Brian Johnston were the sound of leather on willow for radio listeners. This cultured Australian, of French extraction, has made an outstanding contribution to the game for most of his 70-plus years, as a leg-spinner, fielder, batsman, captain, thinker and innovator, as well as a writer and broadcaster.

The key to Richie's success and his charm is his skill as a communicator and competitor. I've not always found a great affinity with former players. The majority, and nearly all of those from Yorkshire (my mentor Brian Close being the notable exception), are frozen in time. When I hear those distinctive Yorkie vowels, I can't help but recall that famous Monty Python sketch with two old-timers trying to outdo each other with how hard their life had been, how they had to walk two miles to the outside toilet, survive on one slice of bread a month, and so on. We young whippersnappers don't know we're born.

Not Richie. He's not stuck in a time warp. He looks for positives, not negatives. There are no cheap shots at today's game or the youngsters. Richie hates sloppy and unthinking cricket, and is not afraid to say so. But most of his stinging criticism has been reserved for those who have the power to run the game, but don't – like the ICC and ECB. Very occasionally, they've sought his opinion. I remember a few years ago a conversation Richie had with Raman Subba Row, then chairman of the then TCCB. Subba Row was complaining about the increasing international schedule and asked Richie what was the solution to playing too many Test matches. 'Play fewer,' was the reply.

Richie's playing career was marked by the same down-to-earth common sense. Younger generations may admire him as the consummate performer behind the microphone, but he was a player of the highest quality and one of the finest cricket captains of all time. His record of four losses in 27 Tests and no losing series as Australian captain is impressive enough, but mere statistics do not do justice to his tenure. He communicated with his players, the media (Richie was the first to invite journalists into the dressing-room for a chat after a day's play) and, probably most importantly, cricket fans and general public. He and the West Indies captain Frank Worrell got together before the 1960–61 series in Australia and declared their intention to entertain. They kept their word, and the public responded. The first match ended with the run-out that ensured cricket's first tied Test –

more than 90,000 people, then a world record, were at the MCG for the second day of the fifth Test.

Richie was also an instinctive sports psychologist, although there were no such fancy titles in those days. One of my favourite stories concerned his handling of Ken 'Slasher' Mackay at Dacca in Pakistan. Richie's instructions were clear: on a unforgiving pitch, the ball must be bowled at the stumps, not outside them. After 40-odd overs in the oppressive heat, Mackay let one slip wide and it was thumped to the boundary. Richie walked over to the bowler. 'What's the matter. Getting tired?' he asked.

A couple of overs later Richie was back, congratulating Mackay for hitting the stumps: 'That's where I wanted it.'

Richie, as cricketer, captain and commentator, is the finished article – polished, poised and precise. But, as is the case with most people who make what they do seem easy, no cricketer worked harder at his craft. He spent more time in the nets than I spent out of them. Nor was he an overnight success. Eventually, his leg-spin brought him 248 test wickets, but his only highlight on his debut tour to England in 1953 came in the final match at Scarborough, when he hit a world-record 11 sixes.

'This cultured Australian, of French extraction, has made an outstanding contribution to the game for most of his 70-plus years, as a leg-spinner, fielder, batsman, captain, thinker and innovator, as well as a writer and broadcaster.'

His elevation to the captaincy in 1958 was a surprise. Ian Craig went down with hepatitis and everyone expected Neil Harvey to get the job. England had enjoyed three successive Ashes series before sailing for Australia in 1958–59 with one of the most talented teams including May, Graveney, Cowdrey, Laker, Lock, Statham, Evans, Bailey, Dexter and Trueman to leave these shores. Australia won 4–0.

His most famous Ashes moment as captain came at Old Trafford where, five years earlier, he had twice been one of Laker's 19 victims. England, having come from 1–0 down, seemed certain to go 2–1 up when going into the final Test at the Oval. England were well on their way at 150 for 1, chasing 256 in four hours, for victory. For most captains, instincts would have told them to slow down the action and waste time. Not Richie; if Australia were going down, they were going down fighting. He went on the attack. After removing Dexter for 76, he bowled May round his legs for a duck in a spell of 5 for 12 in 25

'The key to Richie's success and his charm is his skill as a communicator and competitor.'

deliveries. Australia won by 51 runs and regained the Ashes. For once, I'm forced to agree with Ray Illingworth. In his book, *Captaincy*, this was his verdict on Richie: 'The nearest thing we are ever going to get to a perfect cricket captain. He matches boyish enthusiasm with ceaseless concentration, calculated attack and non-stop encouragement.'

Richie lost credibility and friends in some circles with his involvement in Kerry Packer's World Series Cricket. But he deserves a pat on the back, as far as I'm concerned. Richie put his money were his mouth was; cricket must evolve and go forward. Without Packer and the support of influential cricket folk like Richie, I'm not sure we'd be enjoying the resurgence in Test cricket that we are today. Richie puts some of the credit down to Shane Warne and his impact on the game over the 1990s. Always generous, without handing out accolades lightly, Richie is happy to acknowledge Warnie as 'the greatest leg-spinner of all time'.

I'm rarely intimidated, but I must admit to feeling slightly daunted when I slipped into a commentary chair next to the great man for the first time. I needn't have worried. Richie has never felt threatened by young upstarts and is always willing to help. He's exactly the same on the golf course, where I've been able to gain first-hand experience of his competitive instincts. People forget that 'Botham's Ashes' summer of 1981 didn't start that well ... defeat at Trent Bridge, a pair at Lord's, followed by my resignation as captain. I could sense that there was general satisfaction that I was on that downslope at last. Not from Richie, who interviewed me several times that summer. He knew what I was going through and was very supportive. Always the innovator,

Richie also has an extremely dry, if not arid, sense of humour. During Mike Atherton's 1994–95 tour of Australia, I heard, 'Gatting at fine leg' – then a pause before Richie added, 'that's a contradiction in terms.' Typical Richie. Understated. He taught me that less is more and silence is golden when the viewer can see the action. When he speaks, Richie Benaud is always worth listening to, because he has something to say. That's why he has remained at the top of his game for almost half a century.

Dickie Bird

'Arrived from the planet Loony to become the best and fairest of all umpires. Great bloke, completely bonkers.'

I rarely have occasion to quote myself, but the words I penned about Dickie in my autobiography stand the test of time. Dickie's mannerisms, quirkiness and great good humour are no longer seen on the cricket field following his retirement in 1996, and world cricket is undoubtedly the poorer for that.

But if the ICC are serious about setting up a training scheme for the next generation of Test umpires, I wouldn't hesitate in getting the old nutcase out of mothballs.

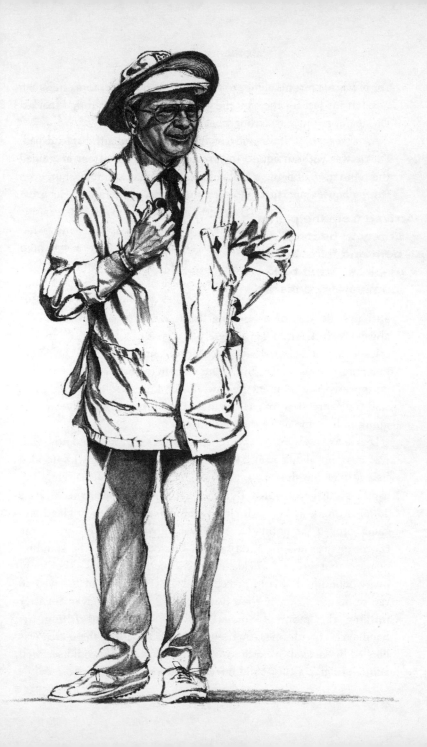

For it was not just his ability to get decisions right far more often than not, but his feel for the way the game should be played that marked Dickie out as the outstanding 'cheat' of my time.

As a reader of lbws and catches behind and off bat-and-pad, Dickie was without equal. Towards the end of his career he gained the reputation of being a 'not-outer', a batsman's umpire, but, even from a bowler's perspective, I felt that was a trifle unfair. His great

'Arrived from the planet Loony to become the best and fairest of all umpires. Great bloke, completely bonkers.'

strength as a decision-maker was his instinct for what was out and what wasn't. Dickie never left a batsman dangling. If the finger wasn't raised by the time you looked up to discover your fate, you knew you were safe. But although he was quick on the draw, his first sight was almost always correct. And I can honestly say that in all my years in Test cricket I never, ever got a bad decision from him. And if Dickie did get one wrong, any hurt the batsman may have suffered disappeared the moment he saw the look on Dickie's face. 'This,' said the expression just as the digit began its journey skyward, 'is going to hurt me more than it will you.'

Dickie had a way of behaving with players that let you know who was boss, but didn't ram it down your throat. Some critics derided him for being a showman, claiming that Dickie liked the television cameras a little too much. But his final, farewell appearance in June 1996, fittingly at Lord's for the second Test between England and India, proved the point that he never allowed the spotlight at the centre of the stage to blind him to the job in hand. The standing ovation that greeted Dickie on the first morning was not only overwhelming, it was unprecedented. Few players had received so rapturous a welcome in their final match; an umpire, never. Yet after milking the moment for all he was worth and filling his handkerchief with tears, by the time the fifth ball of the match was bowled by Javagal Srinath at Mike Atherton, Dickie could see well enough to give a rock-solid lbw decision in the bowler's favour.

Right from his first year as a Test umpire back in 1973, strange things happened whenever Dickie was around. In the second half of that summer, the West Indies played a three-Test series and in two of the matches Dickie was confronted by situations that no one could have forecast in their wildest dreams. First, in the second Test at Edgbaston, his partner Arthur Fagg went on strike in protest at the behaviour of the West Indies captain Rohan Kanhai. Fagg had given Boycott not out to a catch by wicket-keeper Deryck Murray off Keith Boyce, and Kanhai at first slip had spent the remaining two hours of the day moaning about it. The following morning Dickie arrived in the umpire's changing room at around 9 am to find Fagg packing his bag. Fagg had wanted an apology from Kanhai which was not forthcoming; he was at the end of his tether, and argued that the enjoyment had gone out of the game because the players did not respect the umpires' judgement any more, and there was too much at stake. He told a bemused Dickie: 'I'm going home. I'm taking no further part in this match.'

You can imagine how Dickie must have felt. Standing in only his second Test, he had to walk out to umpire at both ends, with substitute official Alan Oakman working from square leg. Fortunately, after deciding one over of protest was long enough to make his point, Arthur came back out to join his fellow umpire. Dickie told me later he had never felt so relieved in his life.

As if that wasn't enough controversy, in the very next Test at Lord's, for which he was a late replacement for an unwell Bert Rhodes, play was interrupted on the Saturday afternoon

'Of all the men in white coats I came across, Harold Dennis Bird was the maddest, by far.'

by a bomb scare. It was at the height of the IRA terror campaign in London, and Dickie suddenly found himself surrounded by 28,000 spectators who had decided the pitch was the safest place to be and wandered out to join him in the middle.

From then on, trouble and comedy followed him like a couple of mischievous minders. But, after that little lot, he was able to take the rest in his stride – overflowing drains, firecrackers as Bob Willis ran up to bowl, newspapers going up in flames while he was reading them, finding his car on four piles of bricks, and a rubber snake in his soup bowl courtesy of Dennis Lillee and Rod Marsh, or having to answer Allan Lamb's mobile phone while standing at square leg in the middle of a Test match. And some of the above I didn't even do.

Meeting royalty, however, was another matter entirely. On days when Her Majesty was due to make her traditional trip to meet the players during a Lord's Test and Dickie was on parade, his performance on the field would be extraordinary. Everything would be twitching and God help you if you got hit on the pad early on because he would be desperate to get one in the bag to relieve the tension. On the day he was due to receive his MBE in July 1986, he pitched up at Buckingham Palace all top-hatted and tailed, nice and early. How early? At 7.30 am for 12 noon, to be precise.

Dickie once told me 'cricket is my wife' and predicted that without it he would be dead in six months. Thank goodness that turned out to be one of his few lousy calls. But the game was, and remains, everything to Dickie, and the players loved him for that enthusiasm. Of all the men in white coats I came across, Harold Dennis Bird was the maddest, by far. But as the world game struggles to deal with increasing pressure on umpires from players and technology, cricket would be madder still not to take full advantage of his wealth of knowledge and experience.

Allan Border

You can trace Australia's rise to the summit of world cricket from the moment Allan Border decided enough was enough.

There are those who identify that moment as the time we secured the retention of the Ashes in 1986–87 under Mike Gatting. Others will tell you that Border hit the wall when contemplating our 3–1 victory in England in 1985, a result that crowned a glorious golden summer for us but represented a severe shoeing for the Aussies.

True, Border was on the end of heaps from the Aussie press after that series, chiefly because they felt he spent more time in our dressing room than in theirs, and it was as much his demeanour on and off the field with the old enemy, and the friendships that he so obviously maintained with guys like me, David Gower and Allan Lamb that antagonized the folks back home as the extent of their defeat. They could handle being beaten by a better side – just. What did not tickle their funny bone at all was seeing the Australian captain seemingly enjoying the company of the Poms who were beating them.

But while the flak he took in '85 undoubtedly fuelled his desire for revenge – 'I had enough of being a nice guy who came last', he told me – I believe the mood was born even earlier. Four years earlier, to be precise.

Talking to Allan over the years, I grew to learn that the one stone he simply could not remove from his shoe was our Ashes victory in 1981. All Englishmen, especially myself and the other players involved in that amazing series, were justifiably proud and elated at what we had achieved that summer. Don't waste too many tears, here. But just try to imagine what it must have been like to be on the receiving end. There they were, one Test up and seemingly cruising to victory in the third of six at Headingley, when Graham Dilley and I embarked on one of the great alehouse slogs in history, setting in motion a chain of events there, at Old Trafford and at Edgbaston that resulted in the reduction of the previously cocksure Australians to psychological basket-cases.

'You can trace Australia's rise to the summit of world cricket from the moment Allan Border decided enough was enough.'

Try to imagine how Allan must have felt to see his side appear to cave in tamely as soon as they were the ones on the wrong end of some real pressure. And try to imagine how he would have felt when after another hammering from the West Indies he later saw and heard the Australian captain Kim Hughes break down in tears when trying to explain away the capitulation of his players.

In drink in later years, and sometimes even sober, Allan would go over the events of that summer with me time and time again; it was as if he felt that by talking about them he would get them out of his system, and they might disappear forever, or, even better, turn out to be nothing more than a bad dream. I wouldn't say he was obsessive about it. He only brought the subject up three or four times an hour.

So when another bashing in '85 gave him and the Australian board the perfect opportunity to clear the decks and start again, the vigour with which he pursued his aims surprised only those who didn't know the man.

> 'Border's famed ruthlessness extended to his own players. They feared him, but because they knew he wouldn't demand of them any more than he would give himself, they not only grew to respect him, eventually they were prepared to run through minefields for him.'

There were setbacks. After losing to New Zealand in the winter of 1985–86 Border was so hacked off that he quit the captaincy, only to be talked out of it by the Australian Cricket Board. And while they were still there for the taking when we arrived a year later, the plan to identify a clutch of new players like Steve Waugh, David Boon, Merv Hughes and Ian Healy, and stick with them through thick and thin, finally brought the rewards Border and Australia craved.

Over the years, Border attracted strong criticism for the way he allowed his team to indulge in verbal assaults on opposing players. True, he was responsible for taking sledging to a new level; using it as a systematic intimidatory weapon with which to undermine an opponent's confidence. But his attitude was that mental toughness was as much a part of the modern game as the technical skills of batting, bowling and fielding. He reasoned that if a guy couldn't take it he shouldn't be out there, and he never moaned if an opponent gave some back to his players.

In 1989 his new approach shocked those players like David Gower and Allan Lamb, with whom he'd been friendly on previous tours, and when Robin Smith asked for a glass of water in mid-innings and received a mouthful of abuse instead, all Lambie's stories about what a great guy AB was sounded somewhat hollow.

On the 1993 trip, when England just laid down and died time after time, he claimed his fielders sometimes sledged because they were just so furious that our players were not putting up more of a fight. Do I believe that? On balance, I think I probably do. It was not for the purists and certainly not for those who liked their cricket nice and creamy, but it worked.

Border's famed ruthlessness extended to his own players. They feared him, but because they knew he wouldn't demand of them any more than he would give himself, they not only grew to respect him, eventually they were prepared to run through minefields for him.

Dean Jones, later my team-mate at Durham, once told me the full story of what took place between him and Border on the field during their partnership in the first Test at Madras on Australia's 1986–87 tour to India, in which Deano compiled the double-hundred that put him in hospital. Suffering from a combination of the heat, humidity

> ## BEEFY ON BORDER
>
> **Born:** 27 July 1955, Cremorne, Sydney
> **Country:** Australia
> **Tests:** 156
> **Hundreds:** 27
> **Average:** 50.56
> **Beefy analysis:** The one batsman you would take to the trenches with you. Ruthless, fearless and tough as old nails left-handed batsman.
> **Beefy moment:** 'Do that again, and you're on the next plane home, son' – Border's response to Craig McDermott's protests at being bowled from the wrong end in a tour game.
> **Do mention:** Sledging.
> **Don't mention:** Ashes 1981.

and the other debilitating ailment this part of the world is notorious for inflicting on foreigners, Dean first reached his maiden Test hundred, then, fighting through cramps, nausea and loss of bodily fluids from all imaginable areas, doubled that and finished with 210 from 330 balls during eight hours and 23 minutes at the crease.

To keep Deano going in the moments when he felt he just couldn't stand up, let alone carry on batting, Border used three tactics: he bullied him, he taunted him, and he scolded him.

Whenever Dean complained about the state he was in, Border would come back at him with: 'I never realized you were a quitter', or 'Okay, mate. You go off. I'll get someone out here who cares.'

The night after the innings was over Dean spent several hours on a saline drip. He cursed Border for the way he treated him, but later grew to understand that his captain was merely demonstrating that this was the level of commitment they all required if they wanted to be the best. Furthermore this was not simply 'do as I say'. Students of the '81 Ashes summer will recall that, amid all the excitement and carnage, Allan ended the series with a hundred at The Oval made with a fractured bone in his hand, which I subsequently hit twice more during the innings.

And players knew he wouldn't stand for any nonsense, as Craig McDermott, the quickie nicknamed 'Billy' as in 'Billy the Kid', found when he protested that the captain was using him at the wrong end in a county game against Somerset at Taunton on the '93 tour. 'Do that again and you're on the next plane home... What was that? You test me and you'll see.' Billy got the message.

Border's attitude was non-negotiable. But players knew that if they gave him and the 'baggy green' everything they had and were prepared to make the necessary sacrifices, the least they could expect in return was unshakeable loyalty. When the Australian Board decided to drop vice-captain Geoff Marsh for the final Test of the 1991–92 series against India, AB was so furious his right-hand man had been axed without his prior knowledge that only Marsh's intervention persuaded him from quitting the captaincy.

The bitter taste of defeat was what fuelled AB's desire to win. And when he retired he passed on the message to his other great mate David Boon. He told Boon, 'Now it's up to you to never ever let these younger blokes know what it's like to get their backsides kicked.'

Max Boyce

Max Boyce may be the royal rugby bard of Wales, but I will always regard him as one of my poorer subjects from my panto days as the King in *Jack and the Beanstalk*. Whether it's on the cricket field, golf course or on stage, Max has always made me laugh. He's also played a big part in my rugby education. Max came to national prominence during the glory days of Welsh rugby in the 1970s, appearing on the TV show *Poems and Pints* and gaining a string of gold records, starting with *Live at Treorchy*. His catchphrase was 'I was there.' Even the sad decline of Welsh rugby has not dampened Max's bubbling enthusiasm. When Wales kicked off the 1999 World Cup in the spanking new Millennium Stadium, Max was there belting out his beloved *Hymns and Arias*.

I first came across Max long before the panto days – in a benefit match for my Somerset colleague, Graham Burgess, at Monmouth School. Max was billed as the demon fast-bowler for the Welsh Invitation XI, and came in off an enormous run that even Michael Holding would have been proud of, something in the region of 80 yards. Unfortunately, by the time Max got to the wicket he was knackered! That experiment was abandoned after an over that took a quarter of an hour. Off a less strenuous run, Max did capture the wicket of I. V. A. Richards with a catch in the deep. Very deep indeed, because the fielder had been shrewdly placed in the field next to the ground. Max celebrated in style, then announced that as he'd done his bit by getting the best batsman in the world out, he was retiring from bowling. This common sense continued when it was his turn to bat and he saw the bowler he was about to face was Joel Garner. We were wondering where Max had got to when he suddenly appeared in a motorcycle crash helmet.

Max obviously had a sense of humour, so I suggested that we cement our friendship with a night out before the next Somerset game in Swansea. This we did in some style, although it can't have been that bad because I got a century before lunch the next day. I kept looking for Max in the St Helen's crowd because he'd assured me that he would be there for the first ball. Instead, when I answered a phone call at lunch-time this pathetic voice croaked: 'I'm still in bed and not very well!'

He got his own back when I turned up at Glynneath Rugby club, which backs onto Max's house, on the Friday night before the 1993 Wales vs England game in Cardiff. Will Carling's England had claimed back-to-back Grand Slams in 1991 and 1992, and were firm favourites to make it a unique hat-trick. Max's beloved Welsh team had not won anything for ages, and the Red Dragons were favourites for the wooden spoon. I made a presentation of a black beret, black scarf, black gloves and even a black leek to Max that night as I kept on about England's domination. So far, so good. During the game I was surrounded by Max and his Welsh mates. Unfortunately, we were sitting right in front of where Ieuan Evans caught Rory Underwood napping and kicked through for the stunning try that was to give Wales a 10–9 victory. The Welsh went mad, and at the final whistle I was presented with the whole lot of black gear back again in front of a packed National Stadium. Not a pleasant experience.

Max was the person responsible for my time as a stage performer – or guilty of causing it, depending on your perspective. I don't really know

'Max Boyce may be the royal rugby bard of Wales, but I will always regard him as one of my poorer subjects from my panto days as the King in *Jack and the Beanstalk*.'

why, but he asked me if I fancied doing panto. I was forever challenging Max to do things and calling him a wimp if he declined, so I had little option. He invented the role of the King for me in *Jack and the Beanstalk*. We opened in Bradford and I've still got my first notice from the local paper. I was so nervous. Max said, 'This can't be any worse than facing the likes of Michael Holding and Malcolm Marshall.' Don't you believe it. Without too much prompting, I somehow got my lines out and waited for a favourable review. After several paragraphs about Max's energetic performance, near the bottom of the article came my mention – 'The only thing more wooden than the Beanstalk was Botham.' Max consoled me by pointing out that things could only improve. 'Theoretically,' I said.

In fact, by the end of our three-season stint at Bradford, Bournemouth and Stockport, I felt reasonably comfortable and competent, and I later went into panto with Robin Askwith in *Dick Whittington* at the Wimbledon Theatre. After my wooden start, Max gave me a valuable prop. It was a toy dog with a weak bladder but an excellent aim, the perfect weapon to deal with hecklers. My favourite story from our days in panto together concerned the guy at the front end of 'Daisy' the cow. Early on in the run Max's funniest speech was interrupted by the sight and sound of the cow's head falling off, rolling down the stage and dropping into the front row of the audience. Having been upstaged during one of his big moments Max told the bloke in no uncertain terms to take the necessary steps to ensure that, from then on, the cow's head stayed attached to the rest of its body. The following night, however, at around the same moment in the performance, Max became aware that the audience's attention was drifting away from him to a point at the back of the stage. Daisy had wandered on, several minutes earlier than she was due, and to the obvious delight of the full house, was stumbling around as though she'd been at the merry milk. Then she ran sideways to the front of the stage and launched herself into Row C. Max was puzzled to say the least, and it wasn't until after the disobedient 'beast' had been helped back to the dressing-room that the cause of the problem became clear. Inadvertently, Daisy had been sniffing neat superglue, used to fix its head on, for the best part of half an hour.

> **'Whether it's on the cricket field, golf course or on stage, Max has always made me laugh. He's also played a big part in my rugby education.'**

Max also provided one of my most bizarre moments on a golf course in the inaugural Max Boyce Classic at the Royal Glynneath Golf Club. It absolutely hosed down and by the time we teed off, some of the greens were flooded. Max hinted we'd all be better off in the clubhouse, but I gave him the 'wimp' line once again. Local rules came into play for any ball landing on a flooded green – pick up the ball and put two putts on your scorecard. But my approach to the 17th green – which was completely under water – disappeared under the waves only about two foot from the hole. I wasn't accepting two putts from there, so I stripped down to my underpants, waded through the water and 'sank' the putt for my birdie. So the members of Royal Glynneath were treated to the sight of I. T. Botham striding down the 18th fairway in his smalls!

Max and I have had some great times, but you need to keep a close eye on him during rugby weekends because, I'm sorry to reveal he's a secret 'tipper'. Sometimes the drinking rate gets rather fierce. That's when he starts visiting the toilet with a full pint and returning with an almost empty glass. I followed him once and caught him pouring his beer away down the pan. Needless to say, severe punishment was exacted as he was made to down the next pint in one.

Despite that filthy habit of wasting perfectly good booze I'm always delighted to see Max, except after Wales have beaten England. Thankfully, that rarely happens these days.

Geoff Boycott

Boycs has never made any bones about it, so I won't. Just about the most self-absorbed cricketer I have ever met. First, the undeniably good things about Geoffrey. Self-motivated and hard-working, you have to respect and admire the man for what he did. He was not a natural cricketer, but he made himself into a very good one. As an opening batsman for England, his record speaks for itself. He was, as he would have said, a 'soooper' player and his cricketing brain was always switched on. The problem was that as colleagues we all felt there were times when he was far more concerned with the needs of the one than the needs of the many.

My first experience of playing alongside Boycs for England contained an incident that told me much of what I needed to know. It happened on my Test debut in the third match of the 1977 Ashes series at Trent Bridge, Nottingham, the home ground of local hero Derek Randall. According to *Wisden*: 'Randall began in great style but he was run out when Boycott went for an impossible single after stroking the ball down the pitch where Randall was backing up. In the end, Randall sacrificed his wicket to save Boycott.' Listeners to *Test Match Special* heard John Arlott comment: 'How tragic, how tragic, how tragic.' The words used in the dressing room were somewhat more pointed.

BEEFY ON BOYCOTT

Born: 21 October 1940, Fitzwilliam, Yorkshire
Country: England
Tests: 108
Hundreds: 22
Average: 47.72
Beefy analysis: Hard-working opening batsman who made himself into a very good cricketer.
Beefy moment: Running out Boycott, on the orders of his vice-captain, against New Zealand in Christchurch, 1978.
Do mention: Geoffrey Boycott, Yorkshire, records.
Don't mention: Anyone else.

To his credit, Boycs made a magnificent hundred and, fittingly, Randall made the winning runs. But the words 'run out' and 'Boycott' were destined to play a significant part in my future career. I didn't realize it at the time, but looking back on events in the second Test against New Zealand on the following winter tour, there is no doubt in my mind that carrying out the orders of vice-captain Bob Willis to run out skipper Boycott did more for my standing within the England camp than any runs or wickets I was in the process of compiling.

Boycs will tell you until you are tired of hearing that his attitude to batting was that it is a selfish business. He sincerely believed that he was the best batsman in the side and therefore, if anyone had to sacrifice their wicket in a run out, for the benefit of the side it should be the bloke at the other end. There is some logic in that, but not enough for me to ever be fully persuaded that when he stood his ground he was doing so for the good of the team.

The thing that really hardend my thoughts on Boycs took place years after we had both retired from the game, during the court case brought by myself and Allan Lamb against Imran Khan for libel over his accusations that our motive for alerting the world to ball-tampering by the Pakistan bowlers was racism.

'Self-motivated and hard-working, you have to respect and admire the man for what he did. He was not a natural cricketer, but he made himself into a very good one.'

Boycs was called to give evidence in what we considered to be a serious matter and he turned the proceedings into a Geoff Boycott Benefit event. He apologized to the court for the fact that he had not had time to change, and so arrived wearing a shirt sporting a logo for Wills, the tobacco company. I'm sure it was an accident, but some observers were convinced otherwise. They pointed out the case was attracting huge publicity in India and Pakistan where Wills have massive interests. Surely that couldn't have had anything to do with his choice of attire.

Then, in the eyes of some, he tried to railroad the case from the witness box by launching an attack on Brian Close, his former Yorkshire and England team-mate. True, Close had cast aspersions on Boycott's character the day before, but his testimony was hardly startling stuff and was probably very much in keeping with the views of the majority of those who had come across Boycs during his career. And anyway Boycott had been summoned to talk about the case at hand, not himself. On second thoughts, some chance. The judge was so incensed by Geoff's performance that he told him to belt up and was very close to charging him with contempt of court.

The way Boycs trampled all over the case made me distinctly queasy and I have to say our relationship suffered as a consequence. Indeed, until he has the guts to apologise to myself and my family, the most he will get from me is bare civility. Great player, strange bloke.

Mike Brearley

It never ceases to amaze me that English cricket failed to find a role for Mike Brearley after he retired from the first-class game. Brearley was without doubt the best captain I ever played under, a man with a billion-dollar cricketing brain. Bearing in mind the numbskulls we had to suffer running the team and the game itself after he packed up, his absence from the decision-making process must go down as the biggest waste of talent in England's recent cricketing history.

Brearley wasn't always right. My early progress in the team was hampered by the fact that he was convinced my team-

mate, the Yorkshire paceman Chris Old, was a far better all-round prospect than I was, once he told me that he felt sorry for Geoff Boycott and he was forever going on at me to retreat from my advanced position at second slip. But his intellectual power and how he applied it to Test cricket was awesome. He spent his entire captaincy two steps ahead of the game, picking the minds of opposing batsmen and bowlers like a master safe-cracker, and, after a while, his reputation for being able to out-think opponents became a weapon in itself.

Quite often, his minor field adjustments would be part of a cunning plan. Sometimes, on the other hand, he would stick someone in an unusual position not because he believed it would work, but because he thought the batsman might think it would. It was kidology, pure and simple, and Brears was brilliant at it.

My first experience of the phenomenon came during my debut Test series, the 1977 Ashes. The victim was Richie Robinson, the Australian wicket-keeper batsman. Brears was struggling to find a way to get inside Robinson's head, and just for something different, stuck a man in short on the offside. For some reason, that was like a red rag to a bull for Richie, who promptly tried to remove the fieldsman with a wild yahoo only to be caught in the slips. From then on, Brears employed a similar tactic whenever Robinson arrived at the crease, and with the same result.

My only real criticism of Brears was that, in terms of his ideas on selection, I felt he was biased towards his own Middlesex men, but I suppose you could hardly blame him for favouring players he knew inside out. That apart, for me he was the complete captain, more than worth a place in the side for that alone.

Naturally, the most often-quoted example of Brearley's abilities as a tactician, leader and motivator is the transformation in our fortunes during the 1981 Ashes series, when he replaced me as skipper. Brears recommended me for the job when he decided to quit at the beginning of the previous summer, and once the chairman of selectors Alec Bedser had put me in an impossible position by announcing I was to be judged on a match-by-match basis, I was only too happy to repay the compliment.

Would Headingley have happened had I still been in charge, or Old Trafford, or Edgbaston? How important was it that I was allowed to concentrate on expressing myself with bat and ball, and that the detail of captaincy was put in the hands of Brearley? Fortunately, and for the sake of cricketing folklore, not even Brears would be able to answer that one. All I do know is that Mike himself never claimed the credit for what took place. Indeed, it's interesting to me that the most famous visual image of Brearley during the Headingley mayhem has always been utterly misconstrued.

'It never ceases to amaze me that English cricket failed to find a role for Mike Brearley after he retired from the first-class game. Brearley was without doubt the best captain I ever played under, a man with a billion-dollar brain.'

At the moment I reached my hundred in the second innings, on the way to the 149 not out that would give us just enough runs to put crucial pressure on the Aussies, television pictures showed Brearley pointing vigorously and calling out to the middle. As the pictures did not show who he was pointing to or what message he was passing on, so various interpretations were put on the incident. Some observers will tell you with utter certainty that Brears was gesturing to me to stay out there and keep going. Others know for sure that he was telling my partner Chris Old to remind me to concentrate. What Brears was actually doing was trying to tell me to get into Chris's ear; to keep him focused on what we were doing. As far as I was concerned, he just wanted me to keep slogging!

But there was no ambiguity in the words with which he sent us out to attack the Aussies in their second innings. With the opposition still needing only 130 to win the match and probably the Ashes, Brears insisted, 'More aggression, more liveliness, and more encouragement for the bowlers. They are the ones who are nervous now.'

Some critics of Brears claim he was over-lenient with me, that too often he allowed me my head, whatever the consequences. He once admitted to me that on one occasion he had done exactly that, to the detriment of the team. In one of my early Tests, against Australia in Perth, I lost my rag when trying to prove that their batsman Peter Toohey could not hook. As I bowled faster and shorter, Toohey kept slapping me to the boundary and I finished the innings with match figures of 0 for 100. Brears' insistence that I should get the matter out of my system angered my team-mates, with Bob Willis particularly indignant that he had allowed me to carry on bowling.

But the key to the success of our relationship was that Mike reckoned more often than not that with me the gamble was worth taking. He never told me how to play, he just let me go. If I got out trying to smack someone out of the ground, or whatever, that was fine by him. And I responded. Yes, I was headstrong, and inevitably, from time to time, I would let my natural cricketing arrogance get the better of me. But he worked out that if he was going to get the best out of me he would have to take me warts and all. He showed that understanding in a crucial discussion we had prior to the Headingley Test of 1981.

'Are you all right, mentally?' he asked me. 'Are you sure you're okay to play?'

'I'm fine,' I told him.

'Good,' he replied, ' because I think you're going to score a hundred and take ten wickets.'

Brearley's success at beating Australia earned him huge respect here. But it turned him into a hate-figure Down Under. With the long beard he grew during the 1979–80 tour there and his occasionally less than helpful response to banal questions from reporters, he gained the nickname 'The Ayatollah'. That never bothered him in the slightest and he actually loved the fun and games with hostile Australian crowds. His favourite story of Aussie antagonism concerns the use of the skull cap he pioneered in advance of batting helmets. One day in Sydney he was struggling to keep the cap in place and a couple of times it actually fell off.

'Hey Brearley!' came a shout from the Hill. 'I've got just the f***in' thing for that f***in' helmet ... A six-inch f***in' nail!' The comedian almost certainly has no idea of this, but Brears kept himself amused recounting that story for the rest of the tour.

Brears never allowed himself a backward glance after he walked away from cricket, preferring instead to concentrate on putting his powers of analysis to use in the field of psychiatry. On occasion, his club, Middlesex, would ask for his help when players were experiencing problems in their private lives, and I know Phil Tufnell is grateful to him for the help he gave him when The Cat was in the pit. There are those who suggest I could have done with something similar when I was going through my mid-80s crisis, and they may have a point.

Finding a way he could contribute to English cricket would not have been easy. But for sure it would have been worth the effort.

Laurie Brown

Laurie Brown played as significant a role as anyone in England retaining the Ashes in Australia in 1986–87. His name may not be overly familiar to cricket buffs, but Laurie was the England physio at the time. We were the side that had only three things wrong with it: 'They can't bat, can't bowl and can't field.' Step forward, Martin Johnson, then on *The Independent* and now with *The Daily Telegraph*. I made sure his drinks bill got a hammering after we won the opening Test at the Gabba, especially as I managed to make what turned out to be my last century for England there. I was less happy following the second Test in Perth, after damaging an intercostal muscle. That's basically a rib injury, which affects most bowlers at some time in their career; it's one of the most frustrating because it takes its own time to heal and simply cannot be rushed.

I was very depressed because I knew this was a bad strain. Laurie confirmed that. 'You've done a good job there, Ian. This could take eight weeks to clear.' Waiting on the sidelines for the remainder of the tour was not in my game plan. I gave Laurie one of my special hugs and informed him gently that we could do better than that. Laurie realized this was not a time to argue, and just nodded. He was brilliant. I can't remember if we had any other injury problems at the time, but other patients hardly got a look in. We had up to half-a-dozen sessions a day, and I always had the last appointment. That's when a bottle of Scotch would appear out of a drawer or out of my cricket coffin. Laurie was a Scot. He played rugby on the wing for Musselburgh, and he certainly enjoyed a dram. Every night we went through the same ritual after three fingers of the liquid gold were poured out.

'Do you want any water with that?' I would ask.

'Water ... water. There's enough water in there already,' was the consistent answer.

Whatever the reasons, these intensive sessions worked. As well as all the ultra-sound treatment and various rubs, I would be in the swimming pool for a couple of hours a day. I only missed one Test, the third in Adelaide, and was declared fit to play after a month, just in time for the Boxing Day Test in Melbourne. England were still leading 1–0 in the Ashes series with two to play. 'Fit to play' was rather a loose term. I was about 75 per cent fit, but Laurie and I reckoned that was about as good as it was going to get in the time available. That was just as well, because my opening partner, Graham Dilley, dropped out on the morning of the MCG Test and was replaced by Gladstone Small. In the end, 'Stoney' and I took five wickets apiece, and the Ashes were retained by an innings inside three days. I would never have made it without Laurie's time and consideration.

All physios play the Father Confessor role to cricketers to some extent – there's a strong and strange bond because you rely on them so much – but Laurie held a special place among England players during my time. The physio hears all sorts of things from players lying on the treatment couch. It's not only physical grumbles that cricketers want reassurance about. The bottom line is trust. You have to trust that the physio's solution to an injury problem is the right one. The best physios are the ones who don't bullshit when out of their depth or dealing with a problem outside their area of expertise. Injuries and strains do seem to be more difficult to diagnose these days, even with all that sophisticated machinery. The good physios are the ones who refer you immediately to an expert consultant or clinic, and are not too proud to admit they don't know the answer. Laurie was one of the good ones.

'Laurie is a very special man. The Botham spirit was always willing, but, towards the end of my career, the body began to let me down. Laurie Brown, as much as anyone, made sure I got as much use out of it as I did.'

Finding a specialist abroad can be difficult and you are often taken to specialists on recommendation. Sometimes you strike lucky, as when Graham Gooch was suffering from a finger infection during the 1990–91 Ashes tour. Laurie soon realized the problem was too tricky for him to solve and within hours of sending him to see the surgeon, Randall Sach, Goochie was under the knife. This quick action probably saved him from losing his hand. On other occasions, cracks and fractures have not been picked up on X-rays. By the time of the 1992 World Cup, Laurie was as familiar with my creaking body as I was. Back, shoulders, knees and ankles had all been heavily strapped at various times. Laurie said that as soon as he bandaged me in one place, it would force the trouble to emerge somewhere else. He was convinced there was going to be a day of reckoning – when some part of me would just explode. Laurie's hope was that he wouldn't be around when it happened.

There was a price to pay for Laurie's friendship and assistance. That price concerns a football team from the Unibond Premier League called Stalybridge Celtic. Laurie lived next door to the ground and had a seemingly interminable supply of stories. If I were ever to go on *Mastermind* – stop chortling at the back there – that bloomin' club would be my specialist subject. For years and years, Laurie boasted proudly that Stalybridge were on their way up. I've waited and waited, but, astonishingly, as yet local rivals Manchester United haven't been threatened.

Laurie was the daddy to the team in my time. He was a generation older than most of the lads, and had been around a bit. When we sought advice, it was offered in that gentle Scottish accent and with that canny way of his. He was always available for a chat. Even I didn't want to go out every night, and Laurie never complained about me or anyone else invading his room for an evening of philosophizing or talking nonsense. He put his life, as well as his career, on the line with me during the 1992 World Cup. He was the management's sacrificial lamb when I wanted a night out. They reasoned that, unlike any of my colleagues, Laurie and his health were expendable. Not as far as I was concerned.

Tom Cartwright

Tom Cartwright was the man who convinced me I could bowl. Had it not been for him, 383 Test wickets would have had to be taken by someone else. What is more, quite a few slip catches would have gone missing as well.

Until the day I met Tom at Taunton – I was a callow youth, he a Somerset veteran and England Test player, regarded as the best of his type of medium-pace bowler in county cricket – no matter how much I thought my bowling was worth persevering with, all the coaches I had come across were equally sure it was a waste of time and effort.

My first experience of this happened at the 1969 England Schools Under-15 festival in Liverpool. In the final trial match to decide who would represent England Schools against the Public Schools, I took six wickets in the innings, a performance I expected would be enough to secure a place. I quickly discovered how wrong I was. My dad, Les, happened to be watching the match near where the selectors were sitting and overheard them describing my efforts as a fluke. I declined their offer of a place as 13th man.

'Tom Cartwright was the man who convinced me I could bowl. Had it not been for him, 383 Test wickets would have had to be taken by someone else. What is more, quite a few slip catches would have gone missing as well.'

The situation barely improved once I arrived to join the MCC groundstaff at Lord's. Chief coach Len Muncer was certain that I should concentrate on my batting alone and although his No. 2, Harry Sharp, was a great supporter of my ability and the way I approached the game, he agreed.

But Tom took notice of my pleas that I should be considered a genuine all-rounder and told me he saw enough in my bowling to believe I might be right. He told me never to give up or get dispirited. It was music to my ears. He always had time, always had faith in me, and I couldn't have had a better man to teach me the art of bowling. Tom's kindness meant that for the first time in my life I was a willing pupil.

The first things Tom instilled in me were to do with the craft of bowling: staying tall in delivery and keeping the seam position upright. Specifically, he stressed the need to get in tight to the stumps when bowling, and aiming the ball wicket to wicket; he saw that I had a natural outswinger's action, and that the straighter I delivered the ball down the other end, the more pronounced the effect of the slightest movement and therefore the more problems for the batsmen.

He also encouraged me to try and get a yard or two of extra pace out of my action, and it was a combination of that pace and swing that enabled me to get out the best batsmen in the world in my heyday. As time passed, he taught me the subtleties of disguising which way I was going to swing the ball; a complete education, in other words.

Later, after the operation on my back forced me to remodel and rethink my action, Tom's advice was more about how to cope psychologically with the real blow of not being able to bowl the way I wanted to, and it helped me to squeeze a couple more years out of my career as a Test all-rounder than would otherwise have been possible. He told me I had to be realistic about what my body would allow me to do, to forget about trying to be the bowler I had been and imagine that I was beginning a new career as though the previous one had never happened. And never to let a batsman think just because I wasn't as quick as I used to be that I didn't believe I could get him out.

He told me that I should concentrate on line and length, keeping things tight and boring the batsman into making an error. He encouraged me to try to think what it would be like to be batting against that kind of bowling. 'Imagine you have not had anything to hit for three overs,' he suggested. 'It wouldn't take much for you to try something different and then the bowler is in business.' It was sound advice, and applying it during the 1992 World Cup helped me to finish the tournament as England's most economical bowler.

As for the slip catching, Tom and I discussed on many occasions the best place for me to stand. Generally speaking, I felt that most slip fielders stood too deep against fast bowling. To me, too many chances went begging because they didn't carry, very few because they sailed over a slipper's head. This wasn't exactly a popular view, and granted, your reflexes needed to be wasp-sharp. I told Tom that I would rather take a chance and drop the ball than stand too deep and the ball fail to carry. Tom simply said to me that if I felt that way I should ignore what others thought and just go out and prove them wrong. I took a bit of stick over the years for adopting that advanced position. But I took a few sharp chances that I'm sure wouldn't have reached me if I'd stayed put.

Sylvester Clarke

Anyone who knew Sylvester Clarke knows there never were truer words spoken than his entry in the *Cricketers' Who's Who*, next to the section entitled 'Relaxations'. It comprised precisely two words: 'music' and 'parties'.

You'll understand, then, why although on the field I rated a meeting with the Surrey and Barbados monster-quickie several places behind sitting naked in a bucket of wasps, I looked forward to the après-cricket with this guy more than almost anyone else.

On one occasion, things might even have got a shade out of

hand, although, in my defence I only ever had the interests of my team-mates at heart. The place was Weston-super-Mare; the event, a county championship match between Somerset and Surrey in the early 1980s; and the result, carnage. The pitch at Weston used to be lively at the best of times. Sylvester Clarke, menacing and almost perversely keen on his work, represented the worst of times. We had won the toss and fielded first on day one. Day two meant us against the Beast on a flyer. Enter Vic Marks, my wily Somerset team-mate with a cunning plan.

'Beef,' chuckled Vic. 'Any chance of you having a little drink with Sylvers tonight?'

'Even from a safe distance, for those of us who enjoyed watching great, fiery fast bowling, watching Clarke bowl was a terrifying experience.'

Thus a convivial pint in the sponsor's tent wandered into a second, a third meandered into a fourth, and by then Botham and Clarke were in love with each other and the world. 'I know,' piped up someone whose voice sounded strangely like Vic's, 'What about a drinking contest, lads? Somerset v Surrey, Beefy against Sylvers?'

And so my double-vodka and rum was matched by his double-rum and vodka. My half-pint of gin and campari was matched by his half-pint of campari and gin until by the time we got back to the hotel the only thing holding us up were the fumes we kept breathing into each other's faces. Kids, do not try this at home. In fact, do not try it at all. The last thing I recall was the sight of probably the most fearsome fast bowler alive, dead to the world laid out unconscious on the pool table and snoring like a walrus.

The next time I saw him I passed him on my way out to bat. He didn't look well, and he sounded worse.

'Beefie, mahn ... Beefie, mahn. What have you done to me ... Beefie Mahn?'

'All in a night's work,' I told him.

No idea what happened in the game. By then, the result was incidental.

Even from a safe distance, for those of us who enjoyed watching great, fiery fast bowling, watching Clarke bowl was a terrifying experience. What struck you was the ambling, rolling gait of around seven paces with which he sauntered to the crease, like a Western gunslinger walking through the doors of the saloon, come to fill some varmint full of lead. The gunshot came from absolutely nowhere. One arm up, the other driven by a right shoulder that seemed about twice the size of his left, through the delivery before you could blink. And the resulting high-climbing missile was almost always unerringly straight. He was simply a terrific bowler; in his day, I believe, the quickest in the world. In any other era, he would have strolled into the West Indies team. It was just his misfortune to be operating at the same time as Malcolm Marshall, Joel Garner, Andy Roberts, Michael Holding and Colin Croft.

'He was simply a terrific bowler; in his day, I believe, the quickest in the world.'

But in county cricket Sylvers was something else, so much so that every time Surrey played at the Oval there were two games in progress simultaneously. The first when Sylvers was not bowling, when the flat, pacey but even-bouncing decks prepared by Harry Brind looked absolutely jam-packed with runs. The other, when Sylvester came on to bowl. Be afraid. Be very afraid.

For a guy who inspired so much apprehension and caused so many niggling injuries to flare up on the eve of a trip to Surrey, mainly in batsmen I seem to recall, the wave of sadness that washed over the game when Sylvester died stupidly young indicated in just how much affection the Bajan was held. For lovers of cricket in Barbados particularly, to lose Sylvers and Malcolm Marshall in such a short space of time must have been difficult to bear.

Brian Close

Another prize nutter. Is it me, or what? Don't answer that. It is something of a minor miracle, in fact, that my career lasted beyond my first few matches under Brian Close's captaincy. It was not that he didn't think I could play. As time progressed, he convinced me that I could achieve anything I set my mind to. No, the problem was his bloody driving.

I've faced the fastest, most hostile bowlers in world cricket, with helmets and without, on minefields as well as shirtfronts. But I never knew what cold fear was until I slipped into the passenger seat of Close's car.

As young players taking our first steps at Somerset under Brian, and being taught everything we knew by him, guys like myself, Viv Richards, Vic Marks and Peter Roebuck would travel to the ends of the earth for him. The only problem was his preferred mode of transport.

Behind the wheel of whichever beaten-up old banger he was scaring to death at the time, Close's performances were legendary. On one occasion he picked up a motor from the garage where it had undergone major surgery, turned left, smacked into the back of a van, went around the next roundabout and drove it straight back in for repair again.

I will never forget my first experience of Close's unique driving style; the first thing that hit you was his need for speed. Come shine or rain, day or night, crystal-clear visibility or pea-soup fog, to him all driving conditions were perfect for cruising at around 100 mph. The next thing you noticed was the open flask of scalding hot coffee pirouetting on the central console. Then there were the beef sandwiches made for him by his wife Vivian, which, while steering the car with his knees and with seemingly little regard for what was happening on the other side of the windscreen, he would open up with both hands to make sure the meat content was acceptably high. And finally, to complete this nightmarish scene, he had a copy of *The Sporting Life*, folded in half on his lap, from which I swear he was studying the form as he drove along.

'Do you want me to drive?' I would ask, hopefully. His reply every time? 'No, lad. Driving helps me relax.'

People who didn't know Closey used to recount the stories of his exploits in the field in tones of hushed amazement. Those of us who knew him took no persuading whatsoever to believe every single word.

His speciality as a fielder was to use himself as a human shield. He

'I've faced the fastest, most hostile bowlers in world cricket, with helmets and without, on minefields as well as shirtfronts. But I never knew what cold fear was until I slipped into the passenger seat of Close's car.'

reasoned that a cricket ball couldn't possibly hurt you because it wasn't on you long enough. And he lived and nearly died by that principle in suicide positions all round the bat, particularly at the shortest of short square leg. Once, fielding in that spot, the ball rebounded from his forehead towards second slip.

> **'A lot of captains talked about leading from the front. With Closey it was more than just talk. He made an art form of it, and I have no hesitation in saying that a lot of what I've achieved in the game is down to the principles he drummed into me as a youngster at Somerset.'**

'Catch it!' he shouted.

After the ball was taken, his team-mates raced towards the stricken Closey to make sure he was okay.

'I'm fine,' he assured them.

'Yes, but what if the ball had hit you an inch lower?' one of them asked.

'Well, lad. He'd have been caught in the gully,' said Closey.

Gary Sobers was another who fell victim to Closey's awesome (some might say foolhardy) disregard for personal well-being. On a featherbed pitch, the best hooker in world cricket was playing John Snow with a stick of rhubarb. Only a madman would have put himself so close at forward short leg. Say no more.

The inevitable moment arrived; Snow bowled a short one, Sobers rocked back and prepared to lever the ball into the middle of the Harleyford Road. Any other cricketer would have hit the deck and hoped for the best. Closey didn't budge an inch. In the event, Sobers was a fraction too early with the shot, and as everyone else in the ground prepared to trace the flight of the ball over the perimeter wall with the fielder's head attached to it, Close kept his eyes open and on the ball that travelled from the bottom edge of the bat to the batsman's hip and into his hands for the catch.

There could be no more graphic proof of his bravery than his performance against a fearsome West Indies pace attack led by Michael Holding in near-darkness on the evening of the third day of the Old Trafford Test of 1976. At 45, 27 years after making his Test debut,

Closey had been recalled by skipper Tony Greig to add some experience to the England batting, and some guts too. In a terrifying barrage and without any protective intervention from the umpires, Close and John Edrich took blow after blow on the body. When Close took his shirt off in the dressing room afterwards his chest was covered with black and blue, cricket-ball shaped bruises. 'Someone take a picture of my medals,' he urged. Someone did and the resulting photo was one of his most-prized possessions.

A lot of captains talked about leading from the front. With Closey it was more than just talk. He made an art form of it, and I have no hesitation in saying that a lot of what I've achieved in the game is down to the principles he drummed into me as a youngster at Somerset. I know that if you asked Viv Richards he would tell you exactly the same.

The first thing he taught us was just how much cricket was played in the mind. Very early in my career at Somerset, when I'd played only a dozen or so matches for the first team, he took me to one side and told me straight out, 'You should be in the England side.' Before Viv had even properly established himself in our first team at Taunton Close told him, 'You are going to be the best batsman in the world.' And those things rub off. Sure, some might say that such talk could have an adverse effect on a certain type of character. Close's opinion was that it would only have an adverse effect on the wrong type of character.

'Closey retained his total enthusiasm throughout his extraordinary career, and was still leading the Yorkshire Academy XI of promising youngsters well into his sixties.'

For the rest, it was always his intention to instil in you the belief that you were the best. As far as he was concerned, all he needed to say was this: 'You are better than the bloke at the other end. Now prove it.' And I recall him saying that to me when I ran in to bowl for the first time to none other than Colin Cowdrey.

Closey retained his total enthusiasm throughout his extraordinary career, and was still leading the Yorkshire Academy XI of promising youngsters well into his sixties. The only two occasions on which I ever saw him anything like flustered had nothing to do with cricket. The first was when I announced that I was going to marry his god-daughter Kathryn Waller when we were both still so young, and the second, at a hotel in Westcliff before a county match against Essex, when I watched him walk straight through a plate-glass sliding-door. It sounded like a bomb had gone off. Miraculously, he escaped with a tiny nick on his hand, just to prove that whether behind a wheel, at madly-close short leg, against Michael Holding's bouncers in the gloom, or whatever the danger, Closey was a born survivor.

Colin Cowdrey

Long after I knocked back Colin Cowdrey's off-stump as an 18-year-old in a Gillette Cup semi-final, it finally dawned on me: I had bowled one of the greatest ambassadors world cricket has ever known.

I was brought up by my old Somerset captain Brian Close to treat all batsmen alike, and never to be overawed by great reputations taking guard at the other end. All the same, it was a great feather in my cap when I won my personal duel with 'Kipper' – later to become Sir Colin Cowdrey, and then Lord Cowdrey of Tonbridge – at Canterbury that afternoon in August 1974.

Sadly for me, there was to be no happy ending, or a trip to Lord's: Kent won by three wickets and went on to beat Lancashire in a low-scoring final. But to be confronted by one of the game's great names, and rearrange his off-stump, was a special moment.

Later in my career, I was fortunate enough to get to know Kipper pretty well. We used to enjoy the odd game of golf, and he was as much fun off the pitch as he was an exemplary character on it. It was a terrible moment when, two days before England's fantastic win at Karachi in December 2000, his son Chris was awakened in the middle of the night with the tragic news that Lord Cowdrey had passed away, and Chris had to fly home from Pakistan.

'Long after I knocked back Colin Cowdrey's off-stump as an 18-year-old in a Gillette Cup semi-final, it finally dawned on me: I had bowled one of the greatest ambassadors world cricket has ever known.'

Just four months earlier, I'd been photographed at Old Trafford with five of the other six Englishmen to reach 100 Test caps: Geoffrey Boycott, David Gower, Alec Stewart, Mike Atherton and Graham Gooch. Colin, the first man to reach that milestone, was unable to attend because he was recovering from a stroke at the time. But to me, he will always be the leader of the magnificent seven.

Colin's love of the game and his conviction that, no matter how high the stakes, it should be played the right way, encouraged him to become the driving force behind a move to define 'the spirit of the game' and have a statement describing it written and included in the laws of cricket. It hurt him deeply when cricketers let themselves down on the field with poor behaviour. And I shudder to think what he would have made of some of what went on during England's tour to Sri Lanka, or when England took on Pakistan at the start of the 2001 summer.

But while his work as an administrator may bear fruit in the long run, it was his skill as a player that made him one of the best-loved figures in the world game. As a batsman, he was one of the most graceful of any era. His textbook cover drive was a work of art: his timing was so immaculate that he appeared to caress the ball to the boundary. With

Peter May, he shared a partnership of 411 against the West Indies at Edgbaston in 1957 which still remains England's record stand for any wicket in Test matches.

He was also a man of extraordinary courage, and the way he walked out to bat with his broken left arm in plaster at Lord's in 1963, to save the game when England were nine wickets down against the Windies, is part of cricket folklore. He thought it was all a jolly jape, of course, and he stood at the non-striker's end for the last over, beaming like a Cheshire cat. On the only occasion I can remember talking to him about it, he told me he would have batted left-handed – using only his right arm – if he'd been called upon to face the bowling.

Only a few months after I'd dismissed him at Canterbury, I can also remember Colin marching out to face Dennis Lillee and Jeff Thomson – at their ferocious peak – in Perth on the 1974–75 Ashes tour, where he'd been summoned as an emergency replacement for England's vast platoon of walking wounded. Thommo greeted him with a few snarls, as you would expect, but Colin just doffed his cap and chortled, 'Good day, I don't believe we've met – the name's Cowdrey.'

'Colin's love of the game and his conviction that, no matter how high the stakes, it should be played the right way, encouraged him to become the driving force behind a move to define 'the spirit of the game' and have a statement describing it written and included in the laws of cricket.'

At the end of that over, he wandered up the pitch for a chat with his batting partner David Lloyd, like two neighbours chatting over the garden fence. 'Bumble' had been ducking Thommo's 99 mph bouncers on a trampoline pitch for dear life, and was somewhat taken aback when Colin, approaching his 42nd birthday, greeted him with the words, 'This is rather good fun, isn't it?' Bumble replied that he'd been in funnier situations, but together they knuckled down to put on 50-odd runs against some of the fastest bowling ever seen. If Cowdrey had a fault, those who played under him as captain will tell you that he suffered occasionally from bouts of indecision brought on by a totally unwarranted lack of self-confidence. When, during the fourth Test of England's 1968 tour to the West Indies, Gary Sobers threw down the gauntlet to England by offering them a target of 215 in two-and-three-quarter hours, Colin was so unsure as to whether to go for the runs that it was only the combined efforts of Ken Barrington, Basil D'Oliveira and Tom Graveney at tea on that final day that persuaded him to do so. In the end, Cowdrey made 71, and England won the match and the series 1–0. Mind you, according to Colin, leading the side, though a tremendous honour, was by no means a driving ambition. Later in his life when he reviewed the circumstances that led to him being given the captaincy, after Brian Close had been sacked following a time-wasting controversy in county cricket, he admitted, 'I felt as if I had come third in an egg-and-spoon race at school and been awarded the prize because the first two had been disqualified.'

'His skill as a player made him one of the most-loved figures in the world game. As a batsman, he was one of the most graceful of any era.'

Cowdrey was enormously proud in 1988 when Chris, the eldest of his three sons, completed only the second father-and-son captaincy double for England, after Frank and George Mann. But he showed just as much compassion towards others who held the post, and I remember getting a phone call from him when things weren't going so well for me as England skipper. He told me to keep my chin up and, coming from a man of his stature in the game, that meant a lot to me. Pats on the back and complimentary headlines are par for the course when results are good on the pitch, but it's at the lowest points when you find out who your real friends are in cricket – and Kipper showed his true colours with that phone call. I know Mike Atherton, for one, also used to receive supportive messages from Cowdrey during the more troubled phases of his reign as England captain, and that's a measure of the man.

Somehow it was appropriate that in the week English cricket lost one of its most celebrated characters, Atherton should score a match-winning century in Karachi, and England should mark Cowdrey's passing with one of their best victories of modern times.

Colin Croft

As anyone who has listened to or read the thoughts of Colin Croft as a commentator on radio or for the cricket website 'Cricinfo' will surely agree, the least celebrated of the great West Indies 'fearsome foursome' is never short of an opinion or five. Try this, about Angus Fraser after the West Indies polished off England in the Guyana Test of 1994: 'His bowling is like firing at F-16 fighters with slingshots. Even if they hit, no damage would be done. Like an old horse, he should be put out to pasture.' Say what you mean, Croftie.

I rarely argue with the big man now. During our playing days, such a tactic was definitely straight out of the manual entitled: 'Test cricket for idiots, Vol. 3: How to get your head knocked off.' For me, the story that best summed up exactly why I back off concerns an incident that took place during England's 1980 Test tour of the Caribbean. Clive Lloyd and I, as captains, were very keen on our players going into the other team's dressing room after close of play – not all the time, but from time to time, to relax and unwind with the opposition over a beer. We both felt this was an excellent way of defusing any conflicts that might be developing, and showing that no matter how hard we were trying to beat each other, we didn't have to be at war off the field as well.

'I found batting against Croft one of the more challenging experiences of my career.'

After one particularly sticky day during which the atmosphere on the field had became a little overheated, Clive thought the time was right to bring his guys in, and in they all came. All, except Croft, that is. Clive noticed he was absent and called back across the corridor separating the two changing rooms: 'Come on, Croftie! There's a beer for you here.' Still he wouldn't budge so, after a while, Clive left our room to find out what was the matter. When he returned he looked a little shaken.

'He was one of those rare athletes who actually seemed to get stronger the more he bowled.'

'Croftie isn't coming,' he said.

'Why not?' I asked.

'Well,' said Clive, 'he told me he couldn't bring himself to drink with fellahs he was trying to kill.'

'Come off it, Hubert,' I smiled, 'He's only having a laugh.'

'I don't think you quite understand,' explained Clive, 'Croftie doesn't have a sense of humour.'

If any of our blokes asked me where Croft was that evening, which otherwise went very well by the way, I told them he was having treatment.

Kiwi umpire Fred Goodall found out what happens when you upset the big man, big time. It was on the notorious West Indies tour of New Zealand in 1980, when Clive's men lot their rag with the officials and at one stage, during the second Test in Christchurch, threatened not to take the field unless Goodall was removed from the action. The incident involving Croft happened after Goodall decided, in his wisdom, to no-ball the fast bowler. Croft's response was nothing if not straightforward. On his way to the wicket to deliver the next ball, the giant paceman sent Goodall flying with a shoulder-charge that would have made Roy Keane proud.

Croftie's mum knew what kind of demon she'd produced. 'When I hear Colin bowl de bounces, I get vexed,' she explained. 'Two bounces an over okay, but when he bowl five I get vexed bad. I tell him, what happen if he hit batsman and he fall dead on de spot?' Sadly for batsmen the world over, Mrs Croft's protestations had no effect.

I found batting against Croft one of the more challenging experiences of my career. Bowling from wide of the crease with an awkward, gangling action he was always at you, it was extremely difficult to pick up the length of the ball – which varied from short to very short – and he never seemed to give you any width to work with. He absolutely detested getting hit, which only happened once in his career, to my knowledge, when Viv

BEEFY ON CROFT

Born: 15 March 1953, Lancaster Village, East Coast, Demerara, British Guyana
Country: West Indies
Tests: 27
Wickets: 125
Average: 23.30
Beefy analysis: Demon fast bowler who delivered from wide of the crease and had the unerring ability to hit batsman with short-of-a-length deliveries.
Beefy moment: Croft sending Fred Goodall flying with a shoulder-charge during the Christchurch Test, New Zealand 1980, after the umpire no-balled him.
Do mention: English batsmen, hard wickets.
Don't mention: A friendly drink.

took him on and destroyed him, playing for Somerset against Lancashire on a real flyer at Southport. And he was one of those rare athletes who actually seemed to get stronger the more he bowled.

After packing up the game, Croft took it upon himself to learn to fly, put in the work, got his pilot's licence and now flies commercially. Normally, when I hear the words, 'This is your captain speaking', deep sleep follows imminently. I think in his case it would be a good idea to make an exception and take notice.

Hansie Cronje

If I bumped into Hansie Cronje tomorrow, there is only one word I can think of saying to him – apart from the obvious smattering of Anglo-Saxon vernacular – after his conversion from a sporting statesman who led South Africa out of apartheid's shadows to become a two-faced, two-bob cheat: 'Why?' We may never know what possessed Cronje to fall into the clutches of bookmakers and become a willing stooge for match-fixers. Nor am I convinced that the full story of his duplicity, deceit and double standards came out at Judge Edwin King's commission of inquiry in South Africa. But one thing is certain: Cronje will go down in history as a devious charlatan who sold cricket's reputation for sportsmanship and fair play down the river.

Why did you do it, Hansie? Why, why, why?

I was as shocked as everyone else when he was sacked as South African captain on 11 April 2000 because he was just about the last person on earth you would suspect of making squalid pacts with the underworld.

Everyone young enough to remember the autumn of 1963 recalls where they were and what they were doing when US President John F. Kennedy was assassinated; and I will always remember being on my way to a Pride of Britain awards lunch in Park Lane when news of Cronje's downfall broke. I was gobsmacked, absolutely dumbstruck.

The previous weekend, Indian police had announced they had tapes of Cronje's mobile-phone conversations with a bookmaker – which they stumbled across pursuing an unconnected murder inquiry – and most people had treated their revelations with a cellar, never mind a pinch, of salt. The allegations seemed to lose credibility when a respected South African journalist, Trevor Chesterfield, claimed he had heard the 'incriminating' tapes – and that neither of the voices was Cronje's. Little did he know that the tapes were merely re-enactments of the transcripts, and the voices he heard were those of Indian actors.

'You have to ask whether any sportsman, alive or dead, has ever fallen from grace so suddenly – and so far.'

Four days later, the dreadful truth was out. Cronje, having lied to his employers about any involvement in dodgy deals with bookmakers, spilled the beans to a clergyman before telephoning Dr Ali Bacher, managing director of the United Cricket Board, at three in the morning.

You have to ask whether any sportsman, alive or dead, has ever fallen from grace so suddenly – and so far. Ben Johnson, who won the 1988 Seoul Olympics 100 metres in a world-record time before he was exposed as a drugs cheat, comes close. But from being a South African sporting pin-up – a God-fearing, clean-cut, successful captain of his country, revered by fans and sponsors – Cronje was suddenly despised worldwide. And he gets no sympathy from me.

When you consider how long South Africa had spent in the doldrums because of apartheid, and the giant strides they had made in the eight years since being readmitted to sport's mainstream, it must have been a crushing blow to their national pride. In 1994, when Kepler Wessels led them to victory at Lord's, and when Francois Pienaar accepted the rugby World Cup from President Mandela a year later, South Africa had regained the respect lost over 25 years

'From being a South African sporting pin-up – a God-fearing, clean-cut, successful captain of his country, revered by fans and sponsors – Cronje was suddenly despised worldwide.'

of blinkered politics. At a stroke, Cronje's greed dispersed that pride and replaced it with dark clouds of shame. What a waste – under his leadership, South Africa had emerged as the likeliest challengers to Australia's domination of Test cricket, and it seemed inevitable that they would have employed him in a coaching or managerial capacity when his playing days were over.

Now he's been banned for life from all forms of cricket. In the summer of 2001, he was even barred from making an after-dinner speech at a benefit function for his old Free State team-mate Gerhardus Liebenberg – and I'm not surprised. I wouldn't want him to open my local school fête.

It still sickens me when I think of the way I applauded his decision to forfeit an innings at the Centurion Test against England 17 months earlier. At the time, like most people, I thought it was a wonderful gesture by Cronje to make a game of it for the spectators after three days had been wiped out by rain and condemned the match to a certain draw. I wrote in my column for the *Mirror* that Cronje's foresight was a great step forward for cricket, only to discover later that he had been following an altogether more devious agenda which was nothing to do with sportsmanship, and everything to do with lining his own pockets.

While England, unsuspecting accessories to the sting, had every right to celebrate their two-wicket win, I felt I'd been duped, conned and cheated when the truth came out. Cronje had not horse-traded and contrived a tight finish for the good of the game, but for a £5,000 backhander and a leather jacket from some bookmaker who stood to lose a fortune if the game petered out into a draw. Mike Atherton said at the time it felt like the cheapest Test win of his career, and now we know why. At the King Commission, more sordid details emerged about Cronje's attempts to draw vulnerable team-mates into his web of deceit. Picking on Herschelle Gibbs, a Cape-coloured batsman, as a target for his scheming was particularly loathsome.

'I could go on to say what a fine batsman and respected captain he was – but who cares now? Nobody will remember him for those things any more.'

In effect, Cronje now lives in exile among his own people. He has to rebuild his life, if he can, knowing the cricket community worldwide despises him. I could go on to say what a fine batsman, and respected captain, he was – but who cares now? Nobody will remember him for those things any more.

Basil D'Oliveira

There have been other examples of how the game of cricket has had an impact on the passage of history. None are so quite vivid as that which came to be known as the D'Oliveira affair.

In these post-apartheid days, when the new South Africa is doing its best to repaint its political landscape in all the colours of the rainbow, it is hard to imagine the context in which the political furore erupted that followed Basil's belated inclusion in the England squad for the 1968–69 tour to South Africa as a replacement for the injured Tom Cartwright, eventually led to the cancellation of the tour, and thrust the republic into sporting isolation for more than twenty years.

But the fact is that, in 1968, governed by hard-line Prime Minister John Vorster, South Africa was still utterly committed to maintaining its hated racist subjugation of black and coloured people. For supporters of the status quo there, the name Basil D'Oliveira represented the kind of independence and strength among what it considered to be its underclass, which they feared and despised. For the rest he became a symbol of hope.

Categorized in those days in his homeland as a Cape Coloured, Basil arrived in England from South Africa in the early 1960s to make a career for himself in professional cricket. His performances with bat and ball, a hard-hitting striker using an immensely heavy bat and a partnership-breaking specialist swing bowler at slow-medium pace, earned him his Test debut in 1966, and by 1968 he was a regular in the side.

After South Africa had refused the New Zealand Rugby Board permission to bring its Maori contingent in 1967 on the grounds that they would not entertain teams of mixed race, and the Kiwis cancelled their All Black tour as a result, fears were raised that Basil's presence in an England touring party might lead to a similar stand-off. Marylebone Cricket Club, under whose flag England teams toured the world, assured Dennis Howell, the Labour Minister for Sport, that their team to tour South Africa in 1968 would be chosen on merit, and that if any player chosen were to be rejected by the host country, then the projected tour would be abandoned.

All year long, mindful of the probability that Basil would be selected for the winter trip to South Africa, and of the South African government's possible reaction, the MCC sought to clarify the position. As early as January 1968, the MCC wrote to the South African Cricket Association asking for an assurance that no preconditions would be made over their choice of players. No answer was forthcoming, but as the time approached for the squad to be picked it looked as though the issue would be avoided for the simple reason that although Basil made 87 in the first Ashes Test, by the end of the series he'd been dropped.

Had Roger Prideaux, himself a replacement for Geoff Boycott, not pulled out of the final Test at the Oval with bronchitis, the D'Oliveira affair might never have happened at all. In the event Basil, drafted in at the last moment, made 158 in a rare England victory and what happened next changed the course of sporting history. First, when the squad was announced the day after the Test ended, on 28 August, Basil's name was not on the list. The selectors and captain Colin Cowdrey insisted that the decision had been made purely on cricketing grounds. Chairman of Selectors Doug Insole attempted to explain by saying that Basil had been considered as a batsman only, and not as an all-rounder. 'We put him beside the seven batsmen that we had, along with Colin Milburn, whom we also had to leave out with regret.' But for the majority of observers, their decision smacked of appeasement, of bowing to South Africa's racial policies.

The stakes were raised when Reg Hayter, Basil's agent (and later mine), arranged a deal for Basil to cover the tour for the *News of the World*. Now that would have made interesting copy.

Then, three weeks later on 16 September, Cartwright was forced to withdraw from the squad through injury, Basil was called up to replace him, and the simmering volcano erupted. In South Africa, Vorster claimed Basil's late inclusion proved that the England selectors had given into pressure from anti-apartheid sympathizers, and he made a speech in Bloemfontein, described by the *Daily Mail* as 'crude and boorish', in which he stated that South Africa was not prepared to receive an England team that had been forced upon them by people 'with certain political aims'. On 24 September, the tour was cancelled and the first shots in the battle to force South Africa to confront real change had been fired.

As I grew to know Basil over the years, and later specifically as our coach when I moved from Somerset to Worcestershire, I found he took no pleasure in being at the centre of the affair. He was proud of the role he was able to play, but on occasions wondered if the long-term benefit to his people was worth what they were having to suffer as a result of South Africa's isolation. At that MCC special meeting on 5 December the main speakers criticizing the MCC's mishandling of the affair were former Test batsman the Reverend David Sheppard, and a young Mike Brearley. Basil never forgot what they did, and he was similarly grateful for the support of friends such as John Arlott and Reg, his agent, who had both helped Basil and his wife Naomi to come to England in the first place. The one thing upon which all commentators were agreed at the time was that Basil kept his dignity throughout. Deep down, I know he was inspired to achieve what he did in the game because of a sense of responsibility he felt to all of the above people, but more significantly to all those fighting for recognition and freedom in his native land.

One incident in a county match between Worcestershire and Yorkshire years later underlined how seriously he took that responsibility. I'm sad to say that, for a period, the White Rose county had a reputation for thinly-disguised racism on the field. Viv Richards was subjected to appalling and unforgivable abuse by certain sections of Yorkshire supporters

'Basil was inspired to achieve what he did in the game because of a sense of responsibility to all those fighting for recognition and freedom in his native land.'

over the years, and on occasion in the late 1960s and early 1970s black players found the atmosphere on the pitch equally vile. On the occasion in question, Basil's ears were burning as a result of the comments coming his way from the Yorkshire fielders, and when finally pushed to the limit of his endurance, he brought proceedings to a halt, pointed his bat at each of them in turn, told them what he thought of them and then told them what he was about to do to them; his revenge was a savage hundred.

And when the curtain of prejudice was finally torn down,

walking on to the pitch at Newlands during England's first post-apartheid tour there in 1995–96 to receive a standing ovation from a packed house was one of the proudest moments of his life. It was almost as if the whole city of Cape Town, if not the whole country, was applauding him.

What struck me most through all the years of turmoil, though, was the man's simple, straightforward love of the game. As a coach at New Road he was always worth listening to, and impressed upon young players the need to maintain the highest levels of concentration at all times. He kept his coaching simple, never wasted words or filled you full of science, and I believe he would have been able to help Graeme Hick cope with the ludicrous expectations placed on him during his early career if he'd been allowed to work with him without interference from members of the England team and management who thought they knew better. I recall taking to Graeme after he had been dropped by England for the first time, and his head was so full of the crap that they had pumped into it that it took Basil the rest of the season to persuade him he could play again. Had Basil been handled properly at Worcestershire, as a director of coaching perhaps, working with other younger men, the club would surely have got more out of him than they did.

'It was somehow reassuring to see that such an important figure in the history of our sport loved nothing better than a session in the nets helping players learn the game, followed by a session in the bar nattering about it to his heart's content.'

Watching Basil going about his business in later years, it was somehow reassuring to see that such an important figure in the history of our sport loved nothing better than a session in the nets helping players learn the game, followed by a session in the bar nattering about it to his heart's content. The whole point of our game is that it crosses all boundaries of colour, creed and race. It's just a crying shame South Africa took so long to get it.

John Davies

In a cricketing context, the name John Davies is probably not widely known. But John is one of the most significant characters in the Botham story, for he is the man who added five years to my playing career. Without him, my back injury would have finished me as early as 1988.

It may surprise some people to learn that my back problem was first diagnosed ten years before that, during my first Ashes tour in the winter of 1978–79. I was just 23 years old with a dozen or so Test matches under my belt when I started to feel odd pains in my lower back. Just as a precaution, I was shipped off to hospital for X-rays, and when the specialist called me in to show me what he had found, I got the shock of my life. There was a deformity of the spine, he told me. The problem was at stage one, he said. When it gets to stage three, you're in trouble, he said.

Deformity of the spine? Stage one, stage three? He wasn't talking about me, was he? I've no idea whether that is normal in such cases or not, or whether I was just born lucky, but I was too young, too keen and had too much ambition to allow myself to be sidetracked. It was a case of mind over matter. The back was going to have to take whatever punishment was in store. So, from then on, I treated the occasional spot of early-morning stiffness as simply that, and put the gloomy prognosis out of my thoughts and I'm happy to say that the condition stayed at stage two for the next ten years.

Indeed it wasn't until I bowled against Australia in England in 1985 that I even allowed myself to acknowledge that the problem might be worsening. Even then I reasoned that if time was running out I was going to make the most of what I had left, and during that series I bowled faster than at any time in my career.

I am grateful that the injury held off long enough for me to play a full part in that memorable Ashes victory under Mike Gatting in 1986–87, and I was doubly fortunate that, when the back finally did pack up on the second day of the county championship match between Worcestershire and my old club Somerset, on 19 May 1988, a surgeon with John's skill and patience was on hand at the local hospital to take charge of the rest of my career.

Many observers at New Road that day identified the decisive incident as the moment I fell awkwardly when diving to stop a ball in the slips. In fact, my recollection is that nothing untoward happened, until some time later. We'd been off the field for a rain break, someone shouted out that the umpires were on their way back to the middle and as I went to rise from the dressing-room bench suddenly and very painfully I realized that I couldn't move a muscle. It was the most frightening moment of my entire life.

John was actually looking through the hospital window when I was delivered by car, and prised out of the back seat locked in the foetal position. He told me later that as soon as he saw me he knew exactly how serious the problem was. He said I had two alternatives: I could pack up cricket there and then because the back had suffered enough; or he could operate to fuse together a couple of vertebrae using donor-bone material from my thigh and hip. Even then, the forecast was not exactly sunny. John said the best chance he could offer me of playing any kind of cricket again was a mere 30 per cent.

'John Davies is one of the most significant characters in the Botham story, for he is the man who added five years to my playing career. Without him, my back injury would have finished me as early as 1988.'

It was not a hard decision to make, though. Sure, I was never again the bowler I had been, and that was hard to take. And the agony of slowly building up strength and flexibility again after the op – which itself had taken two hours longer than normal because of the muscle that had built up around my spine during my recent charity walk over the Alps with reluctant elephants – and the frustration of three months of total immobility, sitting in a plaster cast from my neck to my backside and not even able to put my shoes on, was almost unbearable. Not to mention the fact that when once again able to train, I trained harder than I had ever done in my life, helped by the two French lads who had acted as security on the Hannibal walk – whose speciality, incidentally, was kick-boxing!

But John was able to nurse me through all this, caring for my mind as well as my body and my impatience. 'Don't fight it,' he said. 'Forget about what you can't do anymore. Concentrate on what you can' and those words enabled me to play five more years of cricket, including a World Cup Final appearance in 1992; to experience a Test match win against the West Indies in 1991 for the first time ever; to be on the field when Viv Richards, my greatest friend in cricket, made his emotional farewell from the game; and to have the honour of reaching 100 Test caps, in the third Test of the 1991–92 series against New Zealand in Wellington.

John has my sincere and undying gratitude.

Ted Dexter

Who can forget Dexter Ted, aka Screaming Lord Ted of the Monster Raving Loony Selection Party? It is one of my few regrets in cricket that I never really got to know Ted until after he and I had both departed the Test scene. Prior to that, I admit I had totally misinterpreted the eccentricity that made him such an endearing character. In 1989, while I was still in the process of trying to restart my international career, having worked harder than I thought possible to recover from back surgery, I mistook the quirky side of his nature for something more akin to just plain daftness.

Mind you, there was quite a lot to mistake.

I missed the first two Tests of Ted's four-year spell as chairman of selectors as I was completing my rehabilitation following a year out of the game, but when I returned for the third of the 1989 Ashes series at Edgbaston, my first experience of his unique style left me wondering what planet he had just arrived from. At the team dinner on the eve of the match Ted let his skipper, David Gower, have his say, short and sweet, then proceeded to hand out to each of us a single sheet of A4 paper. At first I thought he was passing on some brief tactical notes or specific pointers concerning our opponents. Er, not quite. What he gave us instead was the words and music to a little number he had penned entitled: 'Onward, Gower's Cricketers'.

'Onward Gower's cricketers', it began, and went on,

> *'Striving for a score,*
> *With our bats uplifted,*
> *We want more and more,*
> *Alderman the master,*
> *Represents the foe,*
> *Forward into battle,*
> *Down the pitch we go.'*

As the psychiatrist observed of Basil at the end of the best episode of *Fawlty Towers*: 'There's enough material here for a dissertation.'

There was more, too. 'Who could forget Malcolm Devon?' he asked the assembled media when responding to their question about what good had come out of the 1989 Ashes series. And as for his comments during and after the end of England's 1993 tour to India and Sri Lanka had ended in four straight defeats (India 3–0, Sri Lanka 1–0), you couldn't make them up.

After a meeting of the Test and County Cricket Board to discuss England's spectacular failure, Dexter, who had earlier been the target of an MCC campaign to oust him over the non-selection of Gower, was asked to put forward some suggestions as to the cause of the national side's malaise. English cricket held its breath and waited for Dexter to go through the list: the mediocre standard of county cricket, the crippling workload placed on our bowlers by having to play a full mixed domestic season as well as international competition, the standard of pitches, etc, etc. Dexter's response was not quite what we were expecting: 'There is a modern fashion for designer stubble,' he explained, 'and some people believe it to be very attractive. But it is aggravating to others and we will be looking at the whole question of people's facial hair.'

'I never really got to know Ted until after he and I had both departed the Test scene. Until that time, I admit I had totally misinterpreted the eccentricity that made him such an endearing character.'

Earlier in the tour, he had sought to soften the blow of defeat in the first Test in Calcutta by announcing, 'The players have quite reasonably talked about levels of pollution and how it has affected levels of performance ... I've decided to commission an immediate report into pollution levels in Indian cities.' The world game awaits the publication of the report with a clothes peg over its nose.

There is no denying that Ted upset me greatly when leaving me out of the1989–90 trip to the West Indies under Graham Gooch. I said at the time, and I'll say it again: the England selectors had been asking me all the previous summer to make myself available for the trip. I also believe he and other selectors misjudged just how much effort I had put into regaining fitness. After having put myself through all that pain, why should they think I would throw all that away by not being totally committed to the cause in the Caribbean? But over the years I have come to believe that while Dexter held the gun, someone else was pulling the trigger.

As for his explanation, halfway through the Ashes series of 1993, of why England were so useless against Australia, I'll leave his remarks about Venus being in the wrong 'juxtaposition' to the other planets to continue their eternal journey around the Universe.

All that having been said – and there is a lot more I haven't touched on – since he and I retired from our active roles, I have come to appreciate Ted for the extraordinary guy he is.

Personally, bearing in mind his less than acute sense of direction, I would have chosen British Airways, but you have to admire a man who decided to fly himself, his wife Susan and two small children Tom and Genevieve halfway around the world in order to be present in Australia for the 1970–71 Ashes series. He piloted the aircraft named Pommie's Progress, a Cessna 172, I think, via a series of short hops through Europe, Africa and Asia and arrived well in time to cover the first Test of the series for his newspaper, the *Sunday Mirror*. And anyone who can come up with the following line – 'I have on occasion taken a quite unreasonable dislike to Australians' – or ride home to Acton from selection meetings at Lord's in full leather regalia on a high-powered motorbike can't be all bad.

'I have come to appreciate Ted for the extraordinary guy he is.'

If it's a novel you expect from your Renaissance man, Ted came up with something called *Testkill*, a murder mystery he co-authored with the sports editor of the *Observer*, the late Clifford Makins. Not a patch on my own novel *Deep Cover*, of course. And I have to award Ted the prize for the best excuse I ever heard for turning up late for nets. Flat tyre? Hit by a passing meteorite shower? Nothing could compare with the reason he offered in 1964 – canvassing for votes as a Tory party candidate in the general election.

As a player, with the ball he wasn't of the highest class but could still hurry the best, but as a batsman Ted was the ultimate buccaneer. He was a stroke-playing batsman and quicker-than-sharp pace bowler. For some, the game seemed to come too easily to him, but that was only because, like all the best players, he seemed to have a tick-of-the-clock more time than the rest. What's more, he had such presence at the crease and batted on occasion with such swashbuckling aggression that observers inevitably felt let down when he was out. His brilliant 80 in the Lord's Test of 1963 against the ferocious West Indies pair, Wes Hall and Charlie Griffith, was a case in point. The match ended with Colin Cowdrey walking to the wicket with his broken arm in plaster, photos of Brian Close's bruised and battered body, and England, thwarted in pursuit of victory, eventually hanging on for a draw. But for me, as a cricket-mad schoolboy, the abiding image is of Ted, standing tall and proud, and coming down the wicket to launch the quicks back over the heads.

Friend and foe used to accuse him, if that is the right word, of theorizing himself down a blind alley. Fellow members at Sunningdale, where Ted's ability as one of the finest of all amateur golfers survived several knee and hip operations, often joke that if Ted is four under par by the tenth hole, his attempts to unravel exactly why will ensure that he finishes the round four over. On the cricket field, colleagues of his such as Ken Barrington told me that when Ted was busy 'in the lab' as they called it, whole passages of play would simply pass him by. If Sky's player-cam had been in operation during the 1960s viewers would have been treated to some extraordinary sights while Ted was fielding, including him practising his short game with an imaginary pitching wedge even as the bowler was starting his run-up. If they were very lucky they might even have been treated to a party trick he used to show off in social cricket. Fielding the ball at cover, he would shape to throw down the stumps at the batsman's end, then actually release it sideways towards the non-striker's end. If he hit, which by all accounts he often did, the batsman running to that end was normally out by yards.

I'm only glad I grew to know Ted well enough in later years to have cause to change some of my more bad-tempered early opinions of the man, and that our relationship evolved from that point. Now, how did that song go again?

Graham Dilley

Whenever I snatch a glance back at the events of Headingley in 1981, the strongest image in my mind's eye is of Graham Dilley, leaning on his bat, braying like a donkey.

When Dill ambled out to join me on that gloomy Monday afternoon in Leeds, the game, the Test match and the series were all gone – no question. After having followed on 227 runs behind Australia's first innings score of 401 for nine, when the 22-year-old Kent fast bowler took guard we could have been in better shape. At 135 for seven, we were still 92 runs shy of making the Aussies bat again and, not unnaturally, the mood in the dressing room was so optimistic that Mike Brearley had already changed into his civvies – although he slipped on a clean cricket shirt for appearances' sake.

'I reckon I'll have a hit,' Dill informed me. The exuberance of youth, I reckoned. Eighty minutes later he left, having made 56 out of our eighth wicket stand of 117 – only seven short of an England record against Australia – that changed Ashes history. It was, quite simply, the innings of his life, and it enabled me to go on to make 149 not out, the innings of my life.

Graham had already shown us he could block the crap out of it. On his debut in the first Test of the 1978–79 series Down Under in Perth, he made an unbeaten 38 in

'Never the most organized of human beings, Dill once equipped himself for a full three-month tour of the Caribbean with one pair of bowling boots.'

nearly three-and-a-half hours, and although clearly picked primarily for his talents as a swing bowler of considerable pace, even in the early stages of his Test career we harboured serious thoughts of converting him into a more than handy all-rounder.

Some of the shots he played on that extraordinary July afternoon eighteen months later represented comedy cricket at its finest – as did a large number of mine, hence the enduring vision of Dill wetting himself whenever one of my cartoon-style heaves carved a hole in pure fresh air. But one or two of his strokes, full-blooded drives, pulls or cuts resembled Sir Garfield Sobers in his pomp. Seriously. It was his success in executing them that sowed the seeds of realization in everyone present, not least myself, that what we were engaged in might turn out to be something more substantial than a private slogging contest. Consequently, the mood of the Aussie bowlers and fielders changed quickly from amused indifference through curiosity to irritation to something approaching anxiety.

Dilley didn't take any wickets when we bowled them out for 111 to complete the miraculous turnaround, but he did make one further telling contribution. Rod Marsh, their brilliant wicket-keeper/batsman was their last recognized bat. Even though their top-order players had come and gone, while Rod was still there they still had half a chance. But when Dill held on to a brilliant catch a few feet in from the fine-leg boundary at 74 for seven to dismiss him off Bob Willis's bowling, that was the moment we all really believed the impossible was possible after all.

As a bowler, I believe Graham suffered considerably from people bending his ear about line and length. When he started, he was genuinely quick, but once the coaches got at him things began to go wrong. Fortunately, he was able to cut through a lot of the nonsense and get back to the basics of what he was good at – generating outswing at genuine pace from a very slingy action, and on occasion he told me, the ball would come out of his hand so quickly that he wondered, 'Did I chuck that?' And his Test career was also cruelly disrupted, then cut short, by a succession of injuries, the worst affecting his neck and back. His problems with anti-inflammatory drugs later served as a timely warning of the dangers of burn-out faced by the top fast bowlers in the English game.

'A naturally laid-back man, he was never happier than when slumped on a sofa exercising his snoring muscles. Other than that, his most obvious characteristic was a dry sense of humour that allowed him to see the funny side more often than not.'

When I revealed in my book *The Botham Report* the fact that Dill's regular use of painkilling pills just to enable him to get out on the field had resulted in a medical diagnosis of liver damage, I hoped the warning of his example would add weight to the argument over central contracts that was finally won with dramatic results at the start of the 2000 English summer.

Dill could come across as a rather lugubrious bloke, but this was only because generally he managed to contain his passions. One time he failed, in spectacular fashion, was at Chrstchurch in the first Test of the 1987–88 tour to New Zealand, when, after having taken his Test-best six for 38 in the first innings, his commentary on less than cooperative umpiring in the second, 'Jesus, sh**, b******s', apparently, earned him a £250 fine.

Never the most organized of human beings, Dill once equipped himself for a full three-month tour of the Caribbean with one pair of bowling boots. When, in Jamaica, the heel snapped off one of them as he ran in to bowl his first spell of the trip, he borrowed a pair of mine which somehow managed to last until we caught the plane home. A naturally laid-back man, off the field he was never happier than when slumped on a sofa exercising his snoring muscles. Other than that, his most obvious characteristic was a dry sense of humour that allowed him to see the funny side more often than not, just as he did that day in 1981, with amazing results.

Allan Donald

His nickname was 'White Lightning', and Allan Donald was undeniably fast. But he was much, much more than just a speed merchant: to me, this guy was the heartbeat of South Africa's restoration to Test cricket's mainstream.

I used to love the way he would smear half a pound of zinc sunblock across his face, charge in and glare with that laser-beam stare at batsmen who played and missed outside off-stump. Donald looked like a warrior, and when he went on the rampage it was like a scene out of *Braveheart*. But I have total respect for the man because he always gave it everything, and as a bowler, he learned to adapt. When he first came on the scene, Allan Anthony Donald relied exclusively on sheer pace – but at Test-match level, speed alone is not enough to succeed, and later he added guile to his formidable firepower. By the closing overs of the twentieth century, he was one of the meanest acts around with a new cherry in his hand.

Always the shire horse rather than a show pony, his perception went beyond things you could do with a cricket ball. It's a little-known fact that Donald toned down his warpaint before South Africa's 1998 tour of England after complaining of headaches at close of play on bright, sunny days. He worked out that the sun's reflection off the zinc oxide protecting his face was forcing him to squint unnecessarily for long periods.

'His nickname was 'White Lightning', and Allan Donald was undeniably fast. But he was much, much more than just a speed merchant: to me, this guy was the heartbeat of South Africa's restoration to Test cricket's mainstream.'

By the summer of 2001, when he had joined the elite band of bowlers with more than 300 Test wickets to their names, it looked as if White Lightning had just about fizzled out. But what a fantastic servant he has been to Free State, Warwickshire and South Africa, and I would be amazed if his country did not make use of his know-how and experience in a coaching capacity for years to come.

In England, of course, he's best remembered for those riveting confrontations with Mike Atherton which, for my money, were among the most scintillating passages of Test cricket in my lifetime. If we really have seen the last of Donald in five-day combat I shall miss his eyeball-to-eyeball battles with Athers, of which three stand out in my memory.

First, there was the England captain's monumental 11-hour rearguard at The Wanderers in December 1995, when Atherton had to survive some torrid stuff from Donald on his way to 185 not out, an innings regarded universally as a masterpiece of concentration and technique.

Then, in 1998, came that white-hot session at Trent Bridge, when Donald's concerted appeals for a gloved catch behind were rejected by umpire Steve Dunne. At first, 'AD' was incredulous when neither batsman nor umpire budged; then he just went ballistic. Channelling all his pent-up fury into the next ball, Atherton got lucky with a streaky inside edge to the boundary – and Donald was so livid he was fit to burst. Atherton went on to finish unbeaten on 98 as England squared the series, and in his autobiography – also called *White Lightning* – AD admitted he was so angry he wanted to 'kill' the Lancashire opener.

Donald was finally able to get his man, for a duck, when England were put in on a greentop in Johannesburg in November 1999 and crashed to 2 for four in the opening 20 minutes. Favourable as the conditions were to the quicks, this was a beautiful piece of bowling – slanted in at the right-hander from wide on the return crease and ducking in late. A perfect illustration of the way Donald learned to 'think' out his opponents instead of just blasting them out.

BEEFY ON DONALD

Born: 20 October 1966, Bloemfontein
Country: South Africa
Tests: 71
Wickets: 329
Average: 22.10
Beefy analysis: Lightning-quick fast bowler who gave it everything and more. Warrior to the core.
Beefy moment: Eyeball-to-eyeball confrontation with Mike Atherton during their thrilling passage of play at Trent Bridge in 1998.
Do mention: South Africa v England, Johannesburg Test, 1999–00 (his match figures 11 for 127).
Don't mention: South Africa v West Indies, Bridgetown, 1991–92 (a pair on his Test debut).

With Shaun Pollock's immaculate line and dangerous movement off the seam at the other end, Donald formed one half of a world-class double act with the new ball for South Africa. Those two were a handful for every top order in the world, although I'm sure Pollock would be the first to put his hands up and admit that he owes much of his success to the hostility and aggression of Donald.

Another string to Donald's bow has been his potency in one-day cricket, where he decided he couldn't control the new white ball and stepped down to come on first change once the shine had gone. Most fast bowlers would have carried on taking the new ball regardless, but that's typical of Donald – doing what's best for his team instead of letting his ego get in the way. In many ways, it turned out to be a smart tactical move because there was no respite for the batsman when he came on and started flinging 90 mph missiles into the blockhole.

'Allan Donald is a major reason why South Africa emerged as the most serious challenger to Australia's domination of both Test cricket and one-day internationals at the start of the twenty-first century.'

Allan Donald is a major reason why South Africa emerged as the most serious challenger to Australia's domination of both Test cricket and one-day internationals at the start of the twenty-first century, and I have nothing but admiration for the uncompromising way he's played the game. Donald? Duck.

Phil Edmonds

One of the strangest blokes I ever played with; someone who could impress you with his ability, amuse you with his wit, but at times, as his Middlesex and England captains, Mike Brearley and Mike Gatting found, leave you speechless with his oddness.

During one of his journeys round the bend, in a county game at Uxbridge, Philippe Henri threw the ball deliberately at Gatt. The reason? The barking mad left-arm spinner had been refused permission by his skipper to leave the field in order to make a phone call, and tried to exact his revenge by launching a return from the boundary straight at his skipper's nut.

He once decided to let everyone know how bored he was with a match that was apparently going nowhere by reading a newspaper in the outfield. His unique method of persuading Gatt to give him a field setting he wanted if it was against his captain's judgement was to ask him to field at short leg then feed the opposing batsmen a succession of balls to sweep, or at silly point, then bowl a few full-tosses outside the off stump, for as long as it took the skipper to come round to his way of thinking.

Perhaps the most hilarious passage of play in the last decade of the twentieth century took place during his comeback match for Middlesex against Nottinghamshire at Trent Bridge in June 1993, at the age of 41, five years after he had turned from first-class cricket to pursue his other interests in the City and elsewhere. With Phil Tufnell recovering after an appendix operation, Philippe answered an SOS from the club to renew his partnership with John Emburey, arriving at the ground by Rolls-Royce, of course, and, according to him, 'bowled exquisitely' to take four for 48.

The problem arose because, after such a long absence from any kind of serious physical activity, let alone six hours in the field and 28 overs, Phil's body started coming apart at the seams. He had been suffering from a chronic back complaint for some time, and when it flared up the day after his long bowl, he decided to chuck a few more painkillers than usual down his neck, reasoning that the more pills he swallowed, the less pain he'd feel. That part of his diagnosis was correct. What he didn't anticipate were the side-effects of the increased dosage.

A few of his colleagues noticed his somewhat unsteady gait as he walked out to field during Notts' second innings, but put it down to high spirits. It was only when Philippe started belting out songs from the shows that the rest of them noticed things were not altogether as they should be. Still, Phil's antics might have gone unnoticed had he not been fielding at square leg at both ends. Between overs, he would sprint across from the position on one side of the wicket to the same position on the other side, and calamity finally struck when, flapping his arms like an albatross and squawking like Donald Duck, he attempted to long-jump the width of the wicket and landed flat on his face no more than halfway across. That evening, he spent two hours in the dressing room bath eating cold turkey.

Henri was also responsible for one of the oddest sights I ever witnessed in Test cricket. In the early 1980s one of the New Zealand batsman we came across, and I cannot for the life of me recall his name, had a habit of running up and down the pitch as soon as he came to the wicket, probably to get himself loosened up. Edmonds went in one day, took guard, stopped the bowler in his run-up, then sprinted up and down the track as though going for quick runs before settling back into his stance and waiting for the bowler to proceed. Gatt believed the best way of handling these moments of madness was to intervene only when he had absolutely no alternative. For the most part, he found Henri's eccentricity as diverting as it could be distracting.

Brearley, though, was far from amused with him, in one of only two moments in his entire captaincy that I witnessed him lose his rag with

'A quite brilliant fielder, capable of making extremely difficult catches look ridiculously easy, he was also more than adequate with the bat, although he rarely made the most of that talent.'

a team-mate (the other time was, inevitably, with Boycott, when he complained of a mystery ailment shortly before the start of a Test match in Australia). Phil had not been selected for the match in question, but instead of carrying out twelfth man duties as anyone in his situation would have been expected and should have been willing to do, he sulked. When we came off for lunch in sweltering hot Perth on the first morning of the game in question, there were no drinks prepared and Phil was making a great show of sitting on his backside reading the papers. Brears went ballistic. While there were occasions when Phil gave us good reason to question his sanity, there was no doubting his ability. Tall in his delivery stride with a beautiful pivot, he was an extremely gifted, orthodox (if that word could ever be applied to him) left-arm spinner. On helpful wickets he could turn the ball considerably and the unpredictability in his nature was mirrored by what he did with the cricket ball in his hand. It was quite impossible to anticipate what was coming next, including the bouncer he used to send down just to keep everyone on their toes, for the very simple reason that half the time he had no idea himself. In many ways, his quirkiness was the perfect foil to the reliable, grinding, metronomic persistence of Emburey at the other end. What's more, he loved the competition of trying to outdo his county colleague. One delivery he sent down to New Zealand's Bev Congdon in a Test match at the Oval stands out in my mind as probably the best ball I've ever seen bowled by a spinner of his type. On a wicket which had played like a shirtfront all through the match, he got one to dip in late, pitch around middle stump and hit the top of off. It was just about an unplayable ball.

'Phil was an utter oddball. He would do things to antagonize people, apparently deliberately, and you never knew what he was going to do next. And we loved him for it.'

A quite brilliant fielder, capable of making extremely difficult catches look ridiculously easy he was also more than adequate with the bat, although he rarely made the most of that talent.

But as a bloke, above all, Phil was an utter oddball. He would do things to antagonize people, apparently deliberately. You never, ever knew what comming next. And we loved him for it.

John Edrich

B ravery seemed to course through the veins of the Edrich
family. John's cousin, Bill, who during peacetime was
inseparable from his friend and Middlesex and England
batting twin Denis Compton on and off the field, attained the
rank of Squadron Leader during World War II. John's courage
above and beyond the call was demonstrated most
memorably on that grim and grey evening of the third day of
the Old Trafford Test between England and West Indies in
1976, when Brian Close, aged 45 and Edrich, a mere pup at
39, were called upon to withstand one of the most frightening

assaults ever launched on a cricket field. In a final session that shamed the game the two batsmen took everything thrown at them by Michael Holding & Co. with no protection whatsoever from the umpires and without helmets. But if the Windies were expecting their opponents to be cowed into submission at the end of it, Edrich's reaction probably took the wind out of their sails. Coming off the pitch, he stopped suddenly in his tracks and burst out laughing.

'What's so funny?' asked Close.

'I've just looked at the scoreboard,' he replied. 'You've been out here for seventy minutes and been clobbered everywhere. Do you know how many runs you've scored in that time?'

'No,' said Close.

'One,' replied Edrich. 'I hope it was worth the pain.'

Typical of the kind of selectorial good manners all England cricketers have been privileged to experience down the years, neither man was ever picked for England again.

As a player, I don't think John ever really received the recognition he deserved. For a start, he deserved quite a lot for putting up with Geoff Boycott's running between wickets. John used to joke that during his days as an England opener, his biggest worry was not the bowler charging in trying

'Bravery seemed to course through the veins of the Edrich family.'

to knock his head off but the guy with whom he was batting. Understandable, really, when you consider that Boycs was to rotating the strike what Hansie Cronje is to the future of challenging declarations.

John was never the most stylish of batsmen, but he was first-class at frustrating opening attacks by nudging and nurdling the ball into the open spaces for ones and twos, and I can't recall seeing a better 'leaver' of the ball outside the off-stump. From the other end I can tell you that the most irritating thing about bowling to a compact left-hander like him is when you produce the perfect outswinger, only for him to play deliberately inside the delivery, rendering all your craft and skill utterly pointless.

Opening attacks also knew that you had to get John out early in his innings. Once 'in', more often than not he made sure he stayed in for a long time, as the Kiwis found to their cost when he milked them for his highest Test score of 310 not out against them at Headingley in 1965.

Ray Illingworth and I didn't often see eye-to-eye on cricketing matters during his time as chairman of selectors in the mid-1990s, but one appointment I had no argument with was his choice of John for England batting coach in 1996, even at the age of 58. I don't think John ever saw himself as a great textbook technician. On his appointment he indicated as much when he said, 'Old ladies of 80 are wishing me well. I can't let them down, can I? Anyone got a coaching book?'

'As a player, I don't think John ever really received the recognition he deserved. For a start, he deserved quite a lot for putting up with Geoff Boycott.'

I do think the age divide between him and the players was probably unbridgable, as was proved in the terrible mishandling of Devon Malcolm by the entire management team who believed misguidedly that they could provoke a response from the fast bowler by bullying him. But from the perspective of passing on first-hand experience, I'm sure one or two of the batsmen would have learned something valuable from John had they been more prepared to listen.

As you would expect from a guy of his character, his response to the news that he was suffering from leukaemia was simple, straightforward and positive. However long he had left, he told me, he was going to live it to the full.

Ernie Els

Provided we salvaged two sets of golf clubs, a few cases of wine and a box of matches – to light the barbecue – from our shipwreck, Ernie Els would be among my first-choice companions as a desert island castaway.

Ernie is probably the most relaxed golfer, and one of the most easy-going professional sportsmen, I've ever seen. That's why fellow players on the Tour nicknamed him 'Big Easy', and Nick Price once said, 'I've taken to calling him 'Horizontal' because he is so laid-back.' Temperamentally, Ernie is a role model for any youngster, from the crazy golf course on Blackpool's Golden Mile to your local municipal pitch-and-putt or a championship links ... and for anyone else who's ever picked up a club. You never see him fling his putter away in a strop, or chastise his caddie for choosing the wrong club.

As a player, he is a colossus. If Tiger Woods had not been around, how many Majors would Els have won by now? I loved his response to a question about what he would need to shoot in order to win another Major, and he replied, 'Tiger!'

In another era, Ernie would be acclaimed as one of golf's all-time greats, but, as he admitted, 'We may be getting our butts kicked by Tiger, but that's not because we're intimidated by him. We are just getting beat because he's a phenomenal player who has been able to pull out something extra special when it's required. I don't think even the greatest heavyweight boxers have ever been so far ahead of their rivals.'

For all that, I can't think of another golfer who has been in the shake-up at the climax of so many big tournaments in modern times more than Ernie.

When he finally won the first of his two US Open titles at Oakmont in 1994, he was still celebrating 24 hours later; although I wasn't there to see it happen in person, I was so pleased for him that I was still raising a glass to him the following week. Somehow I don't think we've toasted the last of Ernie's Major triumphs, and it couldn't happen to a nicer bloke or a more sociable guy.

As a keen golfer myself, I can only envy Ernie's rhythm and timing. His technique is so smooth, you never know whether he's going to hit the ball or just taking a practice swing. We have been mates for quite a few years now, especially since he bought a home at Wentworth – where his barbecues are always a highlight of the calendar, and he is always fascinating company. Els is a well-read guy, and away from the golf course you can often find him watching cricket at Lord's or rugby at Twickenham – especially if South Africa are the visitors – or immersed in a sporting personality's autobiography or bestseller. His bookshelves include a signed copy of Nelson Mandela's biography and, such is the regard in which Ernie is held back home in South Africa, he used to have the number of the direct line to Mandela's office when Mandela was President. Just think about that – I wonder how many of Britain's leading footballers, cricketers, rugby players, golfers or athletes have Tony Blair's private number at 10 Downing Street in their phone books?

If I get the chance, between commentary box commitments, I always try and play in the Ernie Els Invitational Pro-am down in South Africa that takes place just before Christmas and raises a lot of money for his charity foundation. Ernie supports a lot of youth development schemes, and thanks to his foundation there are now a lot of talented young golfers – both black and white – making waves in the amateur ranks. Just imagine how proud it would make him feel, and what a terrific story it would be, if a black kid from the townships was crowned Open champion or measured up for a green jacket at Augusta thanks to the Ernie Els Foundation – not that he is the type to shout it from the rooftops if it happened.

> 'Ernie is probably the most relaxed golfer, and one of the most easy-going professional sportsmen, I've ever seen.'

Ernie doesn't like blowing his own trumpet, nor does he enjoy speaking at functions. He once told me that he finds it more nerve-racking to stand up and say a few words in front of sponsors or corporate guests than a four-foot putt to win a championship. And his career in public speaking may never recover from his experience at last year's invitational event, when his address didn't get past the first sentence.

Ernie had barely risen to his feet when a flatulent diner in the front row whose name for the moment somehow escapes me inadvertently released a gust of wind; and this quite uncalled-for blast of air-conditioning was enough to make the guest speaker break down in fits of giggles. It was like the famous interlude on BBC Radio's *Test Match Special* in 1991, when I was dismissed hit-wicket by Curtly Ambrose at the Oval, and commentator Jonathan Agnew's observation, 'Botham couldn't quite get his leg over,' reduced Brian Johnston to tears of laughter. For Ernie, that was it: speech over.

Fortunately, Els doesn't need to be a masterful orator to increase his public profile. He is already a sensational ambassador for the Rainbow Nation.

John Emburey

Without doubt one of the greatest moaners the game of cricket has ever known. John Ernest Emburey ('Ernie') moaned for Middlesex and England as a player and captain, he moaned for Middlesex, Northamptonshire and England A as coach and for the senior England side as assistant coach. And he was absolutely brilliant at it.

His moaning was not the type that dragged you down; it was thoroughly and consistently entertaining.

When rooming with him on England tours to far-off foreign parts, it was always a delight to find that our particular shoebox

contained no television. That meant I would be treated to hour upon hour of Ernie's moaning and sleep, when appropriate, would come a little more easily and a lot more quickly.

The other verbal speciality for which he is rightly famous is swearing. Ernie has an extraordinary capacity for it. He does it without thinking, much as most of us breathe in and out, and with just as little offence intended. In fact the doctors will be able to tell when Ernie has finally fallen of his perch for it will be the moment he is no longer bombarding them with words beginning with 'F'. Mike Selvey, his Middlesex colleague, once explained: 'A conversation with him would be 50 per cent shorter if he deleted the expletives.'

How true. Consider this response to an inquiry concerning his latest injury concern: 'Well,' he said, 'to be honest, the fackin' facker's fackin' facked.'

Or this offering, after I explained how my dismissal trying to heave Aussie left-arm spinner Ray Bright out of Lord's was caused by my pad impeding the smooth passage of my bat: 'Funny that, Beef,' he said, 'I never fackin' realized your fackin' pad was strapped to your fackin' 'ead.'

'John moaned for Middlesex and England as a player and captain, he moaned for Middlesex, Northamptonshire and England A as coach and for the senior England side as assistant coach. And he was absolutely brilliant at it.'

During our time together with England and afterwards Ernie has been a loyal friend to me, never more so than when he organized my 'great escape' from Lord's following the TCCB disciplinary hearing on 29 May 1986 for, apparently, bringing the game into 'fackin' disrepute'. My crime had been in admitting, in an article in the the *Mail on Sunday*, to using cannabis, and failing to clear the article with the Board in advance. Several prominent ex-players, including Denis Compton had gone into print to insist that nothing short of a life ban would be appropriate punishment. In the event, I was banned from all cricket for two months and in stepped Ernie and his wife Susie to help a friend in need.

First, he managed to spirit me away from the ground under the noses of the waiting media. I just wasn't in the mood to talk, and had I been asked the wrong question I might have said something I would later have regretted. While the media pack was hovering, Ernie told me to get into his car, handed me a blanket and told me to keep my nut down. By the time the press guys realized I'd slipped through their net I was back at Ernie's house with Kath, Liam, Susie and friends, and about to begin a mission to drain a case of very fine claret of which Ernie had just taken delivery.

'He has an extraordinary capacity for swearing. He does it without thinking, much as most of us breathe in and out, and with just as little offence intended.'

Then, while all kinds of thoughts were running around in my brain, including a notion to quit the game altogether, Ernie was one of those who helped to make me think again. Kath and I had had quite a bloody time of things in the previous couple of years, from the moment the *Mail on Sunday* published their 'sex, drugs and rock 'n' roll' allegations about the 1983–84 tour to New Zealand, through my relationship with Lord Tim Hudson in 1985 to bizarre and lurid tales of bed-breaking in the Caribbean a year later. This last controversy was close to breaking the camel's back.

I simply could not see the point of carrying on if it meant the kind of intrusion in our lives normally reserved for mass murderers, Great Train Robbers or, as one of their number later found to her and the nation's cost, members of the royal family. No matter where we went or how we tried to live, we felt surrounded by the headlines. The intensity of the hounding was just plain mad and we had both had more than enough of it.

'Don't give them the satisfaction,' was the gist of Ernie's argument. 'Give it up now and they've won.' And, despite everything, I'm grateful I listened.

As a player Ernie made the very most of his talent. Best, I always felt, when bowling in tandem with the eccentric Phil Edmonds, with both Middlesex and England, he was always buzzing with theories and ideas about how a certain opponent could be winkled out. And, even though the masterblaster helped himself to the fastest Test century of all time in the fifth match of our '86 series in Antigua in the process (off 56 balls in 83 minutes) I'm sure that the one he had for Viv Richards would have worked eventually!

Ernie's batting had to be seen to be believed; the way he squeezed balls from outside off stump behind square on the leg side, and vice versa, made me wonder whether he'd read the coaching manual back to front, but whatever the purists might have thought, he found a method that worked for him and stuck with it. His catching in the slips and his general fielding were at times brilliant and his captaincy skills surely worth more than the two Tests during which he was allowed to employ them against the West Indies in 1988, the completely bonkers summer of five England skippers. 'Fackin' search me,' as he might have said at the time.

David English

Former film extra, with a starring role as a dead German in *A Bridge Too Far*; manager of the Bee Gees; chief executive of RSO Records; creator of the Bunbury cartoon cricketers and the charity cricket team of the same name; organizer and massive supporter of the English Schools Cricket Association festivals and the Under-15 World Cup; Master of Ceremonies for many of my roadshow expeditions; and the funniest man I've ever met.

I first came across 'the Loon' during my days on the MCC groundstaff at Lord's in the mid-1970s when English was a good club player with nearby Middlesex club, Finchley.

He's started to tell me the same joke every time I've been in his company since then, and one day he'll finish it. In the meantime he'll continue to absolutely live for the game of cricket.

The list of young players who appeared in the ESCA Under-15 festivals, then went on to play first-class and Test cricket is impressive indeed. Stars such as Mike Atherton, Alec Stewart, Nasser Hussain and Graham Thorpe all owe Dave a debt of gratitude for the drive that has ensured the event continues to go from strength to strength. Those who run the England Schools Cricket Association will tell you that the festival would have died a death had it not been for David banging the drum to raise sponsorship, interest and awareness.

As for Dave's other passion, the Bunbury XI itself, surely the only way to explain how he has persuaded some of the biggest names from the worlds of entertainment, sport and public life, from Eric Clapton to John Major, from Joanna Lumley to Viv Richards, from Gary Lineker to Rory Bremner to give up their time on a Sunday afternoon to bat at No. 17, out of 29, or to bowl 12th change out of 27, field at eleventh slip to a new-ball bowler running in off 20 paces and sending down a real Jaffa – as in a real Jaffa orange, peel and all – is his puckish enthusiasm.

English has the knack of grinding down resistance with a feather duster. He's just too nice a bloke and too sincere in his support for the causes to be turned down. Once he even persuaded me to go against my word and my better judgement when I was forced to make a brief cricketing comeback in a game of beach cricket just to get him off my case.

Humour is always around the Loon, whether he motivates it or is the butt of it. He'll never forget the first question he pulled out of the hat on the inaugural roadshow. It read: 'My name is Kate and I live above the chip shop in the High Street. Is it true you are hung like a giraffe?'

It came out as: 'My name is Kate and I live above the chip shop in the High street. Is it true you take leg stump guard?'

Such ability to think on his feet made him the perfect MC for the shows I did with Viv and Allan Lamb and, from time to time, to help take my mind off the pressure of performing at the highest level of the game.

I have to admit that David has often had the misfortune to be on the wrong end of one of my practical jokes. Perhaps the most memorable took place on an unsuccessful fishing trip to Ullapool in the north-west of Scotland. Bored with the lack of fish coming our way I grew restless. Stand by your beds. Having come across a dead seagull on one of my trips I decided to give it a proper Christian burial, so I took it back to the house we were staying in and placed it carefully under the covers of David's four-poster. It wasn't until about 3 o'clock the following morning that he noticed he wasn't sleeping alone.

He too has been known to get up to some tricks, particularly in the field of labour-saving. On my inaugural walk for Leukaemia Research, in 1985, one of the many traditions was that the first person to complete the day's march was awarded the coveted yellow jersey. Bearing in mind his flat feet and the oxygen treatment he requires to complete the 300-yard trip from his house to the Tube, when David picked up the treasured garment for the third day in succession I began to get suspicious. While I weaved in and out of traffic on the fourth day something in the aroma of cigar smoke wafting out from behind a newspaper in the back of a stationary black cab rang a bell. Out of curiosity I opened the door, pulled down the paper and found him, Bernard Hinault Anglais, on the end of it.

But give him a charity cause and you'll find no-one better to fight it as he proved when organizing the memorial match in aid of Malcolm Marshall's family at the Honourable Artillery Club ground in the City of London in 2000. The zeal and imagination he demonstrates time and again in this environment persuaded me long ago that if any county wanted to take a punt on his marketing skills they would certainly get more than they bargained for and some of it would even be beneficial.

Nick Faldo

Quite early in my career with Somerset, I happened to be playing in a golf day at Welwyn Garden City when the local professional took me to one side. 'Watch that lad,' he said, pointing to a youngster who was practising near the clubhouse at the time. 'You'll hear a lot about him in the future.'

At the time I was left with little more than the vague impression of a boy, probably in his early teens. I didn't stay around to watch him play. But he later went on to become one of the best golfers in the world, winning six Major titles. The youngster was Nick Faldo.

Once Nick had started to make a name for himself, with my interest in golf and constant travelling around the globe, it was inevitable that one day we'd meet and it was during an early Australian tour, when he was playing the circuit Down Under, that Bob Willis and I went out to dinner with him and started a long friendship.

Although we've yet to play together in a pro-am, over the years I've enjoyed following him down fairways on many occasions at tournaments. Probably the most memorable was during the final round of the Open at Muirfield in 1987. That was the year that he was fighting neck and neck in the final round against Paul Azinger. While the American's nerve seemed to snap over the closing stretch I watched in awe as Nick held his cool to win his first major and saw for the first time the quality he had that separates the great from the good – the ability to stay focused under the most intense pressure.

'While Nick's public image is based on a relentless pursuit of perfection some have described as obsessive, you can take it from me that he is also a man who knows how to enjoy himself away from the golf course.'

If you had to pick one round in his career to date – and more about the use of that phrase later – for which I most admired Nick, it was his great comeback at Augusta to win his sixth and last major the 1996 Masters. To have pulled off that astonishing victory against the Australian, Greg Norman, ranked World No 1, having started the final day six shots behind him, was a magnificent achievement. It also told the whole story of Nick's character, so determined, single-minded, dedicated and stubborn that earlier in his career, even with several tour victories to his name, he was prepared to rip apart the swing of his youth and painstakingly rebuild it under the guidance of David Leadbetter.

His approach and attitude can be summed up in something he once told me. 'There are times out there on the course when you are on your own, utterly. Those are the times when you are tested; when you find out how much you really want it.'

While Nick's public image is based on a relentless pursuit of perfection some have described as obsessive, you can take it from me that he is also a man who knows how to enjoy himself away from the golf course. In particular, I remember him attending one of the six dinners that a group of businessmen staged for me to mark my retirement from cricket in 1993 at the Café Royal in London. Nick ended up sitting next to me on the top table. The whole evening was spent discussing the merits of various Spanish wines, which we both enjoy immensely. So determined, single-minded, dedicated, stubborn and relentless was he in his pursuit of perfection that we went through every single one on the wine list to find it.

The reason I used the words 'to date' when talking about Nick's victory over Greg Norman is that I can't move on from him without making a prediction that I hope will prove just as prophetic as that comment from the pro at Welwyn all those years ago.

Nick's failure to win regularly since his victory with David Carter in the 1998 World Cup at Auckland has led to many claims that he is finished as a golfing force. That I simply refuse to believe. When you have so much natural talent combined with a technically sound game and a clear and decisive mental approach, you just do not lose it all overnight. Sporting form goes in cycles and though many young professionals now hit the ball much further off the tee than Nick does, there is so much more to golf than raw power alone.

It was interesting to read at the start of summer 2001 that Nick, while in America, paired up again with his Swedish caddie, Fanny Sunesson, who was on his bag for ten years at the height of his career. You never know – that just might be the route that leads him back to the top. I'm sure he still has the game to get there.

The Fishermen

To those who have never fished, the art of catching salmon when shown on TV might seem fairly straightforward. Believe me when I say it is anything but simply a case of casting a line into the water and waiting for the fish to bite.

The fact that I now find fishing the perfect way to relax, and would highly recommend a day out on the riverbank to anyone whose stress levels are close to breaking point, is due entirely to one man – Charlie Martin. In the times when things looked blackest, a few hours of gentle relaxation helped to clear the mind and cleanse the soul.

'Take me to your leader, earthling, or I will show you the rest.' Dickie Bird in typically bonkers mood.

Nasser Hussain was a revelation as captain, leading England to four series victories.

White Lightning Allan Donald was the heartbeat of the new South African Test side. Fast, fearless and uncompromising. Donald? Duck.

One of the most eccentric blokes
I ever played with; Phil
Edmonds was an impressive
cricketer, an amusing man and
a complete oddball.

'Now then, Beef, any chance of
writing something for the English
Schools' Cricket Festival brochure?'
David English wears you down with
his humour and sheer enthusiasm.

At Headingley in 1981 Graham Dilley batted like Sobers and brayed like a donkey.

Mick Jagger doesn't like cricket; he loves it.

David, where's yer troosers?

'Listen, mate,' I was told by Dennis Lillee, the finest fast bowler in the world, 'you hold the bat still and I'll aim at it.'

Derek Randall, or 'Rags' as we knew him, was mad as a hatter but good enough to tame the great Dennis Lillee.

Big Bird Joel Garner had a heart to match his giant size, and sometimes a thirst as well.

The best sledger in world cricket and one of the best stumpers as well. Ian Healy and Shane Warne had an almost telepathic understanding.

My soul-mate, the masterblaster Vivian Richards, had a passion for cricket, a lust for runs … and a weakness for preposterous cars.

After Lillee, the best I ever faced. Malcolm Marshall was taken too early.

Rod Marsh and Sunil Gavaskar knew that if cricket wasn't fun before, during and afterwards, it wasn't worth it.

Ask not for whom Curtly Ambrose's mum is tolling the bell.

'I'll be your dog,' Merv Hughes tells the pitch invader. But Allan Border loved his ferocity.

Mike Gatting could have eaten for England. In fact, he could probably have eaten England.

Elton John and I shared a distrust of the popular press and an immaculate off-drive.

Nelson Mandela's lack of desire for revenge against the apartheid regime that caged him for 27 years left me lost for words.

Why did he do it? Only Hansie Cronje will ever know what made him betray his country and his sport.

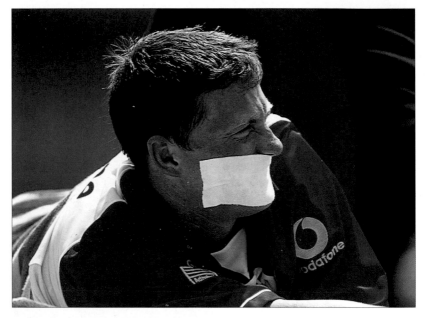

For once speechless, Darren Gough is the original unburstable bubble. How I would have enjoyed sharing the new ball with him at our peak.

'Oy, skippy … got a fag?' Phil Tufnell asks a friendly Aussie.

In fact, I would go so far as to say that fishing almost certainly extended my cricket career by a couple of years at least.

Charlie and I met quite by chance one day when I was in Scotland on a family holiday, trying my luck for salmon on the River Teith. I couldn't have been more than eighteen, and while fishing had fascinated me since my early childhood I really didn't have much of a clue as to what I was supposed to be doing. For a few hours I stood there, naïvely trying this and that without any serious hope of catching anything, and I was on the verge of packing up my rod when Charlie came wandering along the riverbank and started a conversation.

> 'Charlie and I met quite by chance one day when I was in Scotland on a family holiday, trying my luck for salmon on the River Teith.'

It turned out that Charlie was a ghillie, and over the next three or four hours I listened spellbound. In that time I found out that what he doesn't know about catching salmon just isn't worth knowing. He told me where to go for the best chance of finding fish, all about their habits, and the way to tie lures and knots. It was my first-ever lesson and he had me well and truly hooked. Charlie also agreed to join my whole family at our hotel later that night, when his tales of fishing had us all hanging on his every word. From that day he has remained a firm family friend.

From the love of fishing that Charlie instilled in me I have since had so much fun – big-game fishing at sea off Australia and the West Indies and trying my hand at salmon and trout on the rivers and lakes of Zimbabwe and New Zealand. And I like to think I have passed on some of my enthusiasm to guys like Mike Atherton, who now finds fishing the perfect way to unwind after a high-pressure duel with the likes of Glenn McGrath, Allan Donald, Curtly Ambrose or Wasim Akram.

Apart from a continuous stream of lessons on the art of fishing, Charlie has also taken the trouble to make me personalized rods from traditional greenheart wood. They, like Charlie, are priceless.

When we first met he'd never set foot outside Scotland in his life. And his first trip to London to attend the recording of my appearance on *This Is Your Life* in the autumn of 1981 was a show-stopper. Needless to say, he insisted on wearing his kilt from morning until nightfall, which was a sight to behold, and even though hardly anyone could understand his broad accent, he took the place by storm.

In those early days, Charlie also introduced me to another great Scottish fishing pal, Willie Carmichael, also known as the Old Celt. We came across him one day with friends as he was fishing for salmon from pools full of fish leaping all around him. The secret of his success – prawns for bait! These days, that practice is absolutely banned, of course, but Willie, a Glaswegian who once served in the army but has long since been pensioned off, thank goodness, is very much from the old school of angling. When he is not playing indoor bowls, every spare minute is spent with a rod and line in his hands. I don't want to libel a close friend but I have to say that with his knowledge of the many ways to land a fish he would make the world's greatest poacher. I've accused him of it to his face, but he assures me that he's never poached anything in his life except on top of a cooker.

Apart from enjoying every minute of his company, like Charlie, he too has passed on tips that have helped me get the most out of the pastime that helped me become the cricketer I was by enabling me to escape from the game when necessary.

Keith Fletcher

It is hard to credit but prior to Mike Gatting's spot of un-pleasantness with the Pakistan umpire, the late Shakoor Rana, in 1987, the greatest moment of on-field controversy involving an England captain during that decade surrounded the behaviour of Keith Fletcher during the 1981–82 tour to India.

Looking at Fletch it's difficult to believe that the word controversial could ever be legitimately applied to him. Not that as player, captain and coach of both his beloved Essex and England he was ever anything but a tough, ruthless and quick-witted competitor.

It is just that, as the nickname 'Gnome' he still glories in the county he has served man, boy and garden ornament for 30 years implies, his unassuming appearance and demeanour made him look far more at home among the shrubs or on a peaceful riverbank than in the bubbling pressure cookers of world cricket.

Still, at the time, his actions on the first day of the second Test against India at Bangalore in December 1981 caused such a kerfuffle that not only was the incident reported with the kind of tut-tutting displeasure that coloured much of the oceans of copy about Gatt's finger-wagging in Faisalabad, like that unhappy spectacle it also cost the England captain his job. Sad for Fletch, bad for English cricket, and to my mind, just plain mad.

What was Fletcher's crime? Simply that, after having been sawn off by a poor umpiring decision, he let his displeasure at the decision be known by flicking off the bail with his bat. It wasn't pretty, and to be fair, Fletch realized immediately he had overstepped the mark, and later wrote a letter of apology to the Indian Board. To the players it was one of those things that happens when frustration gets the better of you. It wasn't a malicious action, or nasty. He didn't smash down the stumps or abuse an umpire. Yet *Wisden's* report of the match summed up the over-reaction of those back at Lord's sipping their pink gins. 'Fletcher,' stated *Wisden*, 'given out caught at the wicket when he swept at Shastri, so far forgot the standards expected of an England captain that he used his bat to cuff the stumps awry as he turned for the pavilion.'

And when we got back to England after a long and dull series on flat pitches prepared by the Indians to make sure they held on to the lead they'd gained in the first of six Tests, followed by the inaugural Test against Sri Lanka, they made sure Fletch paid the price.

There is no doubt in my mind that Fletch possessed one of the best cricket brains in the game. It served him brilliantly as player and captain of Essex and his country, and listening to him plotting in the slips about just how he was going to engineer someone's dismissal was an education in itself. It could be so disconcerting for the batsman involved that sometimes they worried themselves into an early grave.

He always seemed to be ahead of the game, could identify a player's weakness instantly, was rarely wrong, and was always looking for ways to make things happen. In much the same way as Brian Close turned Somerset from everyone's favourite country bumpkins into steely winners, Fletch, with the help of players such as John Lever, Ken McEwan and Graham Gooch, transformed Essex from the rather quaint poor relations of the home counties to become the dominant force in domestic cricket.

For these reasons, he was an entirely appropriate choice to take on the job when Mike Brearley retired at the end of the Ashes series of '81. But he was always better out in the thick of things than sitting or planning from the sidelines, which is why he did not enjoy the success as England coach that many

'There is no doubt in my mind that Fletch possessed one of the best cricket brains in the game. Listening to him plotting in the slips about just how he was going to engineer someone's dismissal was an education in itself.'

believed he was bound to do when he replaced the retiring Micky Stewart in 1993. Essex colleagues of his told me that when the run chase was on he simply could not bear to watch, preferring instead to experience the tension from trap one of the dressing room water closets, if you'll pardon my French. And one comment he made when coach of the side on their 1993–94 tour to the West Indies indicated just how wrapped up in the fortunes of his side he used to become: 'It's nice to go into the rest day as favourites,' he said, halfway through the third Test in Trinidad (England were trailing 2–0 at the time). 'I might get some sleep.'

But a year later, his commitment counted for nothing, when, at a lunch for sportswriters, Ray Illingworth, his former England colleague and captain, and now chairman of selectors belittled him publicly before the 1994–95 Ashes series had even started. 'He's team manager, isn't he?' chortled Illingworth. 'He nicks a few catches in practice', then levered himself into his position with the help of TCCB chairman, Denis Silk.

As a batsman, Fletch had his own style, and against spin bowling he was a master of waiting until the last moment and playing the ball off the pitch. They never forgave him in Yorkshire for playing in place of their own Phil Sharpe in a Test at Headingley then promptly dropping a couple of the kind of slip catches that Sharpe was famous for pocketing. And they never forgot him in Australia for the distance a Jeff Thomson bouncer travelled to cover point via the peak of his England cap on the ferocious 1974–75 Ashes tour, and the noise it made in the process.

Many other players, colleagues and foes alike, recall Fletcher's other most endearing quality, his unique inability to put a name to a face. On that England tour to India, the skipper was required to introduce his players to Prime Minister Indira Gandhi. All went well until he reached reserve wicket-keeper, Jack Richards at the end of the line-up.

'And this, Madam Premier, this is, er, err … may I introduce, er … erm … I'd like you to meet … er … Tiddler. He keeps wicket.'

Derek Pringle was presented to the Essex committee at the start of his first season as 'er, 'ignell', a name many committee members still know him by to this day. And when England moved to Sri Lanka at the end of the 1981–82 season, he paid homage to the past and present names of the island by declaring his side was 'very pleased to be here in Sri Lon'.

Angus
Fraser

The unluckiest England bowler in modern times, he tells me. And he might just be right. Gus's finest year in Test cricket turned out to be his last, when he took a shedload of wickets in consecutive contests against the West Indies and South Africa, and in the second of those played his full part in their first win in a full five-Test series for more than a decade. During that period, from the aborted first Test against the West Indies at Sabina Park in January 1998 until the last against South Africa at Headingley in August, Fraser took 56 wickets at an average of 19.8, and finished both series indisputably England's most penetrative performer.

In the second Test against the West Indies at Queen's Park Oval, Trinidad, his first on-field appearance for England in two years, he produced the best single-innings bowling analysis for England against the West Indies – eight for 53 – beating his own record of eight for 75 set at Bridgetown, Barbados during the previous tour of 1993–94. In the crucial fourth test against South Africa at Trent Bridge he took five wickets in both innings to help England draw level, then five and three in the two digs at Headingley to bring their comeback to its extraordinary conclusion.

Gus represented the very best of his type of bowler and of his type of cricketer, an impression underlined when he became the first man in cricket history to receive a standing ovation at Lord's for taking the drinks round. Immediately after the Leeds triumph, England took on Sri Lanka and South Africa again in the inaugural triangular one-day tournament and when, the following week at headquarters, he made his way from the pavilion to the Nursery End to deliver some bottled water to Darren Gough on the boundary, the full house of 25,000-plus rose and cheered him every step of the way there and back again. At one stage the applause was so loud that the umpires called a temporary halt to the match.

A few days later *Hello!* magazine bestowed on him and his family what is, of course, the ultimate accolade for sportspeople, when they asked him to invite them into his home in Hatch End, Middlesex for the kind of celebrity picture spread normally featuring pop stars, Popes or princesses. Right up his street, I'm sure. It was heady stuff, and at the time he could have had no inkling of the fact that his next Test, against Sri Lanka at the Oval would be his last on home soil. On the subsequent winter tour to Australia, captain Alec Stewart very quickly came to the conclusion he was past it, and while he figured in the '99 World Cup disaster, that was that.

But how much more might Angus have achieved than his final tally of Test wickets, had he managed to steer clear of the succession of injuries that hampered him throughout his career? How many more wickets might he have taken had Ray Illingworth not got it into his head that Martin McCague and Joey Benjamin were more likely than him to bowl out the Aussies in 1994–95, or that an inability to swing the ball meant his Test career should be ended when England returned from South Africa a year later? And how different his story might have been had those running English cricket seen the light over central contracts at the beginning of the 1990s, rather than at the end, when, sadly for Gus, in terms of his Test aspirations, it was already over.

At his best, when I played alongside him until my retirement in '93, Gus typified the qualities of the old-fashioned English seamer. Nothing fancy, nothing flash, and aware of his own limitations, Gus concentrated on doing what he did best, wearing out a spot on the pitch just short of a good length and on or just outside off stump, at you, posing questions all the time and with a

'The unluckiest England bowler in modern times, Gus tells me. And he might just be right.'

'heavy' ball that seemed to accelerate off the deck and arrive sooner than you anticipated. He never tried to do too much with the ball except keep the seam bolt upright and hope it did something funny when it landed.

It was a simple approach, but it worked beautifully, particularly though not exclusively when the pitch was offering. I recall playing in his debut match, the third Test against Australia at Edgbaston in 1989, when he not only became the first Englishman that summer to get Steve Waugh out (his previous scores had been 177, 152 and 21, all not out) but his nagging line and length meant that the fielders behind the bat were always in the game. I went up to him after a couple of overs and told him, 'If you carry on bowling like this I'm going to take a lot of catches off you at second slip,' and I was embarrassed to learn from him later that these words from someone he had grown up watching and supporting, helped him believe he had arrived at the right place.

In the end, though, the prediction didn't come true, and from his point of view I believe it was his willingness to work, whenever and from whichever end the skipper needed him to, that in the end may have cost him dearly.

To me, he would have been just about the ideal first-change bowler, coming on after the new-ball pairing, wearing the batsman down and creating pressure to make the batsmen make mistakes. But he found to his personal cost that England's need was greater than his, and far too often he not only led the attack but also ended up carrying it as well. More than once he would bowl the overs that should have been sent down by others less gifted or less willing than him, simply because captains like Graham Gooch or his good friend Mike Atherton couldn't trust anyone else to do so. A combination of certain structural weaknesses and a massive workload left him waging an almost unending struggle for full fitness.

'Gus represented the very best of his type of bowler and of his type of cricketer, an impression underlined when he became the first man in cricket history to receive a standing ovation at Lord's for taking the drinks round.'

For all his efforts over the years he more than deserved his later success and I know it cut him up badly that the triumph of Headingley should be tarnished subsequently by suggestions arising out of the Hansie Cronje affair that the England victory might not have been entirely without pre-ordained umpiring assistance. I actually do not believe for one moment that the Pakistan official, Javed Akhtar, was guilty of anything other than a couple of errors of judgement, but, as Gus will tell you, England had their fair share of those going against them during the series and the match, and he is perfectly and rightly entitled to tell those who doubt the legitimacy of his contribution where they can get off.

Gus could be deadly serious about the game, but he also possessed a sense of fun that his hang-dog expression often masked. In response to Colin Croft's assessment of him at the start of the 1997–98 series in the Caribbean: 'Like an old horse, he should be put out to pasture', Gus announced after breaking the record in Trinidad: 'I'm just pleased to have bowled as well in this match as Colin Croft did every day of his career.'

He once moaned to me: 'People complain that when I come off the field at the end of a long bowl I look knackered. How do they expect me to look? I am bloody knackered. I thought that was the whole point.'

And he loved the irony in two stories he told me of his clashes with Brian Lara. The first incident happened when the great man played and missed to a pearler of a delivery that drew him forward into the push-drive then deviated away past the outside edge. Gus said he was going to give him a few words of wisdom 'along the lines of being a lucky bastard', but a glance at the scoreboard at the St John's Recreation Ground, Antigua, made him think twice.

'Lara was 347 not out on the way to the world record and it was the first ball that hadn't smashed into the middle of the bat. I considered sledging him might be considered not entirely appropriate,' he said.

The next occurred when he did manage to remove Brian cheaply in a county match at Lord's and, feeling inordinately proud and relieved, made his way back to his fielding position to receive the generous applause of the Middlesex faithful.

'Oi, Fraser!' came a voice, and Gus prepared to wave politely in acknowledgement of the upcoming compliment. 'You tosser! I paid to watch Lara bat, not you bowl. Thanks very much. I'm off.'

My experiences of playing with and against Angus taught me that what you saw was what you got, both off and on the field; a

---

BEEFY ON FRASER

Born: 8 August 1965, Billinge, Lancashire
Country: England
Tests: 46
Wickets: 177
Average: 27.32
Beefy analysis: Typified the qualities of the old-fashioned English seamer: nothing fancy, nothing flash, but continually posing questions to the batsman.
Beefy moment: Pulling pints at his beloved Stanmore CC.
Do mention: England v West Indies, Queen's Park Oval 1998 (his eight for 53).
Don't mention: Central contracts, Illy, his batting average.

wholehearted trier committed passionately to the cause of county or country but with the social instincts of the club cricketer at heart. It was almost as though he couldn't believe his luck that he was actually earning a living from something he just loved to do. To him, a massive part of the charm of the profession was the chance to enjoy the camaraderie that used to go with it in the bar or restaurant afterwards. As you can imagine, I could identify somewhat with that, and it is sad to think that the demands of the modern international game mean those days may be gone for good.

No matter, when he finally retires from his beloved Middlesex, no doubt you will still find him pulling the occasional pint at his even more beloved Stanmore CC, serving behind the bar as he did when a third XI pup at the very start of the great adventure.

Joel
Garner

We called Joel Garner 'Big Bird' after the loopy, gangling, gentle-giant character from *Sesame Street*, the No 1 kids' television programme of the time, who wouldn't harm a fly. At all times other than when he had a ball in his hand the nickname was perfectly apt.

Joel was an exceptionally talented cricketer in an age when the West Indies ruled supreme in world cricket. The two things were not coincidental. From a batsman's point of view I always thought it a blessing that he operated while Michael Holding, Andy Roberts and Malcolm Marshall were also in their prime.

With these three fighting over the new cherry, the more laid-back Joel was content to bide his time. It was hard to argue with Mikey and Malcolm, but to my mind, had Joel been given first use he would have caused more problems than anyone.

He had genuine pace, he bowled at the batsman with unerring accuracy, and he could make the ball bounce on sand. From his gigantic height and long reach, and with a whippy wrist action, he always got more than anyone thought possible. On surfaces where other genuinely quick bowlers would be struggling to get the ball through above stump height, he would extract another foot or so. And he did all that when he was in a good mood.

> 'He had genuine pace, he bowled at the batsman with unerring accuracy, and he could make the ball bounce on sand.'

When he was riled, maybe by a batter with the temerity to try an attacking shot against him or when he bowled one of the three half-volleys he sent down in his entire career, stand by your beds. Playing alongside him for Somerset, I witnessed this phenomenon more than once. He would crouch at the start of his run-up – the signal for all of us in the slips to retreat by about three yards – then grow taller and taller as he came to the crease. And when he let the ball go he did so with such venomous force that it would devour anything in its path.

> 'For me, not only was Joel one of the true greats, he was simply a great guy as well.'

When the mood was with him on one occasion against Kent in a knockout quarter-final, he destroyed their top-order batting in one of the most fearsome spells I've ever witnessed. Not only was it agonizing to bat against, it was also painful to field to: I caught two catches smack in the palms of my hands, and both times it took about ten minutes for the feeling to return.

On anything other than the flattest of batting surfaces he was quite lethal; if the pitch was offering, forget it, which is why, after Viv Richards and Dennis Lillee, Joel would be the third automatic choice in the best XI I ever watched or played against. Before his shoulder started to play up, his other great attribute was the most amazing throwing arm I ever saw. In one of our first games together, for Somerset against the Australians in 1977 at Bath, I recall him picking up a ball at third man and hurling it in with such force that it snapped a stump in half.

Joel also thought he could bat and, although he was probably in a minority on this one, I do recall the moment he decided to change his approach to the art. After returning to the dressing room one day once again cursing the fact that an otherwise immaculate pull had failed due to the fact that he had missed the ball by

'We called Joel Garner 'Big Bird' after the loopy, gangling, gentle-giant character from *Sesame Street*, the No 1 kids' television programme of the time, who wouldn't harm a fly.'

some six inches, he growled, threw his bat at the wall and declared, 'Man, I'm done swipin.' Not that he had, mind you.

Off the field he was a pussycat. I've seen grown men quivering at the thought of meeting Joel instantly put at ease by his friendliness. He did possess a temper but it only emerged when he was pushed beyond breaking point, like the time he invited Viv and I over to his place for one of his special stews. Home cooking was not the strongest point of the Botham–Richards household in Taunton. The fridge was generally full, but you would struggle to find anything to eat in it. On one of our many visits to Joel's flat he had to go out suddenly to make a presentation at the club. 'Don't worry, boys,' he told us, 'there's a stew on the stove.' Now one of Joel's stews would normally last him a week but Viv and I were feeling particularly peckish that evening and the result was that before Bird had returned we had wolfed the lot, only realizing our error when we hit the bottom of the pan. We knew that Joel would go berserk so we decided bravely to leg it. It was at this point that Viv had a brainwave. We topped up the gravy with hot water and filled the pot with a couple of rocks to give it some weight, so that when Joel lifted it he would suspect nothing. Apparently that is exactly what happened. Half of me wanted to be there when Joel attempted to ladle out the stones; the other half was only too glad to be back in our flat a couple of miles away with the door locked securely and the phone off the hook.

But when Joel fell victim to Peter Roebuck's coup at Somerset that led to the removal of him and Viv, and to my decision to quit the county, his overwhelming emotion was not anger but sadness. Happily, the club has gone some way to repairing the damage by making all three of us life members. But however you look at what happened during those dark days, and whatever the logic or otherwise of the decisions that altered all our lives, the treatment of Joel, in particular was nothing short of scandalous, and it hurt him deeply, because he simply couldn't understand why.

For me, not only was Joel one of the true greats, he was simply a great guy as well.

Mike Gatting

Gatt and I were sharing a private room of a hospital in Kingston, Jamaica. I was keeping him company while a surgeon was stitching back on to his face what remained of the nose Malcolm Marshall had all but removed with a bouncer during England's first one-day international against the West Indies in 1986 – a match I'd had the foresight to be absent from through injury.

The main concern of the doctor was whether fragments of bone had been driven backwards into Gatt's brain. Gatt's main concern, on that hot February afternoon in 1986, was how long the process would take before he could get back to Sabina Park to resume his innings.

I didn't see much point in telling him that this particular avenue of pleasure was closed to him because (a) the ball had bounced from his nose on to the stumps; and (b) he had then trodden on them. Such concerns seemed slightly beside the point while I was studying Gatt's face for the outline of where the nose was going to go. What's more, I thought he was kidding. But when we returned to the ground an hour or so later he kept asking when he could go back in to bat, so someone finally put him out of his misery. His reply was straight and to the point: 'B******s,' he said.

Typical Gatt. The bloke could barely inhale and exhale. He had suffered a blow, the spectacular effect of which brought his assailant Marshall to the point of vomiting on the pitch, a state of health made even worse when he picked up the ball to discover a piece of nasal cartilage still attached to it. It had taken most of the afternoon, first to stop the bleeding, then to replace his nose. Yet there he was, in all seriousness, desperate to re-enter the battle against the most hostile attack in world cricket on a pitch that was corrugated and bare at both ends, grassy in the middle, and would almost certainly have been condemned by the health and safety inspectors.

The fun and games were far from over. A couple of times that night Gatt woke up in a cold sweat, realizing he was unable to breathe properly. Then, when he arrived back at Heathrow with two panda eyes and a criss-cross pattern of fly-stitching plastered all over the middle of his face he had to deal with the most stupid question ever asked by a professional journalist: 'Where did it hit you?'

On his return to the Caribbean, in his comeback match against Barbados, he had his finger broken by a young quick called Vibert Greene. As if that were not enough, the publication of a tour diary by Frances Edmonds, Phil's wife, not only contained rather a lot of information that should have stayed within the dressing-room walls, but also an assessment of a bloke who had just spent three months risking life and limb for the team that could not be described as entirely sympathetic: 'Mike Gatting is the right man to fix your toilet,' wrote Frances.

As later events showed, the stubbornness and extraordinary will that underpinned Gatt's courage as a player and, on England's successful Ashes tour of 1986–87, as captain, occasionally manifested themselves in another, less helpful, characteristic. Some observers described his toe-to-toe row with the late umpire, Shakoor Rana, which brought the second Test of the 1987 tour to Pakistan to a standstill, as pure petulance. With hindsight, even Gatt admitted he went too far. As far as I'm concerned, the only thing he did wrong was to have the row in public. I missed that particular tour, as my mindset over the country and playing cricket there was still stuck in 'mother-in-law' mode, but everything I've heard about the events that day from Gatt and others has convinced me that Mike was provoked beyond reason by nothing short of personal abuse from Rana himself.

'As a player, Gatt was one of those batsmen whom I always felt you needed a front-line bowler to get out and he was just a murderer of anything but the best.'

The facts of the matter were that Gatt, having informed the batsman Salim Malik that he was moving the fielder, David Capel, to a run-saving position, waved his hand at Capel to stop him going up any further. The ball to Malik from off-spinner Eddie Hemmings was already in mid-air when Shakoor came running in from his position at square leg shouting, 'Stop! Unfair play!', and calling the England captain a cheat. After a short discussion, Shakoor had started to walk back to his place when he suddenly decided to let Gatt have an earful, this time expanding on his earlier comments thus: 'You f******** cheating c***!'

You'll probably think it a bit rich for me to suggest Gatt should have tried to contain himself and sort out the mess afterwards, especially as close of play was only a couple of minutes away. And you'd be right, because if Shakoor had said to me what he said to Gatt I would not like to speculate on what my reaction might have been. But if only Mike had been able to hold back until they were all back in the pavilion, none of the ensuing palaver would have happened.

Still, Mike always was inclined to let his emotions get the better of him, as some alleged he did the following summer at Rothley Court, which caused him to be removed from the England captaincy. And while, to my mind, the thorny question of taking part in rebel tours to South Africa has always been a matter of personal choice, I know he made his decision while still in a state of confused frustration at finding out that, while he was the first choice of the England management to lead the side in the 1989 Ashes series, his appointment had been vetoed by a Lord's official named Ossie Wheatley. Few of us playing had ever met him; in fact, most of us had never even heard of him.

Again, incidentally, the courage bordering on naïvety that seemed to get him into strife so often, surfaced on that 1990 rebel tour when, with lumps of concrete being lobbed by protesters determined to stop a match in Bloemfontein, Gatt ignored the warnings of the officials and went out to stand in front of the mob to try and put across his point of view. He totally misread the mood, but was prepared to put himself in the firing line whatever the consequences.

'My best memories of Gatt, mammoth plate-hoovering achievements apart (and nobody had better mention the Madras prawns here, or there'll be trouble), are of our efforts to secure the draw in the Oval Test against Pakistan in 1987.'

As a player, Gatt was one of those batsmen I always felt you needed a front-line bowler to get out and he was just a murderer of anything but the best. As an England batsman, Gatt probably enjoyed both his finest hours and his worst nightmares against Australia. On our triumphant Ashes tour of 1986–87 he was the perfect leader of a team of individuals like myself, David Gower, Allan Lamb and Phil Edmonds, who needed nothing more than encouragement to express ourselves, both on and off the field. During the early games we were pretty appalling, prompting the famous assessment in *The Independent* that there were only three things wrong with us: we couldn't bat, couldn't bowl, and couldn't field. And those who believe we may have allowed our preparation to be blurred by a rigorous search for the best mixer to go with Bundaberg rum may have had a point. But Gatt refused to panic and trusted us to pull ourselves together. There were no naughty-boy nets and no pointless bollockings. Gatt treated us all as gown-ups and got the desired result. It was probably the happiest tour I've ever been on, and he deserves huge credit for that.

As for his return to home Test action in 1993 following his 'rebel tour' ban, nothing really went right from then on. First, he gave the world Shane Warne's ball of the century and then he made a decision to take one last trip Down Under in 1994–95 that I believe was the biggest mistake he ever made as a player. Brought back by Ray Illingworth, who saw him as a ready-made replacement captain should Mike Atherton refuse to come to heel, Gatt should never have gone for the simple reason that by then he was just past it.

He made a brave contribution in Adelaide, with a hundred that actually enabled England to win the fourth Test, but by then the damage had already been done. The sight of him and Goochie plodding around the hard Australian outfield under the hot Australian sun against young, brash and brilliant opponents spoke volumes about the direction in which English cricket was heading and even provoked Atherton to make his public call for younger players and selectors 'more in touch with the dynamics of the modern game' that got him into even more trouble with Illingworth.

In between those two extremes, my best memories of Gatt, mammoth plate-hoovering achievements apart (and nobody had better mention the Madras prawns here, or there'll be trouble), are of our efforts to secure the draw in the Oval Test against Pakistan in 1987. After they'd racked up an amazing 708 all out we folded in our first innings, all out for 232. Following on 476 runs behind when we were 89 for three in the second there was a fair we chance we might lose the Test by the biggest margin ever suffered by an England team. Prior to the start of that memorable final day, a lot of people had written us off, but we lost just one more wicket, and Gatt and I put on 176 in an unbeaten fifth-wicket stand, Gatt finishing with 150 not out.

Many observers spoke and wrote in glowing terms of the magnificent self-restraint shown by two natural-born hitters, all for the cause. The truth was that, after a skinful of curry and lager the night before, neither of us was in any fit state to do anything other than block the vindaloo out of it.

Sunil Gavaskar

T wo emotions came to the fore if you were ever lucky enough to get Sunil Gavaskar out early: delight was the first, and surprise arrived soon after. Sunny was, quite simply, the best opening batsman I ever saw or bowled to. At 5ft 4 $^3/_4$ in he had just about the perfect frame for dealing with quick and slow bowlers alike (Don Bradman, 5ft 6 $^3/_4$ in, once told him, 'These big blokes have the power but we little ones have the footwork'), and he had just about the perfect game to go with it.

He had a fantastic 'eye' which meant that he saw the ball much earlier than most ordinary mortals; wonderful balance to be able to rock and roll with the bouncers, and quite often use his wonderful hook to smash them to the boundary; the footwork of a ballet dancer; and at the centre of all of this were powers of concentration so awesome that when he dug himself in it was like trying to remove a tower block.

His courage and determination were immense. Fired by the desire not only for personal glory but also to prove to the world of cricket that Indian batsmen deserved more than to be patronized as wristy strokeplayers who could not succeed anywhere but on their home pitches, Sunny made it his business to adapt to all conditions and all types of bowling. He used his time with Somerset to learn how to play English seam and swing bowlers on green wickets, and went through hour after hour of specific practice against fast, short-pitched bowling to prepare himself for the might of the West Indies quicks. How well all his hard work paid off can be judged first by the statistics.

'Sunny was, quite simply, the best opening batsman I ever saw or bowled to.'

Of his 34 Test hundreds – Bradman is second on the all-time list with 29 – he made 13 against the West Indies. Admittedly, when he started out on his Test career, they posed a somewhat different threat from that in later years but his performance against them in his first full series in 1970–71 was simply out of this world. Sunny scored a hundred in his second Test, in Guyana; a hundred in his third, in Barbados, and then, in his fourth Test, in Trinidad, he made 124 in the first innings and 220 in the second, and a superstar was born. He finished with 774 runs in the series against Sir Garfield Sobers' finest and earned this tribute from Lord Relator, the Trinidadian calypsonian:

> It was Gavaskar, the real master,
> Just like a wall,
> We couldn't out Gavaskar at all.

Three of his eight more tons against them came in the Caribbean, which goes some way to explaining why he is almost as revered there for his batting as he is at home, and he finished the sequence in 1984 in Madras with his career-best 236 not out.

Watching him from close range as an opponent and a team-mate, the thing that struck me most was his phenomenal concentration. I've seen others seemingly able to switch on and off at will, but nobody did it better than Sunny. You always knew when he was really getting himself sorted for a big one because he would stop at the end of an over, stand in his batting position with his bat resting against his thigh, look down the other end of the wicket, cup his hands around his head like a lookout in the crows' nest and just focus on some faraway point. That was the signal for us to start looking over the horizon as well.

Not that he had things all his own way against me. When I had him brilliantly caught low down by Mike Brearley in the second Test of the 1979 series at Lord's, he became my 100th victim in my nineteenth Test, enabling me to set a new record for reaching the milestone in the shortest time – two years and nine days, apparently. Of all my contemporaries, I believe only the wicket of Viv would have given me as much pleasure.

I dismissed him in both innings of the final drawn Test of that series, although I suppose it only fair to mention that he did manage the little matter of an utterly flawless 221 in the second innings,

> ## BEEFY ON GAVASKAR
>
> **Born:** 10 July 1949, Bombay
> **Country:** India
> **Tests:** 125
> **Hundreds:** 34
> **Average:** 51.12
> **Beefy analysis:** Diminutive batsman with a fantastic eye and wonderful balance. The best opening batsman I have ever bowled to.
> **Beefy moment:** The Little Master being caught by Mike Brearley off my own bowling, Lord's 1979, and becoming my 100th Test wicket.
> **Do mention:** 1970–71 series, West Indies v India (he scored 774 runs in four Tests).
> **Don't mention:** Calcutta.

which meant that with three balls left on the final day all four results were possible and earned him the man-of-the-match award. My knack of rising to the big occasion meant that the next time we met I did the double over him again, on the way to thirteen wickets in the Centenary Test in Bombay, and my first-innings ton meant we were able to win by ten wickets with a day to spare.

But as far as my bowling colleagues and I were concerned, my greatest success against Sunny was accidentally breaking his leg. Even though he had not enjoyed his most productive series against us in 1982, he was still the batsman we most wanted to get out. On the first day of the final Test, at the Oval, I inadvertently hit upon the perfect solution. Geoff Cook and Chris Tavare had laid solid foundations with 96 for the first wicket, and David Gower and Allan Lamb had

'He had a fantastic 'eye' which meant that he saw the ball much earlier than most ordinary mortals; wonderful balance to be able to rock and roll with the bouncers; the footwork of a ballet dancer; and at the centre of all of this were powers of concentration.'

carried on the good work, so that when I came to the crease at 185 for three I figured Lambie and I had a bit of a licence to attack. Lambie reached his maiden Test ton and I went on to make 208, my first and only Test double-hundred. The back-foot drive in question may not have earned any runs, but was rated shot of the series back in the dressing room because it crashed into Sunny's left shin and meant he was unable to bat at all during the match, thus saving all of us a lot of hard work.

Certainly, Sunny had his problems in India. Only those with experience of the particular pressures of superstardom in that wonderfully chaotic cauldron can understand what it entails. But the regional rivalry that colours and sometimes blackens the picture there meant that supposed or real tensions existed, from time to time between him and other high-profile colleagues such as Kapil Dev and Bishen Bedi. But perhaps his most spectacular fall-out came with an entire city – Calcutta. Booed by sections of the fanatical crowd at Eden Gardens for delaying a declaration against England on the 1984–85 tour, Sunny announced that he would never play in the city again. Two years later he proved he was true to his word. In February 1987, just prior to the second Test against Pakistan in Calcutta, Sunny wrote to the Indian Board saying he did not wish to be considered for the Test and for the one-day international to be played there later.

'I am available for the rest of the season. I will not be available for the matches in Calcutta. That is all,' he said.

Sometimes the 'Little Master' could be very stubborn indeed. Then again, that's what they said about Don Bradman.

Graham Gooch

My decision to ban Graham Gooch from jogging on the 1980 tour to the West Indies persuaded some people I was not up to the job of England captain. Others thought it was just a joke. I was convinced then and still am, however, that it was exactly the right thing to do at the time.

Graham's attitude was that for him to be at the top of his game he needed to be as physically sharp as possible. Fair enough. But from where I was looking at it, such activity was leaving him just plain knackered.

To me, the strains and pressures of trying to keep one's head attached to one's shoulders against the Windies pacemen, or attempting to keep some of the greatest batsmen in the world in check with the ball were quite strenuous enough. So when I noticed Graham nodding off in the bar after close of play a couple of times, I told him straight – in my opinion, all that running was doing him more harm than good.

Although some observers might believe he got his own back on me when he left me out of the tour to the West Indies 10 years later, our difference of opinion on the general principle of fitness for cricket was never really resolved. For instance, I couldn't agree with his treatment of David Gower once he became captain because, to me, there was no clearer example of one man's meat being another's poison. If Graham felt he needed to put himself through a gruelling regime of push-ups, press-ups and throw-ups in order to be at his sharpest, that was his business, and we all respected him for it. But I simply did not believe that just because that approach worked for him it was bound to work for everyone else.

'For most of his captaincy of England Gooch *was* the batting. His brilliant unbeaten century against West Indies in the first Test of the 1991 series at Headingley was as near to the perfect captain's innings as you could get.'

How could three laps of Old Trafford possibly make Gower score more runs, or Phil Tufnell to spin the ball more? Of course, all cricketers need to attain a certain level of fitness in order to give of their best, but the point is that all players also need to find their own level, and a way of maintaining it.

In my opinion, Graham, supported by coach Micky Stewart and fitness coach, the late Colin Tomlin, put in place a regime that just wasn't flexible enough, and I firmly believe his insistence on pushing the players to the limit cost us the World Cup in 1992 in Australia and New Zealand. We were by far the best team in the tournament, and early on, when fresh, proved it over and over again. But by the time we reached the semi-final and final too many of us were carrying niggling injuries that needed rest, not exercise, and on that sad night in Melbourne when we came off second best we paid the price.

All that having been said, I have the highest possible regard for what Graham achieved as a player. For most of his captaincy of England he was the batting. His brilliant unbeaten century against West Indies in the first Test of the 1991 series at Headingley was as near to the perfect captain's innings as you could get. Against an attack comprising Malcolm Marshall, the guy Gooch rated as the best he ever faced, Patrick Patterson, possibly the meanest of them all and Curtly Ambrose and Courtney Walsh in their pomp and on a seaming wicket under cloudy skies – in those days typical Headingley conditions –

BEEFY ON GOOCH

Born: 23 July 1953, Leytonstone, Essex
Country: England
Tests: 118
Hundreds: 20
Average: 42.58
Beefy analysis: A class apart as an opening batsman; a great compiler of runs against the best fast bowling attacks the game has ever seen.
Beefy moment: Banning Gooch from jogging on the 1980 tour to the West Indies.
Do mention: England v West Indies, Headingley 1991 (154 not out).
Don't mention: England v Australia, Edgbaston 1975 (a pair on his Test debut).

Gooch carried his bat for 154 out of England's second innings of 252 to which only two others, Mark Ramprakash (27) and Derek Pringle (27) contributed more than six runs. His magnificent effort enabled England to win the match and, finally, earn a share of a series against the West Indies for the first time since 1973–74.

He made bigger hundreds, notably the amazing 333 against India at Lord's the year before that I was convinced he was going to convert into a score to beat the then world-record 365 not out of Sir Garfield Sobers, and proved himself one of England's greats not only in substance – his tally of 8,900 Test runs for England may well never be surpassed – but also in style. And until he packed up Test cricket at the end of the 1994–95 tour to Australia he maintained his status as the England batsman feared by the best bowlers in the world. But the innings at Headingley in '91 had everything. Without it, his team would have lost; they knew it, the West Indies knew it, and he knew it. Yet, while doing his best to squeeze runs out of his less gifted colleagues, his mastery of his own game made you aware you were looking at a special talent expressing itself fully and to full effect. This was real substance with real style.

For all that we had to agree to differ over many issues, the one matter on which we shared absolutely the same opinion was pride in representing our country. Many players talk a good game about being inspired by the three lions on the shirt and so on. For Gooch it was much more than talk. He lived the idea. To people who didn't understand Graham, his decision to take part in the first rebel tour to South Africa appeared to compromise his patriotism. But I know how hard he grappled with the decision to put the financial well-being of his family first, and he was genuinely shocked at the reaction to it. To his credit, he never moaned afterwards because he knew he had made his bed and had to lie in it.

A far truer picture of his priorities was painted when, on the eve of the World Cup final in 1992 he followed me out of the pre-final official dinner when I made my protest at what passed for the 'star-turn' of the evening. With all the subtlety and good taste you might associate with Australian cultural attaché and internationally renowned cheese expert, Sir Les Patterson, someone hired a drag-artist to make offensive jokes about the Queen. Very funny. I walked out and even though the management pleaded with Graham to stay put, he accompanied me out of the hall to make plain his own feelings.

To me, Graham was not the greatest at getting the best out of other players. But no one I played with or against got more out of himself.

Darren Gough

Darren Gough is the original unburstable bubble. On or off the cricket field, 'Dazzler' always lets you know he's around. If he's ever been depressed, I've never seen it. If he's ever thought about letting his chin drop you would never know it from looking at him.

In fact, I've only ever seen him looking and behaving in a self-conscious manner once in the years I've known him, and, to be honest, on that occasion he had good cause for his sheepishness.

The calf-length white shorts he was wearing in the lobby of the Sandton Sun Hotel in South Africa were the kind of fashion item I wouldn't be seen drunk in, and I'll never forget the look on Goughy's face when he realized he was catching admiring glances from a certain member of the waiting staff named David. Apart from that, Darren has always been as straight as a die and totally upfront in his approach to cricket and life. And it was a shame that the England selectors felt the need to change their mind over their agreement that he should miss the tour to India in 2001 with official blessing.

"Dazzler' always lets you know he's around. If he's ever been depressed, I've never seen it. If he's ever thought about letting his chin drop you would never know it from looking at him.'

If there is one incident that sums up his unquenchable spirit it is his dismissal of the Australian batsman, Greg Blewett, in the first Test of the 1997 Ashes series at Edgbaston. Australia were undercooked when they arrived in England for that tour, found themselves on the wrong end of a 3–0 duffing-up in the one-day series and were still waking up to the task confronting them when they reached Birmingham for the opening Test. England's bowlers, tearing into them like men possessed, made them pay the full price for it.

On that first morning of the series, Darren, Devon Malcolm and Andy Caddick were inspired, ripping out the top eight in the Aussie batting order for just 54 before finally bowling them out for 118 on the way to a famous nine-wicket win, following brilliant batting from Nasser Hussain and Graham Thorpe who put on 288 for the fourth wicket in England's first innings.

Although Caddick finished with five wickets in the Aussie first innings, it was Gough who made the early inroads, snaffling three of the first four wickets to fall. And it was the way he took the second of these that emphasized to me the special quality that has made him one of the best bowlers in the world. Both openers, Mark Taylor and Matthew Elliott, were out, Australia were 26 for two and Gough was on the point of popping a blood-vessel with the effort of making another crucial breakthrough when he steamed in, beat Blewett's forward push and heard the crowd erupt as the ball clattered into the stumps.

Imagine how he must have felt, then, to turn and see the outstretched arm of umpire Peter Willey signalling that all his efforts had been for nowt. 'No-ball,' said Willey, and we waited for the inevitable kick of the ground or shake of the head from the disappointed bowler. What happened instead told me all I needed to know. Gough walked back to his mark with a wide smile on his face, turned, ran in and, from the very next ball, had Blewett caught at third slip by Hussain. In terms of my opinion of Gough, and I suspect, not only the opinion of his team-mates, but also of his opponents as well, this was a defining moment.

When I talked to him about the incident afterwards, his words impressed me just as much as his actions had done.

'Why was I smiling? First of all, I thought it was important not to let the Aussies know how frustrated I was,' he explained. 'But the main reason was that I was absolutely convinced that I was going to do it again.'

Goughy showed that same force of will when he took his memorable hat-trick against the Aussies in the final Test of the 1998–99 series in Sydney, the first by an Englishman in Ashes Tests for 100 years, a series of three deliveries which revealed the class he possesses. The first ball, to Ian Healy, reared up front just short of a length and had him caught behind off the glove. The next was a high-velocity inswinging torpedo that gave Colin Miller no chance. How would he react to the pressure of going for three in a row? Like a cat reacts to a dishful of cream. Amid the noise and the hubbub, Goughy kept his nerve and his head, and repeated the exact same delivery. Stuart MacGill was about halfway through the shot when he found himself bowled to death.

It is not just with the ball in his hand that Goughy can make a difference. To me, the turning point of England's entire series against the West Indies in 2000 was his stunning catch at third man to dismiss Sherwin Campbell off Caddick. Beaten in the first Test at Edgbaston, England had conceded a first innings deficit of 133 runs and looked destined for another 'here we go again' routine. But Gough lifted everyone with that effort, and before the day was out, so were the Windies, for 54 runs. Who should be there at the end of an incredibly dramatic win the following evening accompanying Dominic Cork over the finishing line but Gough, with the best four not out he will ever play.

Bowling is his business, though. And when he gets it right there are few better. I think if he was totally honest he might have wished for six inches more height to enable him to become the complete fast bowler, but he has worked damned hard to make absolutely the best use of what he has, and taught himself a whole bag of tricks along the way, including the skills of bowling reverse-swing at high pace that make him, to my mind, the best England has ever produced at this discipline.

This was never more evident than during England's 2000 winter tour to Pakistan. Some quick bowlers I can think of might have decided very early that the bare, grassless and slow pitch conditions in Lahore, Faisalabad and Karachi made it a waste of time them turning up. Gough, on the other hand, set about finding other ways of doing a job. Slower balls, off-breaks, leg-breaks, you name them, he chucked them all in, and consequently finished up with 10 Test wickets in three matches.

And as for his main weapon, the consistently good pace that has made his variations so difficult to handle, English cricket owes a huge debt of gratitude to the former West Indies skipper Richie Richardson. Richie was a controversial choice as Yorkshire's overseas player in 1993, but the few words of advice he passed on to the young fast bowler during the early part of that season more than justified the selection. At the time, Gough was struggling to focus on what sort of bowler he wanted to become and many muttering sages at the club were beginning to wonder whether he would ever make the breakthrough at county, let alone Test level. In a championship match against Hampshire at Southampton, Richie spotted that Gough was going through the motions and let him have a blast. The gist of it was that real fast bowlers actually bowled fast; it stung Gough into action and put him on the path to cricketing righteousness.

Goughy has it in him to be as daft as a brush – he was once asked why his nickname was 'Rhino', and answered, in all seriousness, 'Because I'm as strong as an ox'; and one of his team-mates was more than a little puzzled when he turned to him on a trans-Australian flight and offered the following: 'Don't these planes get low to the ground when they're landing...?'

And he has, how shall I put this, a healthy regard for personal glory. Putting his name on the merit board in the England dressing room at Lord's for the first time for his five-wicket performance in the first Test of the 2001 series against Pakistan meant so much to him, not because of the immediate buzz of the achievement but because it will be there until doomsday.

Furthermore, not only has he had to deal with a series of injuries that might have made a less committed cricketer think twice about his choice of career, but also the occasional grenade lobbed at him by that master of logical positivism, Fred Trueman, who has made no secret of a ludicrous conviction that his bowling action was open to question.

All of which reinforces my feeling that, of the players picked for England since my retirement in 1993, and with all due respect to some fine cricketers, Gough is the man I wish I had stood alongside in an England sweater. I take it as a great compliment that Darren has often been quoted as saying that I am one of his cricketing heroes. I have news for him. He is definitely one of mine.

David Gower

If you want to really hack off David Gower, all you need to do is to tell him he didn't care enough about playing cricket for England.

Viewers of the TV sports quiz game *They Think It's All Over* have been treated to the popular caricature of David as the carefree, cavalier country squire, and he plays the part brilliantly. But those who know him well and have taken the field alongside him understand just how much it annoyed him when people criticized him for appearing too laid-back and uncommitted on the cricket field.

It is true that, in terms of his approach to cricket and to life, David was the last of the 'gentleman' cricketers to play for England. Someone once said that you knew he enjoyed batting because otherwise he would have had someone else do it for him, rather like the brilliant Pakistan strokemaker Inzamam-ul-Haq, who, as a child, used to employ a runner because he simply couldn't be fagged to do it himself. And, as such, Gower would have appeared even more of a museum piece in the snarling, spitting game we had come to expect by the end

'It is true that in terms of his approach to cricket and to life, David was the last of the 'gentleman' cricketers to play for England.'

of the twentieth century. I can honestly say that I never once heard him 'sledge' a batsman, for instance, unless, unbeknown to the rest of us, he did so in his native Latin. But a conversation Mike Atherton recalled to me once indicated that this was not merely because he found it distasteful, as he undoubtedly did.

Athers was stressing the need, as he saw it, to give as good as you got when confronted by verbals, in order to demonstrate that you were not going to be intimidated. 'That's one way,' said David. 'On the other hand, you could just say nothing.' That was the day Athers decided to let his bat and his eyes do the talking.

A truth that is sometimes clouded because of the arguments over David's desire, which came to a head in his stupid and wasteful fall-out with Graham Gooch in the early 1990s is that not only was he an artist with a bat in his hand, he was also highly successful. When you consider his Test record of 8,231 runs (the second highest for England) at an average of 44.25 (higher, incidentally, than Gooch) the charge that he was too much flash and not enough cash is bonkers.

While some colleagues and opponents alike would occasionally seek to get under his skin by questioning the depth of his commitment, the issue only really became significant during what turned out to be David's final Ashes tour in 1990–91, when the tension caused by his personality clash with Gooch rumbled under the surface throughout before finally erupting in spectacular fashion.

Following the disastrous series against Australia in 1989, when just about everything that could have gone wrong did – inserting Australia on the first morning of the series, recruitment for the South African rebel tour taking place all summer and then major injuries to key players – not only was David replaced as captain by Gooch for the 1989–90 tour to the West Indies, but, along with yours truly, he was dropped altogether.

Graham had had some success with his more methodical approach to training and preparation with a narrow 2–1 defeat in the Caribbean being followed by wins over India and New Zealand, but he knew that to have any chance Down Under he needed the class of Gower. On the field, David duly obliged, making two hundreds and finishing the series with 407 runs at 45.22. But Gooch, deflated by the general ineptitude of some of his players and the 3–0 scoreline, somehow figured that what he perceived as

BEEFY ON GOWER

Born: 1 April 1957, Tunbridge Wells, Kent
Country: England
Tests: 117
Hundreds: 18
Average: 44.25
Beefy analysis: Reinvented the word 'class' with his silky batting. Never given enough credit for his contribution to England.
Beefy moment: Pulling Pakistan's Liaqat Ali for four from his first ball in Test cricket – at Lord's.
Do mention: Ashes series 1985 (captained England to last Ashes victory of 20th Century).
Don't mention: 1992–93 tour to India.

David's laid-back approach was among the root causes of the defeat and dropped him again. Don't get me wrong. On occasion David did have a tendency to behave as though he'd sprinkled Valium on his breakfast cereal and, on that tour, the golden-haired one may have been pushing things with his 'Monty Gower's Flying Circus' routine, when he hired a tiger moth to buzz the ground during England's match against Queensland in Carrara, especially as he had borrowed the cash to do so from the unsuspecting tour manager Peter Lush. But the reaction of Gooch and his coach Micky Stewart did indicate a rather profound sense-of-humour failure, even by their totalitarian standards. Gower did not play again for England for more than a year.

Then came the final indignity. After bringing him back into the side for the series against Pakistan two summers later, watching Gower overtake Geoff Boycott as England's highest Test run scorer in the third Test at Old Trafford and helping to win the fourth at Headingley with an ice-cool second innings 31 not out amid the carnage of Wasim and Waqar wreaking havoc with reverse swing, Gooch rewarded Gower by leaving him out of the 1992–93 tour to India.

A group of MCC rebels, under Dennis Oliver, put voice to the indignation of the cricketing public, proposing a vote of no-confidence in the England selectors among the members, but Gooch never budged, and Gower never played for England again. Tragic, stupid stubbornness.

David did give his response to what most people understood to be appalling treatment in his autobiography, but it was rather muted and apologetic in tone. I for one, seeing how upset and hurt he was, how passionately he cared, and how he hated and feared the public being given the wrong impression, urged him to be more outspoken: 'Tell the truth,' I urged him, 'and let the public decide.' His reaction? 'I don't think it would be helpful.'

Any batsman with his timing, grace and wonderful strokeplay is bound to look as though the game comes a little too comfortably. No matter how much he protested that it was anything but – 'It's hard work making the game look easy,' he once joked – and he described the phenomenon as similar to the behaviour of a swan gliding across the water: 'serene on top, paddling like f*** underneath'. And when you compare one of his seemingly effortless square-cuts or cover-drives, or even the gorgeous pull for four from the first ball he faced in Test cricket back in 1978 from Pakistan's Liaqat Ali – at Lord's, of course – to the more prosaic style of a trademark shot from Mike Atherton or Steve Waugh, for example, it is clear that Gower had beauty on his side. Where there is beauty, however, there is also the potential for jealousy. What is beyond argument, though, is that, at his peak, Gower was simply one of the greats.

Players who know me know that I was a lousy watcher of the game. My preferred method of preparation was to try to relax so that when I got to the wicket I was not psychologically tired out with worrying about what was going to happen. But I always made an exception when David was on his way to the crease. I would go so far as to say that David was the one England player I would drop everything to watch.

Anyone doubting his physical bravery should have watched him batting against the West Indies quicks on a corrugated Sabina Park pitch and, as captain, he was not afraid to take a colleague to task if he felt it was necessary. I recall his reaction when I got out against the Aussies in 1989 at Old Trafford trying and failing to hit Trevor Hohns over the Pennines. 'Sorry, mate,' I offered weakly. 'Crap,' he replied. 'Don't do it again.' And I didn't. Not for a while, anyway!

To my mind it's a crying shame that his greatest achievement as skipper, leading us to the last Ashes victory in England of the twentieth century, should be overshadowed by the fact that he was also in charge for the two 'blackwashes' against the West Indies that followed. David took a lot of stick for the way he apparently allowed things to drift on the field, and was criticized roundly for introducing the concept of voluntary nets, for instance. Baloney.

Leaving aside all controversy, one overriding image remains fresh in my mind: of a quite magnificent batsman who cared more about what he did more than some people could ever comprehend.

Tony Greig

'If the West Indies are on top, they're magnificent,' explained the England captain. 'If they are down, they grovel. And with the help of Closey and a few others, I intend to make them grovel.'

Oops. In the list of things Tony Greig wishes he'd never said, his welcome to Clive Lloyd's West Indies side at the beginning of their 1976 tour to England stands proudly at No 1.

By the end of it, with Closey battered black-and-blue by Andy Roberts and Mike Holding, Greig's players were the ones grovelling.

Greigy tried to concede the point by dropping to his knees on the parched Oval outfield at the end of the 3–0 series defeat, but to Clive, Viv Richards and their colleagues, the word 'grovel' sounded a bit too much like some of those his ancestors had heard in their hated colonial past, and it cut too deep to be shrugged off. Even as long afterwards as 1990, fourteen years on the wounds had still not healed, as I learned subsequently from one of the technicians working for Sky television during their first exercise in live Test cricket coverage, the England tour of the West Indies. After England's against-the-odds victory in the first Test at Sabina Park, the Sky director wanted an interview with Viv, the losing captain. Viv readily agreed until he was told that Tony would be doing the interview, at which point he refused point-blank.

'Like Closey, Greig simply believed that on a cricket field he was invincible and that he could single-handedly win every game he played.'

Those who don't know Greig might be under the impression that No 2 on the list of verbal faux pas would be: 'Howzat?', or to be more specific, the appeal for run out against West Indies batsman Alvin Kallicharran that almost forced the abandonment of a Test between the two sides at Port-of-Spain, Trinidad on England's 1973–74 tour. They'd be very wrong.

The incident in question happened when Tony threw down the stumps at the non-striker's end off the final ball of the day with Kalli, who had set off for the pavilion, already yards down the wicket and out of his ground. When the umpire, Douglas Sang Hue, gave him out, as the rules stated he must, the home crowd erupted in protest. Then, against a background of threats from the crowd that, if Kalli was not reinstated the following day there would be a riot, it took top-level talks between the captains, the England manager Donald Carr, the West Indies Board, and some frantic phone calls back to Lord's to find a diplomatic solution.

But when a formula was finally found whereby England could withdraw the appeal without any suggestion that the umpire had been wrong to give Kalli out in the first place, Greig, typically, was dead against it. As far as he was concerned, the wicket was taken fair and square and if Kalli hadn't had the sense to stand his ground until the umpire called 'time', that was his problem. For the sake of peace, Greigy was eventually persuaded to pose for a kiss-and-make-up photo with Kalli, but no one within the England side bought it.

'Immensely brave, he stood up to the barrage from Dennis Lillee and Jeff Thomson on the England 1974–75 tour Down Under that reduced other grown men to quivering wrecks.'

If this was the first example of the abrasiveness and ultra-competitive approach to everything he has ever done which has ensured that the life and times of Tony Greig have been so full of controversy, it certainly wasn't the last. Indeed, by the end of the Ashes summer of 1977, Greig was at the centre of events that turned the cricketing world upside down.

In some quarters, notably St John's Wood, London NW8, Greig will never be forgiven for his part in the formation of the Packer Circus. No matter what his motives, and some still refuse to accept that they were anything other than selfish, the depth of their outrage was not so much the idea that a leading player had secretly been recruiting defectors to join Packer's Australian Channel Nine-funded breakaway movement. What they hated more than anything else, I suspect, was that the player in question should be the England captain.

Greig himself regretted that he'd had to do most of his work undercover, and he made no bones of the fact that he stood to gain personally from his role as Packer's chief recruiting officer for World Series Cricket, under floodlights, wearing coloured clothing etc, but after being sacked by England he took his punishment without whingeing about it.

Although it took a court case brought by Packer against the Test and County Cricket Board and the International Cricket Council to lift their ban on World Series players and some friendships were never restored, the simple fact is that the Packer Revolution was inevitable. At the time, International cricketers were so poorly paid in comparison to other sportsmen and women that they were easy targets for someone with a big enough cheque book. Many England players had full-time jobs during the winter months just to tide them over until their counties rewarded them with tuppence ha'penny for a summer's employment. So when cricketers of the modern era next think about how they have become so well rewarded for playing with bats and balls – if they ever do, that is – they should know that none of it would have happened without the intervention of Packer and Greig.

As for Greig's talents on the field, they were all you would expect from a bloke prepared to take on all-comers off it in the way that he did. From a selfish perspective, I'm only sad that my first season in Test cricket turned out to be his last. We played together in a couple of one-day internationals at the end of 1976, and in two Tests, at Trent Bridge and Headingley, for which Mike Brearley replaced Greig as captain while the TCCB worked out what to do about his role in the Packer business. I regret that because I'm sure I could have learned a lot from operating under his wing and that the challenge of proving myself against him all the time would have been inspirational. What's more his unquenchable energy and at times almost reckless lust for adventure made him my kind of captain.

Like Closey, with whom he shared many characteristics, Greig simply believed that on a cricket field he was invincible and that he could single-handedly win every game he played. Immensely brave, he stood up to the barrage from Dennis Lillee and Jeff Thomson on the England

'The man regarded as probably the best Test all-rounder of his generation.'

1974–75 tour Down Under that reduced other grown men to quivering wrecks. Helmetless, he put himself in the firing line of their bouncers and even devised a new way of trying to score runs off them, deliberately slicing short-pitched balls over the slips and gully time after time. And his unorthodoxy made him hellishly difficult to bowl to. At 6ft 7in and with gangling legs and arms he had such a long reach that you never quite knew where to bowl to him. With the ball, he was a more than useful medium-fast seamer who hit the deck hard from his height and was flexible enough and good enough to win a Test match in Trinidad bowling off-cutters. In the field he caught everything.

People say that young players like myself and David Gower benefited from the absence of the Packer defectors during the early days of our careers. Maybe so, but I'd like to think that we still did okay when they came back from exile. Whatever else the Packer affair did for the world game, though, and however Greig himself will be regarded by history, I'm disappointed that the revolution they conspired to effect did deprive me of the chance of playing more international cricket alongside the man regarded as probably the best Test all-rounder of his generation.

Richard Hadlee

Richard spent a lot of his career dominated by the 'corridor of uncertainty', either bowling in it, or according to him, living in it.

In cricketing parlance, the 'corridor' was a term I grew to dislike intensely through its sheer overuse. But initially, when it was first used by Hadlee's Nottinghamshire team-mate, Clive Rice, to describe his approach to pace bowling, it could not have been more apt.

Basically, what it amounts to is aiming to pitch the ball just short of a length in an area just outside the off-stump to the right-hander, thereby putting doubt in the batsman's mind first over whether to leave it or play it, and second whether to play forward or backward.

BEEFY ON HADLEE

Born: 3 July 1951, St Albans, Christchurch
Country: New Zealand
Tests: 86
Wickets: 431
Average (bowling): 22.30
Hundreds: 2
Average (batting): 27.16
Beefy analysis: The complete all-rounder: a pace bowler with absolute mastery of line, length and seam movement; and a destructive lower order batsman in his early career.
Beefy moment: Hadlee recovering from his physical and mental breakdown.
Do mention: 1983–84 season (batting and bowling in England v New Zealand series, and 1000 runs and 100 wickets for Notts).
Don't mention: Paddles.

In the years after 'Paddles' cut down his run-up and pace to concentrate on line, length and seam movement at a pace that was still more than handy – and suffered extraordinary criticism from the Kiwi press for doing so, incidentally – he was the absolute master of this style of bowling. When conditions were in his favour, as they often seemed to be when he was bowling Nottinghamshire to the county championship on the greentops of Trent Bridge (coincidence, I'm sure), or for New Zealand in Auckland, Wellington, or Christchurch he could make the ball obey his every command. And even when you were batting against him on a flat one, his mesmeric consistency meant that you took liberties against him at your peril.

And his batting could be much more than a thorn in the side of opposing attacks. In the twelve-month period commencing in August 1983, the year of his greatest triumph, he emphasized his all-round qualities over and over again; first, in the second Test at Headingley he made 75 as New Zealand recorded their first-ever victory in England, following seventeen defeats and eleven draws. Next, in the second Test at Christchurch, he made sure our ill-fated 'sex, drugs and rock 'n' roll' series in New Zealand would be remembered for all the wrong reasons, scoring 99 in their only innings of 307 then taking three for 16 and five for 25 as they bowled us out for 82 and 93 to win by an innings and 132 runs and secure the first Kiwi series victory over England. He followed up that lot by doing the 'double' of 1,000 runs and 100 wickets for Notts, the first time the feat had been achieved in county cricket since Fred Titmus managed it for Middlesex in 1967.

'As a competitor and a member of the all-rounder's club that also included myself, Imran Khan and Kapil Dev, I had the utmost respect for Richard.'

But the twist in Richard's tale is that in the midst of this purple patch he suffered what he termed 'a mental and physical breakdown'. Not only that, but he actually ascribes the success he then achieved to the motivational therapy he received as a result of the illness.

Being a member of a cricketing dynasty – his father Walter was the captain of the 1949 New Zealand tourists in England and his brother Dayle also won Test caps – meant that Richard's career had always been in the spotlight. Being the best-known cricketer in New Zealand gave him professional and commercial credibility in a sports-mad country, so that he was treated with the adulation normally reserved for All Blacks, but over the years that high-profile existence, and the burden of carrying the Kiwi attack, also created their own pressures.

Not to put too fine a point on it, by the time he returned to New Zealand after the 1983 series in England he was physically knackered and mentally close to breaking point, neurotic, depressed and obsessive. According to him: 'At home, every tiny problem was magnified out of proportion. If a picture on the wall wasn't straight I had to straighten it; if there was a smudge mark on the window, I had to get up and clean it. It was the same with my cricket trophies – I was constantly polishing them. It was ridiculous.' And the meltdown came during a festival match at Rotorua against an Invitation XI that included Mike Gatting and Norman Cowans, a game he started but couldn't finish: 'I came off the pitch in a daze, wondering what the hell was happening to me. I couldn't see properly and my head was splitting.'

Richard was fortunate that in his hour of greatest need he chanced to meet a motivation expert called Graham Felton. Felton had asked if he could run a course for the Canterbury team to help them prepare for the domestic season. Hadlee listened, and during a three-hour version of a course that normally takes twelve, his mood was transformed utterly. He heard Felton talk about goal-setting, the need to dispel fear, visualization techniques which – although commonplace by the end of the 1990s, may have sounded like so much psychobabble to the cynical-minded cricketing fraternity in those days – targets and rewards. And the result was that not only did Richard get his game back together, he also found a way out of the dark and back into the light.

As a competitor and a member of the all-rounders club that also included myself, Imran Khan and Kapil Dev, I had the utmost respect for Richard. And the way he confronted then defeated the demons inside means I have nothing but respect for him as a man.

Ian
Healy

In recent years, the Australians have produced three wicket-keeper/batsmen who deserve to be rated world class.

Rod Marsh was already setting a high standard when I started out on my Test career and most recently the dual roles played by Adam Gilchrist were to prove highly influential while the Aussies were establishing their world record run of 16 straight Test victories. But in between them came Ian Healy, to my mind the best of that kind of cricketer Australia has ever produced.

Ian was just breaking into the Queensland side during my time playing Sheffield Shield in Brisbane, and his attitude and approach to his job impressed me immediately. But even in that hard environment, what made him stand out immediately was his determination to improve himself. This was a quality that remained with him throughout his career.

Although at the time Queensland had a useful leg spinner in Trevor Hohns, it would be fair to say that much of Ian's time was spent standing back, because the attack was very much seam orientated, with people like Carl Rackemann, Craig McDermott, John Maguire and myself in the team.

However, when Ian got into the Australian side he found himself playing a very important part in the success of Shane Warne.

Standing up to a bowler with so many subtle variations could not have been easy. If batsmen were often fooled by Warne, so too could Ian easily have been, but they set about devising a series of signals so that each knew what the other was up to – a bit like a baseball pitcher and catcher, in effect – and how handsomely that hard work paid off.

Early on, standing alongside Ian at slip I quickly realized how determined a competitor he was, but where that came through more than anything was in his batting. He never stopped working at it, and how Australia

BEEFY ON HEALY

Born: 30 April 1964, Spring Hill, Brisbane
Country: Australia
Tests: 119
Hundreds: 4
Average: 27.39
Caught: 366
Stumped: 29
Beefy analysis: World-class wicket-keeper/batsman who proved his mettle time and again for the Aussies.
Beefy moment: Putting Ben Hollioake in his place after his Lord's debut, 1997.
Do mention: Pakistan v Australia, Rawalpindi, 1998 (Healy breaks the world record for a keeper with his 365th victim, Wasim Akram).
Don't mention: The Barmy Army – not keen.

benefited. I lost count of how many times Ian came to Australia's rescue with the bat during his Test career. Often the opposition, and particularly England, thought they might have had the Aussies on the rack with three or four early wickets, but the truth of the matter was that the back of an Australian innings was never really broken until Healy's wicket was in the bag.

His batting wasn't based on sheer obstinacy alone, because he always reckoned that the best form of defence was attack. He was a good one-day performer too, able to up the tempo of his game to suit the game situation and I know how disappointed he was to be left out of their one-day team a couple of years before he retired from Test cricket, when Gilchrist first appeared on the scene.

> 'Early on, standing alongside Ian at slip I quickly realized how determined a competitor he was, but where that came through more than anything was in his batting. He never stopped working at it, and how Australia benefited.'

People will always find some reason to knock a guy like Healy. In his case there is no doubt that he became probably the best Australian sledger of his generation. And take it from me, ladies and gentlemen, to be regarded as the best Australian sledger of his generation took some doing. For my money, the best he ever came up with was pure poetry. Ben Hollioake, making his international debut for England in 1997, at the age of 19 and at Lord's might have thought his innings of 63 was a feather in his cap, particularly as it included some divine boundaries off Glenn McGrath.

As the young star began his walk back to the pavilion and the England supporters rose to their feet to cheer

> 'There is no doubt he became probably the best Australian sledger of his generation.'

him every step of the way, he heard the voice of Healy calling out from behind him.

'Hey, Ben ...' cried Heals.

The young star, suitably moved that his opponent would take the trouble, duly prepared for a gesture of respect from one international cricketer to another but got rather more than he bargained for when Healy finished the sentence with the words: 'Get back to the nets, you idiot.'

A world-class sledge from a world-class cricketer.

Richard Hibbitt

To reach the top in any field of sporting endeavour you need luck, loads of it. Perhaps one of the greatest slices of good fortune I enjoyed was to meet Richard Hibbitt at a crucial stage of my cricketing life. Richard was the deputy head of Milford Junior School, Yeovil when I arrived in September 1962, a couple of months before my seventh birthday, and my first-ever games master.

For me, it was a happy coincidence that such an animal still existed during my formative years for, along with others like Graham Gooch, Mike Gatting and John Emburey, I belonged to the last generation that had the opportunity even to play regular organized competitive sport at a state school.

Soon after we'd passed through the system, such activities were phased out as a result of a combination of mad government education policies that insisted competition was a dirty word, followed by the selling-off of school playing fields – crimes against the youth of this country for which those politicians responsible should be thoroughly ashamed.

Kids need to be able to let off steam. Give them a chance to do so with a ball or bat, and as part of a team effort in which they can develop a sense of shared responsibility, and you increase the likelihood that the habits they learn will be good ones. The results of an alternative approach to sport in state schools, i.e. don't have any, have been clear for all to see for too long. Not only is there a risk of laziness, indolence and ill-health developing; but the psychological effects can be deeply damaging as well. I've never pretended to be an angel, and on occasion I may have been less than a model citizen.

'Richard was the first really to acknowledge my cricketing ability and to encourage it.'

I'm certain the discipline instilled in me by my parents went a long way towards teaching me right from wrong, but I'm also sure that sport helped me to channel and focus some of the aggression within me in those early years and gave me an outlet through which to express myself.

My second stroke of luck was that the man responsible for running our games was someone like Richard, not only prepared to give up so much time for our benefit, but also able to spot some talent worth taking a bit of extra trouble over.

Richard was the first really to acknowledge my cricketing ability and to encourage it. The equipment at our disposal wasn't the greatest, but Richard was so keen that he even went out and bought a couple of bats for our use out of his own pocket. And I like to think I paid back some of his investment almost straight away, when, during my first big innings in a proper match – 80-odd, I think, but no idea who against, I'm afraid – I picked up a ball pitching on my leg stump and hit it clear and clean over the school building, a carry of some 60 yards. Aged nine.

Not that Richard allowed me to get carried away. The aspect of his help and guidance that I most remember was his knack of instilling confidence and making you believe in yourself without letting you get too big for your boots – an approach I tried to stick to throughout my career, with varying degrees of success.

Graeme Hick

'When Graeme Hick made his England debut at the age of 24, it was already clear that cricket had found a batsman to rival the legendary Don Bradman.' By no means the only example of someone burdening my Test and county team-mate with unrealistic expectations – Lord knows there was enough of it – and some came from otherwise reasonably sane observers.

But the jacket copy on the cover of *My Early Life*, a book published to coincide with the end of Graeme's seven-year qualification period and the start of his Test career against West Indies in 1991, neatly makes the point.

When Graeme looks back over his years in cricket he will be entitled to be somewhat puzzled by the generally accepted assessment that his career has been something of a failure. If failure is scoring more than 120 first-class centuries for Worcestershire, ranging from some murderous and bludgeoning assaults on top-quality bowling including the destruction of Curtly Ambrose in a game against Northamptonshire that I will never forget as long as I live, to some merely sublimely faultless displays of controlled aggression – and all of them fashioned in the positive style that made him the most feared batsman in county cricket – then most of us would settle for the disappointment.

From time to time Graeme did demonstrate at Test level exactly how good a player he was. His big hundred against India on the 1993 tour, a wonderful ton against South Africa at Centurion Park in 1994–95, a clattering sixty-odd against Australia in Perth on the 1998–99 Ashes tour and several exhilarating one-day tons spoke for themselves.

Yet although he had earned 60 Test caps prior to the start of the 2001 summer, it must be said that an average of just over 33 at the highest level indicates a lack of consistent success that has been as frustrating as it has been mystifying.

True, for some in our game Graeme has too often been a convenient scapegoat. When England have failed it seems that Hicky's neck has been the first on the block, an impression underlined by the number of comebacks he has been invited to make – nineteen at the time of going to press. And as time and the story progressed I do believe he became so concerned about the consequences of failure that he occasionally retreated into a strokeless shell of his former self.

But there is no escaping the fact that too many times when England have needed him to rise to the occasion and to express his talent fully, something has been missing.

I often wonder how different Graeme's career at Test level might have turned out had he not had to wait so long to qualify for England; spending those seven long years in the waiting room of English domestic cricket hardly helped him push himself to the limits. Just imagine what Hicky might have been had he been given the chance to learn Test cricket at the age of, say, 18; to find out what he needed to improve on and be given the chance to do so. Could he have emulated the progress of a player like Sachin Tendulkar, perhaps?

And one can only speculate on what might have happened had he gone out and hit a century in his first Test match, like Graham Thorpe managed against Australia two summers later.

And there is one more 'what if?' that has to be considered. The place was the Sydney Cricket Ground, the occasion the third Test of the 1994–95 Ashes tour. England, 2–0 down after two, had fought back well to establish a first innings lead of 193 and, at 255 for two in their second, were preparing to set Australia a final innings target. This is how *Wisden* described what followed: 'In what was thought to be the last-but-one over of the innings, Hick, on 98, blocked three successive balls, and Atherton (the

BEEFY ON HICK

Born: 23 May 1966, Salisbury, Rhodesia
Country: England
Tests: 65
Hundreds: 6
Average: 31.32
Beefy analysis: Destroyer of county attacks but often found batting for England too much to cope with.
Beefy moment: Hick sending Curtly Ambrose to all parts during a county game against Northants in the eighties.
Do mention: Somerset v Worcestershire, Taunton, 1988 (Hick's 405* was the highest score made in England that century).
Don't mention: Australia v England, Sydney 1995 (captain Mike Atherton declares England's second innings on 255 for two, with Hick 98* and on the verge of his first, and as it turned out his only, Test century against Australia.)

captain) lost patience and ungenerously declared; he had batted far more slowly himself.'

Those who were present in the dressing room at the time said Hicky was absolutely devastated by Atherton's decision. Would one over really have made such a difference to England's chances of bowling out Australia to win the match? But what benefit might England have gained by allowing Hick to make his first Ashes hundred and, as it turned out, his only one?

Indeed, what has always struck me even during those formative years was the amount of reassurance Graeme seemed to need from those around him. He once complained to our great coach Basil D'Oliveira that he was frustrated that Basil was quite mean with his praise of him. Basil had to explain that the fact he didn't think he needed to praise him was the biggest compliment he could pay him.

Some have even suggested Hick was just too nice a bloke to succeed at Test level; that the kind of aggression and selfishness you need to do so were simply not part of his make-up.

I have no answers. All I can do is wonder how much more English cricket might have got out of Graeme Hick had he been handled differently. I know he does as well.

Michael Holding

To some observers, the image of Michael Holding that lingers is of the frightening and merciless barrage he and Andy Roberts unleashed on Brian Close and John Edrich in that infamous passage of play during the Old Trafford Test of 1976. Not only does that do an injustice to one of the finest fast bowlers who ever lived by obscuring the enormity of his magnificent talent, but it also gives a completely false impression of one of the true good guys of the game.

As a lifelong mate of Closey, I had been one of those who felt the West Indies quicks had gone too far over the top in proving their point to the England captain, Tony Greig, who'd welcomed them to England in 1976 with the promise of making them grovel. But the depth of their feeling was genuine, as they demonstrated by making the sign of the cross on their foreheads when following through after bowling to Greig himself.

Make no mistake, Michael played for wickets, not for fun. And he was prepared to be ruthless when he felt it was necessary or justified. Just how terrifying that Old Trafford experience was for all concerned can be measured in the words of Greig himself, who later admitted, 'When my turn came to bat, it was the first time in my career I felt frightened. For tuppence I'd have given up the game there and then. I felt as though my world had collapsed. The quick men had got to me.' But one little-known story may help those who still criticize Holding for the working-over he and his colleagues administered in the Manchester gloom to look a little more kindly on this proud Jamaican.

For what I witnessed in Hobart during the match between Tasmania and an England XI during our 1982–83 tour Down Under changed my view of Michael for good. The wicket was a shocker and it took about four balls of Michael's first over to show that hospital food might be on the menu. The ball just flew everywhere. Now I can think of some bowlers who, seeing these conditions, would have thought to themselves this was a priceless opportunity to have some fun and even to enhance their reputation. Not Mikey. At first he all but refused to carry on. Then he did something quite extraordinary. He rocked up and bowled nothing but half-volleys. We, grateful for the gesture, declined to take advantage. His figures in the match were nought for 43 off twenty-one overs, it was probably the first and only time he had ever gone wicketless in a cricket match in his life, and *Wisden* wrote: 'Holding, the West Indian Test bowler, was seldom at full pace.' His attitude was straightforward: 'I don't play cricket to hurt people. That is not what this game is about.' And he passed that sense of sportsmanship down to his successor as the pride of Jamaica's pacemen, Courtney Walsh. Far from intimidation, what Michael's game was about was rhythm, agility and high pace. We called him 'whispering death' for a very good reason. Mikey was a superb athlete, formerly a high-quality 400-metre runner, and he had an unusually long run-up. It wasn't a kick-off-the-sightscreen job, mainly for effect. He ran in that far in order to build up the momentum he needed. The difference was that you could never hear him coming. With most of these blokes you could hear the pounding as they approached the crease, like the steps of some not yet visible carnivorous beast in *Jurassic Park*. With Mikey, you

'Michael played for wickets, not for fun. And he was prepared to be ruthless when he felt it was necessary or justified.'

never heard a thing. He seemed to caress the surface with his feet and that was a nightmare when you were at the non-striker's end, because you never knew when to start backing up. Mind you, not many of us backed up too far, because the best place to face him from was the other end.

Michael was responsible for one of the few moments in my career when I almost fell out with King Vivian. One of the greatest tactical moves of my brief spell as England captain was to inform the public that, unless our batsmen started to knuckle down and apply themselves after a couple of defeats on the 1980–81 tour to the Caribbean, heads would roll. In the next Test in Trinidad, I set the perfect example by going down the wicket to Viv and toe-ending an attempted lofted drive straight to Mikey at long-off. By the time Michael had pocketed the catch, Viv had circled me about four times, kindly reminding me 'heads will roll, maan, heads will roll'. I don't mind a bit of banter, but when Viv then decided to accompany me halfway back to the dressing room just to make sure I didn't get lost, I did feel that might have been going a little too far.

The overriding memories I have of Michael concern two examples of his quite brilliant bowling. The first was against England in the final Test of that 1976 series at the Oval. On a gorgeous flat wicket and a parched outfield, Viv set the tone with a glorious 291 out of the Windies' first innings 687. Dennis Amiss replied in kind, with 203 from England's 435. The rest of the match was all about Mikey. He took eight for 92 and six for 57 to help his side to victory by 231 runs in the match and 3–0 in the series. The pitch was a featherbed so Michael ignored it, doing the job with sheer pace through the air instead; in the first dig, five of his victims were clean bowled and two lbw, in the second innings three more were bowled, and one leg before. Greig, who had his stumps rearranged in both knocks, said afterwards that although he saw the deliveries in question all the way, they'd hit the stumps before he was halfway through the shot.

BEEFY ON HOLDING

Born: 16 February 1954, Kingston, Jamaica
Country: West Indies
Tests: 60
Wickets: 249
Average: 23.68
Beefy analysis: His bowling style was all about rhythm, agility and high pace. A natural, graceful athlete, he has now made a successful career as a cricket commentator.
Beefy moment: 'The batsman's Holding... the bowler's Willey' – another Johnners classic.
Do mention: England v West Indies, The Oval, 1976 (his match figures of 14 for 149).
Don't mention: Anything that might upset him.

The second selection is that famous over he bowled to Geoff Boycott in Barbados in '81. It was awesome. Boycs played at every single delivery ... and missed every single delivery, the last of which uprooted his leg stump and sent it cartwheeling madly towards the boundary.

I once asked Michael why he didn't get more involved in the running of West Indies cricket after his retirement. He gave me two reasons: although he was always happy to help with advice to young fast bowlers on a one-to-one basis, the idea of full-time coaching was about as appealing as a four-sweater day in Dunedin; and he was having far too much fun with one of his other great passions –

horseracing. A close friend of the trainer, Sir Michael Stoute and the owner, Robert Sangster, Michael carried his form guide with him wherever he went, calling it his 'bible'.

The only time his tips totally failed me happened when we went to the races together in Jamaica one day. He marked my card, took my money and placed it on eight sure-fire winners. The only problem was that someone forgot to tell the horses. All eight left the stalls quite happily, but not many of them came back. But when I returned to my room that night, I found my entire stake placed carefully on the dressing room table. Now that's what I call class.

Merv Hughes

If you were to ask Allan Border to pick just one player from among all those who played for him while he was compiling his world record of 93 Tests as Australia's captain, Big Merv is the one I'm sure he would go for.

Bearing in mind the great players AB had charge of, such an assessment might surprise a few people. Take it from me, however, that whatever he might have looked like from the boundary – and Merv was larger than life in every sense of the phrase – the burly fast bowler from Victoria was a captain's dream.

Whatever the time of day, however hot it was, however old and dead the ball, or however stubborn the partnership being built by opposition batsmen; even when his side might have been heading for a trashing, Merv would answer his captain's call to bowl without a moment's hesitation. And he would be just as competitive, aggressive, and blood-vessel burstingly enthusiastic as if he had been given the new ball on the first day of a match on a green top after a month on the beach.

'Merv was larger than life in every sense of the phrase – the burly fast bowler from Victoria was a captain's dream.'

Carrying around that massive and powerful bulk took its toll on Merv's joints and bones, though. He would never show it in public, and never hinted at complaining about it in private, but he rarely bowled without some kind of pain keeping him honest. Shane Warne told me recently that on the 1993 Ashes tour here the sight of him repairing himself after a day's play was an inspiration to the whole team – sitting there in the dressing room with ice packs on knee, shoulder, groin or whichever part of his anatomy was currently feeling the most strain, Merv realized how comical he looked. But no one laughed when he was in full flight on the pitch. Ian Healy once said Merv was the quickest Australian bowler to whom he'd ever kept wicket. The mystery to his team-mates was how he kept going as long as he did.

'And he would be just as competitive, aggressive, and blood-vessel burstingly enthusiastic as if he had been given the new ball on the first day of a match on a green top after a month on the beach.'

When Border first came up with the nickname 'Fruitfly' many were non-plussed. Looking like a cross between Ned Kelly and Giant Haystacks, the last thing Merv reminded anyone of was an insect. But when he explained that the insect in question was known as Australia's greatest natural pest, everything fell easily into place. If ever a team-mate started getting ideas above their station, for instance, agreeing to a live television interview in the dressing room or such like, that was the signal for Merv to administer the Foster's shampoo. No one, not even the skipper, was safe.

As for irritating the opposition, Merv was one of the greatest competitors I ever played against. Of course he was as aggressive as he looked from the boundary and he sledged – boy, did he sledge. Merv, along with all the Australians who played their cricket since AB's conversion from nice guy to winner, sincerely believed that getting under an opponent's skin was a valid part of the psychological battle. He let Graeme Hick know that he thought so too, on more than one occasion. Incidentally, I loved Merv's response when Dickie Bird asked him why he gave Hicky such a hard time. 'He offended me in a former life,' Merv informed him, and for once even Dickie was rendered speechless. But the great thing about Merv was that any aggro always stayed out on the field where it belonged and he was quality entertainment over a beer at the end of the day's play. What's more he would always help a mate.

'Whatever the time of day, however hot it was, however old and dead the ball, or however stubborn the partnership being built by opposition batsmen, even when his side might have been heading for a trashing, Merv would answer his captain's call to bowl without a moment's hesitation.'

My final game for Durham was against the 1993 touring Australians and when all the clamour had died down at the end of the day I asked Merv if he would consider writing a piece for my testimonial brochure. I'd expected Merv would get someone to knock out a piece for him and me having to chase him up for it months later, so imagine my surprise and delight when he went and found himself a pen and some paper and wrote the piece out there and then. The game has always needed colourful characters to survive, and you don't get much bigger in this game than Merv. In fact you don't get much bigger than Merv, full stop.

I'll never forget some of the scenes in front of the old Bay 13 at the Melbourne Cricket Ground before they built the massive new stand that dominates everything. That was where you found some of the game's most animated fans, not to say some of the most pissed, and Merv had them eating and drinking out of his hands. Merv doing his warm-up exercises with 5,000 Australian supporters behind him wearing fake Merv moustaches aping his every stretching movement in perfect unison was one of the funniest sights I've seen in sport, and I'm sure cricket Down Under today owes him a huge debt of gratitude for its mass popular appeal.

The question is sometimes asked as to whether Merv's expanding waistline would have found a home in the professional game as it moves into the twenty-first century, with international players surrounded by a whole army of fitness and dietary gurus. Not unnaturally, this is a subject close to my heart. Given that any captain would give his right arm to have Merv Hughes in his side, I am sure he would have found a way of coping. As he once said, 'Wickets are more important than inches.'

'A genuine cult figure,' according to Warney. 'A child in an adult's body.' And the game is fortunate that he never really grew up.

Nasser Hussain

There was a time when, depending on the company you were keeping, the very mention of the idea that Nasser Hussain should become captain of England would have earned you sympathetic glances, hoots of derision, or the offer of strong drink. There was a time? Make that almost all of the time prior to him taking on the job in 1999 and for a little while afterwards as well. And I have to admit that I would have been one of those pouring out the brandy.

I hold up my hands and say that I simply did not believe Nasser could ever become as good a leader of the national side as he has been. He's proved me wrong big-time.

Surly, selfish and stubborn, a fully paid-up member of the 'brat pack' – those are some of the descriptions that had become the constant companions of this Madras-born son of cricket-mad Joe Hussain, who had played up to zonal representative level in India, and his English wife Shireen – and they were among the more flattering. And those who have charted his career will recall some of them were first used as early as his England debut, back in February 1990. Then, the peaceful island idyll of St Kitts reverberated to the spectacular eruption of Mount Nasser disputing whether a catch he had hit to silly point actually carried, first with the fielder in question, next with the captain of Leeward Islands, Richie Richardson, and then with the umpire who had given him out. In the event, Nasser's protestations were so passionate that all of the aforementioned decided the best course of action was to reinstate him before he blew up again. But when he finally did agree to leave the field after being caught again some time later, his showstopping display brought less than rave reviews from skipper Graham Gooch who headed him off before he got back to the pavilion – and the waiting media – to take him on a long and instructive walk around the outfield.

To be fair to the young Nass, you could understand the reasons behind the frustration that subsequently built up within him, and occasionally boiled over. Dumped after that first senior tour, which he ended batting with a broken wrist in the fifth Test in Antigua, Nass had to wait another three years before getting a second chance, against Australia in 1993, then another three before being given his third and final invitation to claim a long-term place in the side, against India in 1996. For a guy who has since proved just how much it means to him to play for England, and in later years to lead them, and a player with so much natural ability, this object lesson in how not to run a selection policy must have been beyond a joke.

But ever since he grabbed his opportunity, almost everything he has done has been impressive enough to persuade his erstwhile critics – myself included – that there was more to Nasser than the cliché of an angry young man. Anyone who scores a double-hundred against the kind of Aussie attack at Mark Taylor's disposal in the first Test of the 1997 Ashes series, including Glenn McGrath, Jason Gillespie and Shane Warne, can bat. But when Mike Atherton gave up the job the following year at the end of the 1997–98 Caribbean tour, he was not the only one convinced that Nasser, the only other serious contender to Alec Stewart, was not up to the task. In my unofficial capacity as adviser to the selectors, privately I too expressed the same view.

'I hold up my hands and say that I simply did not believe Nasser could ever become as good a leader of the national side as he has been.'

I had an inkling that Nasser might prove to be a shrewder tactician than Stewart, but still the doubts about his temperament persisted. Eye witnesses in the dressing room would often comment on the fact that when Nass got out cheaply or was sawn off by a bad decision he would sit alone for hours in his own private world – not exactly the kind of behaviour that helps team spirit. I just felt that if he remained so self-absorbed and unable to see through and outside his own problems, the business of leading ten others and carrying their burdens on his back would be quite beyond him. By now I was not worried so much about the possibility that in heated situations he might blow his stack, although I have to say I thought that still existed. But I was concerned with the question of whether, when necessary, he could take himself out of his own world successfully enough to command the loyalty and respect of his team-mates.

It took him time to do so. After the disaster of the 1999 World Cup and the pay dispute that had so disrupted England's preparations, Alec was removed and Nasser's first experience of the job he had craved for so long ended in the defeat against New Zealand that cemented his side's unofficial position as the worst side in the world. To my mind, there were several mitigating circumstances. First, Nass was hampered by lack of clear thinking among the ECB who, having lost the services of coach David Lloyd, decided insanely that they could wait until after the series against the Kiwis before Lloyd's successor, Duncan Fletcher, need take on the job. Then the confusion over selection priorities – whether to pick a side to beat New Zealand, or start planning for the future – meant that the selectors ended up doing neither.

By the time a panic-inspired squad for the winter tour to South Africa was picked under strong direction from the ECB powers-that-be to come up with some new faces, Nasser found himself in charge of a clutch of unknown quantities such as Chris Adams, Darren Maddy, Graeme Swann, Chris Read, Gavin Hamilton and Michael Vaughan, only the latter of whom subsequently showed he had what it needed to succeed at Test level. But it was here that he and Fletcher started their quiet revolution, getting into the hearts and minds of players to identify who had the right stuff, as a story told to me by Darren Gough illustrates perfectly.

Nasser and Phil Tufnell go back a long way. Both castigated as rebels and trouble-makers, they were brought together by a mutual disregard for some of the more rigid and unimaginative aspects of discipline and authority, and became firm friends. But Nasser knew that one thing he could not afford was anyone within the side thinking he was an easy touch for his mates. According to Darren, Nasser came out for a net at St George's Park in Port Elizabeth on the eve of the second Test and asked

BEEFY ON HUSSAIN

Born: 28 March 1968, Madras, India
Country: England
Tests: 66
Hundreds: 9
Average: 35.15
Beefy analysis: Has proved to be a shrewd and inspirational captain for his country after early doubts about his temperament.
Beefy moment: Nass' rearrangement of the dressing room in Rawalpindi after a dubious lbw decision.
Do mention: England v Australia, Edgbaston, 1997 (he scored 207* against an attack including McGrath, Warne and Gillespie).
Don't mention: 'Heads or tails, Nass?'

where his left-arm spinner was. Tuffers, he was informed, had done ten minutes and was off for a fag and a cuppa. Nasser instructed someone to fetch him. When he finally arrived, the captain made his bollocking very public and very pointed. In front of all the other players and loud enough so that everyone could hear he bawled him out, saying, 'Tuffers, I put my job on the line to get you on this tour. You're a great bowler, but you do not take the p*** out of me. There will not be a next time.' Darren said that the players' respect for Nasser went up several notches there and then.

It is ironic that the real turning point for Nass as captain came in his absence, as Stewart deputized for him in the second Test against West Indies at Lord's, when the dismissal of Brian Lara & Co. for 54 and the batting heroics of Dominic Cork won a memorable three-day match. But the resilience they showed in coming from behind there reflected the fact that the principles he and Fletcher were trying to instil into their players had begun to take hold. Put simply: give them responsibility and a feeling of belonging, and they will respond. In this new, 'inclusive' regime, players whose opinions were largely ignored, are now asked to make a full contribution to team thinking.

In Pakistan in the winter of 2000, then in Sri Lanka at the start of 2001, these ideas bore fruit in spectacular fashion. Even though he was struggling badly for form himself, a situation that in the past could have been catastrophic, he kept his players going with constant encouragement and, when necessary, the odd kick up the backside. Only once did the old Nass surface, when a dressing-room fridge door received the full treatment in Rawalpindi, but the lbw decision in question would have tried the patience of a saint. But he didn't hold back on his team-mates if he felt he had to step in and his treatment of Goughy when he lost his rag in a one-day match in Dambulla that he probably felt he shouldn't have been playing in, was an object lesson in captaincy. Nasser stepped in before the umpires did, ushered Gough from the field to cool off, then, when confronted by a hot and bad-tempered press corps afterwards, backed his premier strike bowler unequivocally and defused the issue totally.

Nass never lost sight of the fact that every single member of the side needed to be treated differently, as individuals, with individual problems and individual needs – and Andy Caddick's brilliant form testifies to how successful he was in that particular aspect of man-management – and they paid him back.

Pakistan, thrillingly, thwarted England's efforts to win five consecutive Test series by taking the second Test of the 2001 home series prior to the Ashes contest, and how his absence from the second Test and later two more Tests in the Ashes series adversely affected their chances, but Nasser's position in the top rank of modern England captains was already assured by a run of historic victories – over Zimbabwe, over West Indies for the first time in 31 years; over Pakistan for the first time in Pakistan; and over Sri Lanka – that took his side from rock bottom to third in the world rankings in less than a year.

I never thought you had it in you, Nashwan. I'm very glad I was wrong.

Imran Khan

The era when I was playing my best cricket for England bucked the trend of cricketing history. Never before had so many Test teams contained such high-class all-rounders.

Cricket-lovers of a certain age, for instance, will tell you that Keith Miller, the brilliant Aussie all-rounder of the post World War II era was entitled to be called the best of all time.

Maybe so, but he was a minority of one at the time. Later, the world of cricket was lucky to be graced by the wonderful Sir Gary Sobers, a supple, graceful and occasionally brutal batsman with the bowling talent to send down the quick or the twirly stuff with equal menace, and a close-to-the-wicket fielder to rank alongside the best. But even his reign as the world's number one all-rounder was never under any threat because of the paucity of the competition.

How different it was during my career, and how we all thrived on trying to out-do each other. To be compared day-in and day-out to India's Kapil Dev, New

'There was an awful lot in his game that had to be admired.'

Zealand's Richard Hadlee, and Pakistan's Imran Khan created a special and unique rivalry within the game. I don't know about the others, but if there was a Test match being played anywhere in the world I would want to know how those guys were doing. If any of them had bagged a 'five-for' or hit a fifty, it definitely spurred me on to try and match or beat that the next time around.

The statistics were astonishing – Botham 383 Test wickets, Hadlee 431, Kapil 434, and Imran 362. I can just about remember when Fred Trueman was the first to break the 300-wicket barrier, and it was said at

'As a captain he was clever and proud. Imran got the Pakistan team of his day performing more as a unit.'

the time that no one else would ever do this. Yet all four of us did, by some margin, as well as being frontline performers with the bat: me 5,200 Test runs with 14 centuries, Hadlee 3,124, Kapil 5,248, and Imran 3,807. Had apartheid not intervened, I wonder whether Mike Procter might not also have been right up there with us.

I mention all these statistics for one other reason, however, because, sad to say, in the case of Imran I believe they have to be recorded with a big question mark against them.

The differences expressed between Imran and myself in our long-running High Court battle are long since dead and buried. However – and this is not said with bitterness because I lost the court case but with a genuine feeling for the basic traditions of the game – I have to question the methods he used in order to achieve everything he did with the ball.

Imran has admitted publicly that during his career he tampered with the condition of the cricket ball to help him create movement, a revelation that left me wondering just how many batsmen lost their wickets as a result of his illegal practices. His argument is that the methods he said he used – deliberately roughing up one side of the ball, or scratching the surface, to encourage reverse swing – had always been an accepted aspect of the game. All very well, but the cold and indisputable fact is that they were, are and forever will be against the rules of the game, and if you disregard those rules you are not treating the game with the respect it deserves. Call me old-fashioned but, once you start tampering with the ball and tampering with the rules and then saying it is acceptable to do so, you are setting dangerous precedents for future generations to follow; not to put too fine a point on it, it's cheating.

All that having been said, there was an awful lot in his game that demanded admiration.

As a captain he was clever and proud. Pakistani cricket teams have always been fragmented by politics and personalities. But just as Clive Lloyd was largely instrumental in unifying the many island factions in the West Indies, Imran got the Pakistan team of his day performing more as a unit; even succeeding in getting Javed Miandad to play for him more often than not!

'My lasting memory will be of a superb cricketer, a more than worthy adversary, and someone who, overall, made the game of cricket better for his presence.'

When Imran first appeared on the Test scene he was a medium-pacer who batted at No. 9 and was not that effective at either discipline. Over the years, however, he developed the ability to bowl quickly with deceptive pace and plenty of variation. His leap prior to releasing the ball enabled him to get extra bounce from the most docile of pitches. With the bat on his day he could destroy teams.

Furthermore, even though his cricketing reputation might be tainted by his own hand to a certain extent, no one should forget the tireless work he has done in setting up Pakistan's first cancer hospital in memory of his mother. Imran and I may have had our moments, but my lasting memory will be of a superb cricketer, a more than worthy adversary, and despite my reservations someone who made the game of cricket better for his presence.

Mick Jagger

Mick Jagger knows more about cricket than some of the old farts who have ended up picking the England team over the years.

In both of my careers, as a player and TV commentator, I've bumped into Mick all over the world during Test matches – and for 25 years it's been a privilege to share his passion for the game. And, yes, I like the Rolling Stones' music, too; in fact, I'm not sure whether Mick loves his cricket more than I enjoy driving along with Jagger's vocals blaring from the car stereo.

Away from professional sport, one of the biggest thrills of my life was dropping in on the Stones' recording studio in Paris when they were producing their most recent album. I had nipped over the Channel to the Paris Air Show with Alan Dyer – an experienced round-the-world pilot who is also godfather to my youngest daughter, Becky – and the open invitation from Jagger to call in and watch the band at work was too good an opportunity to miss.

Jagger greeted us like long-lost brothers when we pitched up at the studio. Until midnight, not a great deal happened: these rock-and-roll legends strummed a few chords, tested the sound systems, and their production crew twiddled a few knobs on dashboards in the mixing suite. Then, suddenly, at about 2 am, it all came together. While Paris slept, the Stones belted out track after track. To watch the world's greatest band in their element was simply incredible.

Our enjoyment of this little soirée was lubricated by the delivery of Jagger's customary nightcap for the band – a case of Jack Daniels – and by the time we'd polished off one for the boulevard it was 5.30 am, and I wasn't sure if the huge metal edifice piercing the skyline in the distance was the Eiffel Tower or the Blackpool Tower.

Although the following day was one long round of refuelling with several gallons of strong black coffee, that memorable, mind-blowing weekend had been worth every moment. It's not often you get a ringside seat while some of the planet's most revered rockers cut a new album. To be afforded such lavish hospitality and VIP treatment from the likes of Jagger is a great compliment, not least because rock stars tend to be cocooned in their own little world, and it's reassuring that, when you strip away all the razzmatazz, they are as mortal as the rest of us.

As for Mick, let's just say that if there's a Test match on and England are playing, don't be surprised if he turns up. I remember getting back to my hotel room in Georgetown, Guyana, one evening, during a tour of the West Indies, to find a note from him slipped under the door. On another occasion, during the 1986 tour of the Caribbean, he beckoned me into one of the stands at Bridgetown during lunch on the Saturday of the Barbados Test and invited me to dinner at his house on the island that night. Needless to say, I was very happy to accept, and we spent most of the evening discussing cricket and England's prospects of regaining the Ashes the following winter. By his own admission, Mick doesn't see as much live cricket as he would wish these days, because the Stones' recording and touring commitments are still absolutely phenomenal, but he still loves coming to watch England play whenever he can and, where possible, I've tried to reciprocate his hospitality.

Back in the early 1980s, he paid a flying visit to London which coincided with the Lord's Test, and my former agent, the late Reg Hayter – who ran a sports agency just behind Fleet Street and coached many budding cricket writers – managed to conjure up a pair of tickets for him. Mick was so chuffed that he asked his office to send Reg a gift as a token of his thanks, and a motorcycle messenger was duly despatched across London to deliver it. Dear old Reg, who would have been pushing 70 years old, and whose pop music tastes were, shall we say, antiquated, must have got the shock of his life when he opened up the envelope and found a signed copy of the Rolling Stones' latest album, *Emotional Rescue*!

There has been the odd occasion when I wouldn't have minded swapping places with Jagger. On the day he was rocking the planet at Live Aid in 1985, I was being summoned to a kangaroo court at Lord's for allegedly bringing cricket into disrepute during an Ashes Test at Trent Bridge, where umpire Alan Whitehead reported me for blowing a gasket.

But it's been great to know someone of Mick's standing worldwide who has such an intimate knowledge and deep-seated love of the game. He runs his own team in France, while his brother Chris has one in England, and they are very much a family of cricket-lovers. Perhaps I see a bit of Jagger in myself – after all, there's a bit of the rebel in him, and that's what attracts a lot of people to the Stones' music.

If I have one regret about Jagger, it's that I never had the chance to play against him in a showbiz charity match or a benefit game. Fellow

Stone Bill Wyman still turns out for the Bunburys XI, and he looks like he knows the thin end of a cricket bat from the business end, although his habit of smoking and batting at the same time can be a little off-putting for opposing bowlers.

But if Mick Jagger's stage persona is anything to go by, watching him appeal for lbw or a catch behind would be a sight to behold.

Javed Miandad

It was Imran Khan who came up with the following verdict on his fellow countryman, Javed Miandad: 'He has tended to symbolize the strengths and defects of our batting in recent years – exotic strokeplay mixed up with suicidal tendencies.'

Those suicidal tendencies were never better demonstrated than when Javed, as captain of Pakistan, squared up to Dennis Lillee during the WACA Test in 1981.

Even with bat in hand, Javed was giving away so many inches and pounds to DK that not even Don King would have dared to promote that contest. Javed had turned the ball for a single and was obstructed by DK. In the ensuing scuffle, Dennis kicked him. Umpire Tony Crafter then got between the pair as Javed tried to thump DK with his bat. Lillee received a two-match ban after the umpires objected to the £120 fine being too lenient. To nobody's surprise, there was never any sign of the apology requested from Javed. That was Javed, finding any way he could to get under the bowler's skin and exploit the situation.

He thrived on controversy and confrontation, and refused to be intimidated by anyone. Often smiling in the tensest of situations, the width of Javed's bat seemed to increase with the fielding side's growing frustration.

DK wasn't on his own. Javed and I had our little spats on several occasions. Our last time in earnest competition came during Pakistan's tour of England in 1992, the summer of the ball-tampering allegations, when the powers-that-be decided to stage the one-day tournament either side of the Test series. England and I were keen to put one over on the tourists after losing to them in the World Cup Final at the MCG a few months earlier. Pakistan had only sneaked the last semi-final spot of that World Cup because our group game against them had been abandoned after we'd bowled them out for 74, their lowest-ever total in one-day cricket.

BEEFY ON JAVED

Born: 12 June 1957, Karachi
Country: Pakistan
Tests: 124
Hundreds: 23
Average: 52.57
Beefy analysis: An instinctive, inventive batsman and thinking captain, a superb player on awkward wickets and a great accumulator of runs.
Beefy moment: Handbags-at-five-paces scuffle between Javed and Dennis Lillee, Perth, 1981.
Do mention: Pakistan v New Zealand, Karachi, 1976 (his 206, at the age of 19, remains a record for the youngest player ever to score a double century in Tests).
Don't mention: Umpires.

Yet it was Pakistan that took the trophy by 22 runs as I collected my second World Cup Final loser's medal. We had Pakistan on the ropes at 24 for two when Derek Pringle had Javed for as plum an lbw as I've ever seen. Nearly a decade on, Pringle still can't come to terms with umpire Steve Bucknor's reluctance to raise the finger. Javed hit 58 before I caught him of Richard Illingworth, but the 139 he and Imran put on for the third wicket turned the final.

Instead, England had to make do with the Javed lbw that Philip DeFreitas was granted in Rawalpindi during the previous World Cup. It nearly started a riot when Australian Tony Crafter raised his finger to give Javed Miandad out. We soon found out why. Javed had been playing first-class cricket since 1973, and test cricket for 11 years. Would you believe it, he had never, ever been given out lbw in Pakistan in all that time. Even then, Javed was reluctant to go, and a few words of encouragement from the likes of Daffy, David Capel and others only increased his feelings of grievance.

'Not only was he an inventive batsman, intuitive cricketer and instinctive captain, Javed was also one of the great thinkers of the game – as well as being as good a cover fielder as I've ever seen.'

Back to 1992 and the Oval, and yet another Javed lbw appeal. There are certain wickets I've prized more than others. Not only because I regard them as the best batsmen in the world, but because those players never give their wicket away, no matter the match situation or how they are feeling. Viv Richards was at the very top of that list, with Allan Border and Javed close behind. I always got an extra thrill when they were walking back to the pavilion when I was bowling because getting them out had taken something special.

Javed had made 38 that day, and Pakistan were 220 for four chasing our 302 when I rattled the ball into his pads. I wasn't sure Merv Kitchen would raise his finger to my wholehearted appeal, but up it went and I started my normal restrained celebrations by declaring 'You f****** beauty!' That's when the troubled started. Javed heard the 'F' word and thought it was directed at him. He had a few words with Kitchen. I thought he was complaining about the decision, when he was actually objecting to my behaviour. Now the ball was rolling. Soon the Pakistan manager Intikhab Alam, and the match referee, Bob Cowper, were involved and those wise heads came up with this statement: 'Misinterpretation of what was said, leading to a misunderstanding.'

That was Javed Miandad, defiant and argumentative to the end, a cricketer whose competitive edge has not been blunted by age. Since retiring (he was the only man to play in every one of the first six World Cups, as well as scoring 8832 runs in 124 tests, with 23 centuries), Javed has enjoyed – if that is the right word – two spells as Pakistan coach, although he is now involved with the Bangladesh national side. His style has not changed. He was even brave enough to go on the record to the Qayyum Report about what he suspected had been going on in the Pakistan dressing-room regarding match-fixing and gambling.

Not only was he an inventive batsman, intuitive cricketer and instinctive captain, Javed was also one of the great thinkers of the game – as well as being as good a cover fielder as I've ever seen.

We were both named 'Cricketers of the Year' in the *1982 Wisden Almanack* – me for my Ashes exploits the previous summer, and Javed for his 1981 summer with Glamorgan. He's loved in Wales because of the way he inspired that county. Javed's finest moment came in a 13-run defeat against Essex towards the end of the season. Glamorgan, set 325 on a dusty Colchester track, looked history at 44 for four. Javed finally ran out of partners, but the Pakistan right-hander was unbowed and undefeated on 200. That was his seventh century of the season. Another in the final game at Sophia Gardens against Leicestershire took him past Gilbert Parkhouse's record, as well as becoming only the fourth player from the Welsh county to reach 2,000 runs.

'He thrived on controversy and confrontation, and refused to be intimidated by anyone.'

I suppose I should let him have the final word, even in this tribute. Once again, we are locked in battle at the Oval – this time in 1987.

Mike Gatting and I saved that final Test with a fifth-wicket stand of almost 200 on the final day after England had followed on. We had narrowly missed that safety mark by the small matter of 277 runs after Pakistan's first-innings 708, their highest-ever in Tests. That huge total included 260 from Javed, who batted for over 10 hours and looked odds-on at one time to beat Sir Gary Sobers' 365. Javed had come in at 40 for two and left at 573 for five. It was a masterful knock, full of all the Javed qualities – improvisation, stubbornness, defiance, and undoubted skill. All Javed Miandad left me with that weekend were the worst bowling figures, in terms of runs conceded, of any England bowler in cricket history – three for 217 off 52 overs. He was still smiling about that in Pakistan during the 2000 winter tour! For all our scrapes and confrontations, Javed is great company and an extremely generous host.

Final word? Javed is the subject of the world's worst cricketing joke, namely: Which father and son played together for Pakistan? Javed, Me and Dad...

Elton John

During the many years that Bill Beaumont and I enjoyed as opposing team captains on TV's ever-popular *A Question of Sport*, half the humour was generated by seeing our team-mates (or, more often, ourselves) stumbling to find answers that would be blindingly obvious to primary schoolkids. The sight of the country's top sportsmen and women making complete and utter fools of themselves was one of the reasons why the show always attracted an audience of millions and lasted so long. With nothing more at stake than personal pride, *A Question of Sport* was never meant to be taken very seriously. However, had it been a matter of life and death each week, there is no doubt as to who would be my first choice as a team-mate: it would have to be Elton John.

When it comes to sports knowledge there just isn't anyone to beat the man. Obviously, as chairman of Watford, and with his love of the game, you would expect Elton to know a fair bit about soccer. But his knowledge goes far further than that. I've lost count of the times when I have been sitting opposite him over dinner and been left open-mouthed as he's talked with total authority, not only about football, but on every sport under the sun, from athletics to water-polo. Don't even mention tennis!

'When it comes to sports knowledge there just isn't anyone to beat the man. Obviously, as chairman of Watford, and with his love of the game, you would expect Elton to know a fair bit about soccer. But his knowledge goes far further than that.'

It was through his love of cricket that I got to know him in the winter of 1982–83. We were in Australia battling away to try to keep the Ashes while Elton was in the same part of the world for his *Too Low For Zero* tour, and don't tell me it was just pure coincidence that he was performing down under at the same time as the Test series. Barely a day went past without the Channel Nine cameras zooming in on Elton's features as he sat in the stands watching.

For the Sydney Test, we found ourselves staying in the same hotel as Elton, the Sebel Town House, and at night he would join the boys for drinks or invite us to a party, and we also saw quite a few of his concerts. It was during that week that I discovered just how generous a friend Elton can be.

'He's talked with total authority, not only about football, but on every sport under the sun, from athletics to water-polo.'

One night, after play, when I was particularly knackered after bowling too many overs in the heat at the SCG, I arrived back at the Sebel to find a stretch limousine waiting outside the hotel, with the doorman insisting it was for me. I knew absolutely nothing about it, but when I got back to our room Kath told me that it was Elton's. He'd put it at our disposal to go out and have a quiet dinner, and he was going to spend the evening with our nanny, Diane, looking after the kids.

When we returned we found that Elton had invited Diane, along with the young Liam and Sarah up to his suite for a party. What a night they'd had, stuffed full of jellies and ice creams, and Elton had been entertaining them all evening on the piano. That was typical of his generosity.

During that tour Down Under, he and I would discuss the nature of celebrity, and how to handle it. Typical of the guy, although he had been through so much in his life and suffered so much lurid publicity as a result, he was only too willing to offer help and guidance.

The highlight of our tour on the field was our nailbiting win in the Melbourne Test. Unfortunately for Elton his tour came to a shuddering stop in Perth. We'd been together that lunch-time at a barbecue hosted by Graeme 'Foxy' Fowler, who was playing grade cricket in Western Australia. It must have been a hell of a bash because that evening's concert was cancelled, and Elton didn't sing again for several months because of a throat problem.

Through my friendship with Elton, I also got to know Bob Halley, known around the world simply as 'PA.' There are millions of personal assistants, but only one who looks after Elton John. Bob has had that job for as long as I can remember, and remains an integral part of Elton's set-up. Elton spends a lot of time in the USA these days, so I don't see as much of Bob as I used to, or would like to, but we've had some great times over the years.

A couple of years prior to the victorious Aussie tour, on our way from New Zealand to Pakistan, we had diverted to Sydney for an overnight stop because of engine trouble. I knew Elton was in Melbourne, so I called Bob when I got to the team hotel and invited myself over for a glass of wine. 'No problem', said Bob. 'I'll send the private jet to fetch you and we'll take you back to Sydney in the morning in good time for you to catch the onward flight to Pakistan.' So off I headed for a quiet night with Elton, Bob and the gang. Next morning, things went precisely according to plan right up to the moment we realised the private jet wouldn't start. Eventually, with panic rising, I made that plane for Pakistan by about five minutes. The lads thought I was just being super cool as usual, but I was really sweating on how I would explain away missing the team flight.

You've probably heard that Elton has a fairly extensive wardrobe, but Bob's is not far behind. There's no more fussy dresser than Bob. He is the only person, other than Viv Richards, who will not wear a shirt if it has the slightest crease or mark on it. The smallest imperfection and back it goes to the laundry.

Elton expects great loyalty from those around him. So when he decided to give up alcohol, they knew what was expected. They all had to go on the wagon, too, especially when Elton was around, even Bob. At the time, I was in pantomime with Robin Askwith at the Wimbledon Theatre doing *Dick Whittington*. One night there was a knock on my dressing-room door. When it opened, there was a beaming Bob Halley, bottle of champagne in hand. This founder member of Elton's temperance club was going off the rails for one night at least, and couldn't be happier.

Kapil Dev

Kapil Dev was the first Indian cricketer to experience the Bollywood treatment. From the moment the 'Haryana Hurricane' started to brew up his storm, his approach was pure box-office, and how the Indian fans idolized him for it.

I count myself extremely fortunate to have played the bulk of my international cricket in the company of a clutch of outstanding all-rounders. It was quite a freaky time in that respect, and the fact that Kapil, Imran Khan and Richard Hadlee were vying with each

other and myself for the unofficial title of 'the best in the world' undoubtedly spurred us all on. Clearly, every single one of us was a born competitor. To look around the world and see that Kapil or one of the others had turned in a match-winning performance was just the nudge in the ribs the rest of us needed to step up a gear. And when we came face to face, although the interests of the team were obviously of paramount importance, if I told you that we weren't waging our own battles within the war I would be lying.

'I enjoyed my tussles with Kaps more than most. I loved his attitude to the game – attack at all times except when defence is absolutely the only option – because it mirrored my own.'

I enjoyed my tussles with Kaps more than most. I loved his attitude to the game – attack at all times except when defence is absolutely the only option – because it mirrored my own. We were winners because we didn't fear losing, and the overriding principle for both of us was that playing cricket had to be fun, or it wasn't worth the candle. Maybe he could afford to be so gung-ho in his approach, because as the son of a successful building and timber contractor in Chandigarh, Kaps never had to play cricket for a living. Still, having such an opportunity is one thing, taking it is another matter entirely.

Early on in our careers, whenever we met our desire to outdo each other would make for moments that both of us might look back upon and cringe at our naïvety. We first collided during the 1979 series between England and India, and neither of us could resist the challenge of taking on the other. At Lord's, Sunil Gavaskar became my 100th Test victim in my 19th match for England, but just as memorable for me was snaring Kaps for the third time in three innings.

In the first Test at Edgbaston I dismissed him for one and 21, and, in the second Test at Lord's, his desire for revenge was almost jumping out of his skin. I got myself wrapped up in the fervour and gave him four pretty awful deliveries to start with. The fifth was even worse, a wide outswinger not fit for man nor beast, but Kaps was so intent on making a positive statement that he launched himself at it and promptly sent a thick edge to Geoff Miller in the slips. In the final Test of that series at the Oval, he underlined how impetuous he could be. Sunny was in the process of crafting a wonderful double-hundred as he led their chase for 438 in 500 minutes, but when Kapil came in to join him, instead of pushing the ball around in support, he slogged one up in the air and India had to settle for a draw in one of the wobbliest final sessions I can recall.

We may have got older and a shade more mature as the years have passed but the keen sense of rivalry never dimmed. Whereas with most opponents, for me success or failure lasted no longer than the next innings or run. Both of us had long memories when it came to the detail of our skirmishes. With the bat, when the force was with him, Kaps could be utterly devastating and the bigger the occasion the more he thrived on it.

Again at Lord's, on India's next tour to England in 1982, Kapil took the match into a fifth day single-handedly, with an extraordinary knock of 89 in 55 balls. By the time I had him caught by Geoff Cook, he'd hit 13 fours and three sixes and was well on course for what would have been the fastest Test hundred of all time. In a World Cup qualifying match against Zimbabwe at Tunbridge Wells the following season he went in with India struggling on 9 for four, lost another partner at 17 for five, then proceeded to smash an unbeaten 175 out of 266 for eight, and, as captain, eventually led his country to a shock win in the final over the mighty West Indies at Lord's.

And it was at Lord's once more (where else?) in the first Test of the 1990 series, also made memorable by Graham Gooch's 333, that Kapil proved that while he was prepared to play the same game as the rest of the mortals, on occasion what he really needed to make it all worthwhile was a shot at the impossible. India needed 24 to avoid the follow-on when Kaps was joined by last-man and confirmed walking-wicket, Narendra Hirwani. Knowing full well that his partner was as good as dead as soon as he took strike, Kaps resolved to settle the issue there and then. He blocked the first two deliveries of the next over from Eddie Hemmings, then hit the remaining four back over his head into the building site at the Nursery End. From the next ball of the innings, Hirwani was lbw to Angus Fraser.

As a bowler, Kapil's performance in collecting 434 Test wickets, only surpassed by the amazing Courtney Walsh, is even more remarkable because for long periods he carried the Indian pace attack single-handedly. He had incredible stamina and troubled the best batsmen with his ability to swing the ball away from the right-handed batsman at pace. His run-up was a thing of beauty, economical and easy, and he had the ability to change pace with no discernible change in action. His bouncer, well disguised, was rarely wasted. It was at you and straight, and said, 'Go on, take it on if you want.'

'And in everything he did, Kaps had the swank and swagger of the cavalier about him.'

In everything he did, Kaps had the swank and swagger of the cavalier about him, the magic ingredient that elevated him to the status of a sporting demi-god in his homeland. Once, while he was enjoying himself on the championship circuit with Northamptonshire, I suggested to him that being at the centre of attention in such a cricket-crazy country as India, with its film-star treatment and *National Enquirer* intrusion as far removed from the gentle existence of the average English pro as it was possible to imagine, must be quite hard to handle.

'Are you kidding?' he laughed, flashing an Oscar-winner's wall of white teeth. 'How awful it must be not to be the centre of attention.'

Karim
Din

Karim Din is the owner of the best Indian restaurant in England, an accolade that would probably be enough on its own to warrant a place in this book. But, much more importantly, Karim has been a very good friend of the Botham family for about 25 years. You find out who your real friends are when you're in trouble; they're the ones left when the hangers-on and fair-weather types have gone for a powder. During my High Court clash with Imran Khan, Karim, who is from Pakistan, was prepared to come to court on my behalf.

I have always been a curry man. Is there anyone who doesn't like a good curry on a Friday night? In the old days, I'd wash it down with a few pints of beer; nowadays it's wine. I like all types – from fruity, to spicy, to very hot. Karim's restaurant is the 'Indus' in Doncaster, near where Kath's family live; that's how I got to know it, and it's always been the first place we eat when we're in the area.

I'll always remember his first appearance on my first Leukaemia Walk. When a group of Harley Davidsons came roaring into view, driven by guys in full leather regalia, I thought we might be in for a spot of bother with the local chapter of the Hell's Angels. But when the leader of the pack got off the back of one of the bikes and removed his helmet, the mood changed completely. It was Karim, with a couple of weeks' supplies of curries – all my favourites – for the walk. They were loaded into the mobile home, and just when our rations were looking thin, this motorbike cavalcade would reappear with more. From that day onwards, until the end of my last Leukaemia Walk in 1999, we never ran out, and his arrival heralded the culinary high point of the walks.

Karim provided something much more valuable than curry during the Imran Khan action, though. When he heard about the case, he called me and offered to go into the witness box as a character witness. I replied that he didn't have to put his reputation on the line for me, but he wanted to do it. When the news got out, Karim received death threats. He dismissed them as cranks, but no one is ever sure, and it must have been a worrying time for him. Although he was never called to give evidence, Karim sat in the High Court for three days. His offer took a lot of courage, and his gesture is something I will always appreciate.

Alan Knott

As with every career, however distinguished, there are a few gaps in my CV – like a World Cup winner's medal, all 10 wickets in an innings, a year when I wasn't on the front pages of the tabloids for some reason or other, or sharing a room on tour with Alan Knott. I'm not sure who is more relieved by that final omission – me or Knottie. In terms of barking mad, even Jack Russell was a poodle compared to Knottie's Great Dane. Alan Philip Eric Knott is cricket's great eccentric of modern times and, for me, the greatest wicket-keeper, ahead of Bob Taylor, Rod Marsh and Ian Healy.

Knott and Botham in the same room would have been a cocktail for disaster; by the end of a week, one of us would have been talking to the walls, and I've a feeling that would have been me!

But I was always pleased to see Knottie at breakfast, lunch or dinner – though, preferably, not at the same table. His food was sent back more times than Allan Lamb returned the red wine. His menu was limited – meat (no sauces), vegetables and potatoes – but everything had to be cremated. He rarely drank, just the odd glass of sherry. At the end of the day, he'd sit there sipping his half-pint of lemonade. Just when I thought I was used to all his little ways, including a shower and complete change of clothing at each interval, he pitched up for a tour of India with his own pillow to ensure a good night's sleep. Even on the field, Knottie looked like Inspector Gadget – collar up, dark glasses, floppy hat (it had been a cap, but after injuring his neck during a crash on the Brands Hatch circuit, the floppy allowed him to see the ball without bending his neck), creamed-up, stretching, bending, never still, up and down, neck twisting right and left, and keeping immaculately.

BEEFY ON KNOTT

Born: 9 April 1946, Belvedere, Kent
Country: England
Tests: 95
Hundreds: 5
Average: 32.75
Caught: 250
Stumped: 19
Beefy analysis: The finest wicket-keeper in the game's history, whose lightning reflexes allied to an unorthodox approach made him such a unique talent.
Beefy moment: Knottie's half century against Australia at Old Trafford in 1981, which was just as vital as my innings of 118.
Do mention: England v Australia, Trent Bridge, 1977 (his 135 was his highest Test innings).
Don't mention: Being normal.

We might have joked and taken the mick about all his strange mannerisms and habits, but every England cricketer I knew had the utmost respect for this wicket-keeper from Kent, a county with a great tradition of England stumpers, most notably Les Ames and Godfrey

Evans. The old-timers have told me that Godfrey was the best, mainly because of the way he stood up to Alec Bedser. I've always countered that with Knottie's time behind the stumps dealing with Derek Underwood, never easy on a normal wicket, almost unplayable and untakable on a juicy or flying surface. As a catcher, he was brilliant, usually with a minimum of fuss. I will never forget his dismissal of Rod Marsh at Headingley in my first series: breathtaking.

Those lightning reflexes were also put to good use when batting. His unorthodox approach made him extremely dangerous, and I regard him as one of the best players of spin I've seen. He was good enough with the bat to have earned a place on that skill alone.

'Lightning reflexes were put to good use when batting. His unorthodox approach made him extremely dangerous, and I regard him as one of the best players of spin I've seen. He was good enough with the bat to have earned a place on that skill alone.'

Yet, while most of us were locked into the coaching manual in varying degrees, Knottie seemed to start from scratch each time. In his own intuitive way, he would assess the situation and come up with his individual game plan. More often than not, it worked. It was great to watch the opposition's growing frustration as this little man undid all their earlier good work with intentional cuts over the slips. His finest hour with the bat was that century on the 1974–75 Ashes tour against Lillee and Thomson. It was typical Knott... complete concentration and clever improvisation.

I suppose in many ways his batting was an extension of his wicket-keeping. Extremely light on his feet, picking up the line and length of the ball was second nature to him, as was staying focused for ball after ball, over after over, and session after session. His maiden Test hundred should have come at Karachi on the 1968–69 tour of Pakistan, but after a pitch invasion, the match was abandoned with Knottie stranded on 96. When he finally raised his bat to acknowledge his first Test century, at Auckland, another two years had passed. It's a shame Knottie failed by four runs to add another in the second innings because, not only did he hit 116 in his next Test knock, at Edgbaston against Pakistan, but he would have become the first wicket-keeper to score 100 in each innings of a Test.

Knottie looked on course to break all wicket-keeping records when I joined the England set-up in 1977, but his record run of 65 consecutive appearances came to an end at the conclusion of that Ashes series when he joined Kerry Packer's World Series circus. He returned, under my captaincy, for the 1980 West Indies series, aged 34; his last two Tests were the final pair in that amazing 1981 summer. This time he headed for South Africa on the rebel tour and, with a three-year ban announced for that excursion, there was no international comeback, although he played for Kent until 1985.

Knott's record of 250 catches and 19 stumpings is naturally what you would expect from someone Kent signed as a youngster who wanted to bowl off-breaks. His 95 Tests also brought him 4,389 runs, including five centuries, often valuable runs that rescued England from dire positions. And, not many people might know this, but Alan Knott was the first England captain I played under, when he took over the job for a one-day international against West Indies at Scarborough in 1976, my international debut.

Knottie broke and held many Test records, several of which are still standing. But those statistical achievements are not what stick in my memory. That's not why Knottie played the game and behaved in the weird way he did. Knott wanted to be the best, and his every waking moment – and quite a few of the sleeping ones – was spent ensuring that no stone was left unturned in his preparation. It was not the Botham method; likewise, I wouldn't have been much good to England if I'd been tucked up in bed by 10 o'clock the night before. But I have always respected his dedication, determination, talent and right to be different. And the proof of that pudding is that Alan Knott is the benchmark by which I judge every other wicket-keeper.

Allan Lamb

After all the thrills and spills Lambie and I have been through together, I feel like I have known the guy all my life. We've had our fun times on so many England tours and out on the road with our roadshow, and we've had some tough times together, battling it out against the West Indian fast bowlers and fighting together in the same court-room to defend ourselves against Imran Khan's allegation that we were racists. And the characteristic that oozes out of every pore of Lambie is courage bordering on insanity.

This was never more obvious than when I watched him take to the ski slopes for the first time. The idea of going to ski school, learning how to snowplough before graduating to paralleling daintily down to the piste did not figure in his plans at all. He simply took himself to the top of the first slope he could find, put his head down, tucked his poles under his arms and headed off like Eddie the Eagle, with no regard for his own safety or, for that matter, the safety of those below him on the mountain.

Such a gung-ho approach to life and to cricket – almost certainly borne of his experiences doing National Service in the South African army – goes some way towards explaining his extraordinary success in the face of the West Indies quicks, against whom England got the best service out of him.

More than any other type of bowling, he thrived on taking on the pacemen, relishing every moment of it, and his technique was ideally suited to the job. In the mid-1980s it was no mean feat to score runs against a West Indian attack containing the likes of Malcolm Marshall, Patrick Patterson, Joel Garner, Colin Croft and Courtney Walsh, and later Curtly Ambrose. For many batsmen, the night before an innings against that little lot would have ensured sleep was not an option. But Lamb simply loved the psychological and physical challenge of putting himself to the test against the fastest bowlers in the world. He considered standing up to the barrages a matter of personal pride.

Lambie's technique was similar to that used by India's Gundappa Viswanath and Sunil Gavaskar. All three of them worked out their games very quickly. Lambie had quick feet and since, like them, he was on the smaller side of tiny, he didn't have to go down too far to duck under anything pitched short.

Unlike many who cowered in their presence, Lambie would set out to dictate the way the West Indian bowlers bowled to him. If the ball was short and heading for his chest he would simply let it pass by, and if they gave him an inch of width he could cut with power and pull the ball as well as anyone. That would force the bowlers to try to pitch it up, at which point, playing the ball late, he would drive with just the same force. That sort of ingenuity and ability to 'work' the bowlers made him a brilliant one-day player as well, and one of the many highlights of our wonderful Ashes tour in 1986–87 was his assault on Bruce Reid in the final over of the last one-day game against the Aussies in Sydney, which brought him 18 runs to secure victory. The fact that he and David Gower had thrown a drinks party to celebrate the tour the night before might have had something to do with his relaxed approach. The fact that a friend of his wife Lindsay, a girl called Liz Cattrell, had spiked some of the canapés certainly did.

'Away from the cricket field he remains as competitive a person as I have ever met.'

The three hundreds he made against the West Indies at home in the summer of 1984 – at Lord's, Leeds and Manchester – cemented his place in the England middle order for several years.

Born in South Africa to British parents in 1954, he had to wait until 1982 to make his Test debut, ten days before his 28th birthday. But he marked his first summer with his maiden international century against the Indians at the Oval. And though he waited four years to score his first century on an overseas Test ground, the two he made at Kingston and Barbados on the tour to the Caribbean early in 1990 were the innings of a true master. His final tally of 14 hundreds in a 79-Test career left him 15th in the list of England's all-time highest run scorers.

The main subject on which we often disagreed was his atrocious running between the wickets. Now he always was a hard trainer, but when it came to batting together we had some terrible mix-ups, and they often resulted in one or other of us being run out. Needless to say, he would always insist the blame lay with me, but I know the real truth. It was in those little legs of his. Sometimes they never seemed to get going, and he ended up getting stuck in best cartoon-style running-on-the-spot.

The only other issue where our habits differed was taking care of money, because he used to carry two crocodiles in his pockets at all times. He may have hated to spend it, but that's not to say he didn't like making it. From the moment he walked into the England dressing room he was always wheeling and dealing, working on some scheme or other that simply couldn't fail. If mobile phones hadn't existed, they would have had to invent them just for him.

But just how careful he was soon hit home when we started to room together. Lambie suggested that rather than spend hours going through every hotel extras bill, deciding who had spent what, we would simply divide up the total 50:50. It was not until halfway through our first tour of the Caribbean together, when I kept being asked to fork out between $150–200 for phone calls at the end of each hotel stay that it dawned on me what was happening.

I decided to check one particular hotel bill and it confirmed the truth. The records showed that while I might occasionally have given Kath a quick ring back in Yorkshire to check how she and the children were, Lambie was ringing some farm in the middle of the South African veldt to speak to Lindsay every day.

Away from the cricket field he remains as competitive a person as I have ever met. But he still can't hold a rod to me when it comes to fishing, and as for the time when we decided that he should take up golf, I very soon wished we hadn't. Etiquette has never been his strongest point.

The occasion – one of our early rounds; the place – the famous old Leeds club of Moortown, venue for the first Ryder Cup on British soil in 1929; and the outcome – he was very lucky not to be thrown off the course. Lambie had turned up proudly carrying a brand new bag of clubs – provided by a grateful sponsor, of course. So new were the clubs, in fact, that the heads were still wrapped in polythene. I happened to be playing in the four-ball behind him and

'Lambie was a great cricketer, a pocket battleship at the crease and, despite his occasional resemblance to Titus Minimus, still one of my greatest mates.'

for the first few holes I could tell exactly where he had played from and what club he had used because he had simply unwrapped each club as he needed it, thrown the wrapping on the ground and left those of us following to pick up the debris.

Lambie was great cricketer, a pocket battleship at the crease and, despite his occasional resemblance to Titus Minimus, still one of my greatest mates.

Christopher
Lander

I have always enjoyed a love–hate relationship with the media. They've loved me from the minute I picked myself off the floor, spat a couple of teeth out after chewing a short ball from Andy Roberts to win that 1974 Benson and Hedges quarter-final, while I have generally hated them, mainly for the fact that I've not been able to call my life my own for the past 25 years. Any top sportsman has to cope with his time in the spotlight. That is expected. But my every move has seemingly been under the microscope for nigh on a quarter of a century. Even becoming part of the 'media' as a Sky commentator has not changed that. Yet there was one cricket writer whose company I sought and enjoyed for most of that time. He was one of the few journalists I did care about and who genuinely cared about me. Sadly, he died in 2000. I was only one of many who grieved the passing of the *Daily Mirror's* Chris Lander.

We started working together at the *Mirror*, then he followed me briefly to the *Sun*, then it was back to the *Mirror* again. During my playing career, I got into more than my fair share of scrapes with the blazers at Lord's. Whenever I needed to put my side of the story, Chris 'Crash' Lander was the one person I could always turn to. Ours was much more than a working relationship. He was a loyal and trusted friend. Crash and I shared secrets that no one else ever knew about – and never will.

'Ours was much more than a working relationship. He was a loyal and trusted friend. Crash and I shared secrets that no one else ever knew about – and never will.'

For all my sporting achievements, few compare with Crash's effort on my first Leukaemia Walk from John O'Groats to Land's End in late 1985. I had moved to the *Sun* and Crash was still at the *Mirror*, but such was our bond that he refused to let me start my 800-mile journey without spending one day at my side. What followed next has become part of newspaper folklore. Crash got the taste for it, and, while the *Sun* reporter was hospitalized in a matter of days, Crash was still by my side when we dived into the sea at Land's End 35 days later, dressed in top hats and tails. Some days I would return to cover the route in the van because he was so far behind. Part of that was due to the pain he was going through; the rest down to his socializing. I walked quickly, then played hard. Crash played hard and walked slowly, but he refused to give in. The *Mirror* received fantastic publicity for his effort, though it was slightly taken aback when he presented his massive car park bill for what had been a scheduled overnight stay. He repeated the first leg on my 1999 walk less than a year before his death. In all, Crash walked more than 2,500 miles with me on the Leukaemia Walks. I remember *Private Eye* once described Crash as 'Rambotham Toady'. Not true. Chris was one of cricket and journalism's great characters in his own right. Once met, never forgotten, he toured the cricket world causing laughter, chaos and confusion. Any time I thought my life was spinning out of control, a brief examination of Crash's domestic situation made me realize that I was living rather a humdrum existence.

His last tour was England's Millennium trip to South Africa, but my abiding memory of Crash had come in the Caribbean two years earlier. Asked to cover the final morning of the second Trinidad Test from the Sandals pool, he threatened to resign at first. The press box rallied round. Fancy Bermuda shorts, a Caribbean cocktail and a bevy of beauties were provided, and I made sure the Sky cameras were primed and ready. The reluctant bather was no more. Now the centre of attention and, with the girls holding his mobile phone and copy of *Wisden*, Crash was in his element, playing to the crowd and cameras for all he was worth.

Crash, Devon-born, was a product of local newspapers who honed his skills under another great Fleet Street figure, as a reporter at Reg Hayter's Sports Agency. Both Crash and I benefited greatly from the caring guidance of Reg at the start of our careers. Those offices in Gough Square are where the legend of Lander began. Various summonses and notices would be served through the front door while Crash, hearing the establishment step on the stairs, would leg it out the back. Ducking and diving was very much the Crash way.

His first love was rugby and his fondest sporting memory was the 1974 British Lions tour to South Africa. On that final tour there in 1999–2000, in a Port Elizabeth bar, we came across a big blow-up of the article he wrote when the Lions clinched the series, headed 'The Godfather' – a reference to the influence of Willie John McBride. Crash was a great help to me when my son Liam decided to embark on a professional rugby career. The intricacies of cricket might have been pretty much a closed book to him, but he knew his rugby.

If there has been a more disorganized person around, I have yet to meet him. And as the media world plunged headlong into the era of new technology, it was with great reluctance that Crash handed back his typewriter. Anything with buttons, flashing lights or passwords left him bemused. Almost every day, some story of Lander's technical incompetence would seep out of the Press Box. And there were occasions when Crash let his enthusiasm and passion get in the way of his judgement. Once, after a particularly bad day against Australia, Crash declared the selectors useless and announced that he was going to the back of the box to come up with the eleven names that would put some pride back into English cricket. After less than five minutes, a list was pinned to the wall. His colleagues gathered round, there was about 40 seconds of silence, and just before the group dissolved into laughter, one voiced remarked, 'Crash, will this be the first time England have gone into a Test without a wicket-keeper?'

'Saddened as I was by his untimely death, I can't think of anyone who crammed more into, or got more enjoyment out of life as Crash did.'

But when a story needed extracting there was no one with better contacts or sounder judgement. That's why, when Allan Lamb and I felt the cricketing public needed to be told the truth about ball-tampering, and, specifically, why the ball used in the second Texaco Trophy match between England and Pakistan in 1992 was changed, Lander was the man we contacted.

As well as Reg Hayter, another strong influence on both our careers was Brian Close. He and Crash spent a memorable afternoon on the first walk before Closey was taken to hospital. Closey often appeared in Crash's *Mirror* stories. When, one afternoon in the Lord's Press Box, he asked if anyone had seen Brian, Crash was told he was working for Rapid Cricketline, an automated telephone score service. Once again, the journalists were left in hysterics as Crash spent several minutes on the phone trying to interrupt Closey's recorded message in order to engage him in conversation.

There was never a dull moment with Crash, or a wasted one. He was, arguably, the most enthusiastic golfer I've ever played with.

Unarguably, he was the worst. So bad was he that he was actually sacked once by his long-term playing partner, Reg's son, Peter Hayter of the *Mail on Sunday* during the annual match between the cricket writers and Edgbaston Golf Club during the Birmingham Test, when Lander managed to lose three holes in three successive shots. Playing foursomes, hitting alternate drives and shots, Lander first managed to scuttle Hayter's perfect drive along the ground and into a brook no more than five yards in front of him, then he hooked his tee-shot on a par three wildly out of bounds before smacking another second shot on to the lip of the green on a difficult par four, only to be told he had played the ball last hit by the Edgbaston club secretary, Peter Heath.

As a rugby player, he was once famously described as a long-distance winger, and he was equally hilariously useless at cricket. Every July he led his Fleet Street Wanderers on tour to the West Country, with suitably catastrophic results, and they capped a decade at the bottom with a magnificent 10th anniversary tour to Monte Carlo in the year before he died, the low point of which was the discovery that Lander's golf bag contained no fewer than 17 clubs. On the annual Devon tour a few months after his death, the Wanderers placed a full-size cardboard cut-out of the great man at first slip. Someone rather unkindly commented that there was little difference in mobility from the real thing. Saddened as I was by his untimely death, I can't think of anyone who crammed more into, or got more enjoyment out of life as Crash did, nor can I think of him without smiling.

Dennis Lillee

My friendship with DK goes back years, but my admiration for the man as a cricketer goes even further. I have always said, and I have never had reason to change my mind, that he was the finest quick bowler I have ever seen. And that is a big statement, when you think of the calibre of contemporaries such as Andy Roberts, Michael Holding, Bob Willis and Joel Garner, or more recently the likes of Malcolm Marshall and Glenn McGrath.

Considering that he had such serious back problems during his career it's astounding that he managed to maintain his almost perfect delivery action but what made him stand out above all the others was his cricketing brain. Whatever kind of wicket he was asked to bowl on, he was able to adapt to it. If it was one of the old Melbourne Cricket Ground wickets where the ball used to keep slow and low, he would produce off-cutters, leg-cutters and changes of pace. But when we got back to his home ground at Perth, where the surfaces have always been quick and bouncy, he knew exactly where to put the ball there with real hostility. He was a thinking bowler, and without wishing to upset too many of my old chums it has to be said that bowling with the brain is quite unusual among pacemen.

In many ways, though, DK was the typical Australian cricketer, particularly among those of his generation. He was hard and tough on the field. In every game he played, whether it was club cricket, interstate or a Test match, he didn't give an inch and didn't expect an inch. But once the final ball of the day had been delivered he was also the first to go into the opponents' dressing-room to have a glass of wine or a beer and chew the cud.

He did so much for Australian cricket, he brought the crowds to life. Among later generations we were to see the same thing with Merv Hughes, but DK was the first bowler who, when he was running up to the crease, would be accompanied by the Aussie

---

BEEFY ON LILLEE

Born: 18 July 1949, Subiaco, Perth
Country: Australia
Tests: 70
Wickets: 355
Average: 23.92
Beefy analysis: The complete fast bowler who could adapt to any type of wicket. DK had an aggressive temperament and was never far away from controversy. My type of player.
Beefy moment: Facing Lillee at his prime in Perth in the late seventies.
Do mention: His reign as Australia's leading wicket-taker lasted for 16 years until Shane Warne surpassed him in the summer of 2001.
Don't mention: Premature baldness.

crowds roaring 'Kill, kill, kill'. The partnership that DK enjoyed with Jeff Thomson in the 1970s was probably the most feared combination of all time. They were formidable. You had Thomson, unorthodox but lightning-fast and effective at one end, and DK, the perfect machine, at the other.

I'll always remember one game against DK in Perth. He steamed in and when I played and missed at the first ball he came running down

'What made him stand out above all the others was his cricketing brain.'

the wicket with the old medallion around his neck swinging from side to side. He always did the same thing when he'd just beaten the bat. He used to stand there staring at you, wipe his forehead with his finger, flick the sweat on to the floor, kick the earth, and then turn round and walk back to his run-up mark.

The next ball exactly the same happened. I played and missed, he followed through again only this time he came another couple of yards down the pitch before flicking away the sweat, kicking at an imaginary ball on the ground and walking back.

After I missed the third ball, he got even closer, and when he beat me again with the fourth delivery he followed through so far that he was standing less than a couple of feet away from me. There was still the same old exasperated wiping of the forehead and flicking of the sweat but this time it was onto my shirt with the words, 'Jesus Christ, Beefy. Do me a favour mate – you hold the bat still and I'll aim at it.' He was an enormous man and a great opponent, which is why I rate my two centuries against him at Headingley and Old Trafford during that unbelievable series of 1981 as undoubtedly the most satisfying of my career.

My lasting memory of DK has to be of that wonderful action. It was the one you would show to every kid who wanted to be a quick bowler. It had everything – control, rhythm and pace, and the ability to produce swing or seam virtually on call.

For many years since his retirement DK has been travelling regularly to Madras in Southern India where he has established a fast-bowling academy, and the Test teams of India, Sri Lanka and even New

Zealand now contain his pupils. The authorities at Lord's have so far shunned the idea of paying for some of our young bowlers to go over to India and benefit from his tuition. Surprise, surprise. But even if their pride won't let them use facilities on the sub-continent it still amazes me that, when you have someone as good as DK willing to travel over all over the world to coach, he has not been invited over here officially to look at our young quicks for a month or two. Okay, so it would cost money, and DK might not possess 28 coaching certificates, but I know who I would rather listen to if I was setting out all over again to be a fast bowler.

'The lasting memory of DK has to be of that wonderful action. It was the one you would show to every kid who wanted to be a quick bowler. It had everything – control, rhythm and pace, and the ability to produce swing or seam virtually on call.'

At his home in Perth, 'Wot' – he used to be called Fot in his playing days but now he really is the 'world's oldest teenager' – Dennis Lillee keeps a wonderful stock of some of the most famous Australian wines. But he is equally famous for wanting to drink them all himself, preferring to share only the lesser vintages with his mates.

It was never a case that any wine served in the Lillee household would be rubbish, but unlike when he was bowling, you always felt that he was keeping something back. However, over the many years that I have known him I've developed a strategy which gets me into that wonderful cellar of his to lay my hands on the best stuff. I never visit Perth without getting an invite to the DK household, and nowadays I always try to make sure I arrive before him to get among his better bottles.

I would never have taken such liberties during our playing days. Revenge would have been swift and pretty merciless.

Clive
Lloyd

Many holidaymakers are quite shocked when they fly to the Caribbean for the first time. They are usually unaware that most of the islands are individual nations, with their own flags, governments, cultures, in some case languages, and in almost every instance a deep sense of their own national pride.

Those who choose to visit two destinations often get upset when they arrive at an airport for a short island hop and discover they have to go through the whole rigmarole of customs and immigration at either end of the trip.

They cannot believe that all this could happen to them in that idyllic haven of sunkissed beaches and palm trees they had read about in brochures or dreamed of while listening to radio commentary of Caribbean 'calypso' cricket.

'Lloyd created a West Indies team that performed as a single body. He appealed to a sense of nationhood by reminding the players of their history, their 'roots' and the responsibility he felt they owed to the coming generations.'

But it is only on the cricket field that the West Indies actually exists. It is a composite team drawn from more than 50 islands in the Caribbean (plus, of course, Guyana, which sits on the north-eastern tip of the South American mainland), and for many years the fact that they did not share a national identity was pretty obvious for all to see.

For instance, if a Test match was being played in Jamaica and there wasn't a Jamaican in the West Indies side or a particular player the Jamaicans thought should have been in the side, the crowds didn't bother to watch the cricket. It was same for the Bajan people and their heroes from Barbados, and so on through Trinidad and Antigua. For years, bitter inter-island rivalry was rife. Then along came Clive Hubert Lloyd, the man I would credit with uniting the people of the Caribbean.

Lloyd created a West Indies team that performed as a single body. He appealed to a sense of nationhood by reminding the players of

'For years, bitter inter-island rivalry was rife. Then along came Clive Hubert Lloyd, the man I would credit with uniting the people of the Caribbean.'

their history, their 'roots' and the responsibility he felt they owed to the coming generations. Give them a sense of pride, an identity to believe in, he urged, and see what they might be capable of doing. He persuaded them that if they could come together

with the single purpose of putting Antiguans, Bajans, Jamaicans or Trinidadians on the world map, then the people they were representing might see a way forward for themselves. As a result, and perhaps for the first time, people throughout the Caribbean began to go and watch their

West Indian team, not just the man from their island. Lloyd's actions paid off in terms of their performance on the field as well. Because he managed to unite the crowds and the players, the West Indian team of Clive Lloyd's era was arguably the best side in the history of Test cricket worldwide. Not only that, but in the late 1970s and early 1980s there was a lot of talk about whether cricket was a dying game, and I think Clive Lloyd and his team should get a pat on the back for the way they entertained wherever they went in the world and attracted new audiences to the game.

Some critics believe that Clive was responsible for the surfeit of bouncers and intimidatory bowling that dominated the game for a while. But they forget that it was only after his side found itself at the receiving end of similar tactics on their 1975–76 tour to Australia that Clive decided to find some young quicks who could give as good as they got. As for the scenes at Old Trafford in 1976 when Brian Close and John Edrich had to put up with some terrifying stuff in dim light despite their advancing years, Clive was quick to acknowledge that his guys 'might have got a bit carried away'. But in understanding the motives behind the assault it is important to remember the context in which that series was played, and most particularly the infamous comment from Tony Greig about making the West Indies 'grovel' that inflamed their efforts to make him eat his words.

BEEFY ON LLOYD

Born: 31 August 1944, Georgetown, British Guyana
Country: West Indies
Tests: 110
Hundreds: 19
Average: 46.67
Beefy analysis: Master tactician as captain of the all-conquering West Indies side from the late seventies to early eighties, and a hard-hitting batsman and brilliant cover fielder.
Beefy moment: Lloyd managing his four fast bowlers to wreak havoc on opposition batsmen.
Do mention: India v West Indies, Mumbai, 1974 (he hit a Test-best 242*).
Don't mention: Spinners, Caribbean inter-island rivalry.

People talk about the current Australian side in their pomp as the modern-day invincibles. But what I wouldn't give to witness a five-Test series between them and Lloyd's West Indies sides, both at their peak. Think of the one-to-one match-ups: Shane Warne against Viv Richards; Glenn McGrath against Gordon Greenidge; Michael Holding, Malcolm Marshall or Andy Roberts against Mark and Steve Waugh. The result? My money would have been on Clive.

'His ability to pick the ball up and deliver it in one seamless, feline movement had you rubbing your eyes, while his flick-throws into the wicket-keeper or at the stumps were just too fast for the naked eye to pick up at all.'

But Clive was not just a great captain/politician. He was also one of the most beautiful batsmen to watch in world cricket, and one of the most destructive. With his long reach, an almost languid stance at the crease and a wonderful eye (thanks to spectacles that transformed him from being blind as a bat to eagle-eyed), it was all too easy to believe his approach would have been more to caress the ball than clobber it. But the enormous strength he possessed in his huge arms and hands, and the heavy 4lb bat he used to harness it meant that when he hit the ball it went very far, very very fast.

In the early days too he was like a panther in the field, along with South Africa's Colin Bland, a man who brought a new dimension of enjoyment to a part of the game that most players, and all bowlers, had considered none of their business. His ability to pick the ball up and deliver it in one seamless, feline movement had you rubbing your eyes, while his flick-throws into the wicket-keeper or at the stumps were just too fast for the naked eye to pick up at all. When he lost a bit of his athleticism he switched and became an exceptional slip fielder. You had to be good against their quartet of quick bowlers.

He was outstanding ... in almost every respect.

David Lloyd

It was only in the years since he quit as coach to the England side at the end of the 1999 World Cup and moved into the commentary box that I got close to David Lloyd. I just wish I had made more of an effort earlier.

'Bumble' is a bundle of nervous energy, his brain is constantly buzzing, and this combination of ingredients adds up to a very clever, sometimes slightly dotty, but very funny man. Some of the off-the-cuff stuff he comes out with has me doubled up, and it's no wonder he is a very sought-after figure on the after-dinner speaking circuit. He seems to have a tale to suit every occasion.

In my early days at Somerset I played against Bumble whenever we had games with Lancashire, but I also played with him for England and it was in the summer of 1980 that I, as captain, recalled him for the one-day international against the West Indies at Headingley. We got the impression that he had been in good form, scoring two centuries in the Benson & Hedges Cup, though he would quietly admit to me later that one was against a very weak Derbyshire attack and the other against Scotland!

Anyway, Bumble turned up in Leeds and probably soon wished he hadn't. On a typical Headingley terror track he tried to cut a fast short ball from Malcolm Marshall only for it to jag back and smash him on the point of the elbow. It didn't take much of an inspection from our physio to diagnose a possible break, and Bumble was whisked quickly into an ambulance. As a caring captain I thought it my duty to go down and see how he was, but rather than moaning about the tremendous pain he simply looked up at me and said, in all seriousness, 'Thanks for picking me, Beef.' Mad. At least this time he was only in danger of losing an arm. Back on the 1974–75 Ashes tour down under a delivery from Jeff Thomson hit him so hard in the 'groin area' that it bent his pink litesome box inside-out.

Events that have happened since Bumble and the England team parted company suggest that he might not have been as bad a national coach as some people tried to make out. One criticism was that he was too gimmicky. Some said it was going too far over the top by introducing patriotic songs like *Land of Hope and Glory* before games, but I saw nothing wrong in a bit of 'Pomp and Circumstance' to get the lads going in the dressing room. And as for his ideas and methods to promote team bonding, well, maybe getting the lads to drive Land Rovers blindfolded at dead of night might have been going a tad far, but you've got to admire his imagination.

Though England's Test record left a little bit to be desired under his management, and pales somewhat further when compared with that under Duncan Fletcher, he shouldn't be blamed totally for that. First, he was hamstrung, as all England coaches prior to the appointment of Duncan Fletcher in 1999 had been, by having to share his top players with the counties. Many of us believed that central contracts for England players were an absolute necessity if we were going to be serious about competing with the best in the world. It was surely no coincidence that the team which beat the West Indies during the summer of 2000 to record England's first victory against those opponents for more than 30 years contained a four-pronged pace attack of Darren Gough, Andy Caddick, Craig White and Dominic Cork that managed to stay fit and sharp through all the series – free from the demands and stresses, not to mention the mileage, involved in playing county cricket at the same time. Bumble was one of the most vocal supporters of those contracts and I'm sure the passion with which he argued the case with his employers made him some enemies at Lord's.

'Bumble found himself engaged continually in wasteful battles against the (cricket) heirarchy.'

Secondly, he suffered in the very early days from uncertainty over the level of support he enjoyed from his bosses. England and Wales Cricket Board chairman Lord MacLaurin's comments about the shambles England were in during Bumble's first tour in charge – the 1996–97 'we flippin' murdered 'em' tour to Zimbabwe – were justified up to a point. And Bumble should not have allowed himself to rise to the bait set by the Zimbabweans on more than one occasion. But I was amazed by the fact that, among all the blathering criticism of him, neither MacLaurin nor Tim Lamb offered a single word of support, nor even bothered to hear his side of the story.

Understanding very early in his career as a coach just how the land lay, Bumble found himself engaged continually in wasteful battles against the heirarchy. In the end, he gave up the unequal struggle. A shame, I believe, because with a bit more support from above, Bumble might have been able to put England on the right track at least two years earlier than Fletcher, Hussain and central contracts finally managed it.

Nelson Mandela

I'm rarely lost for words, even in the most extreme circumstances – such as Allan Lamb picking up the bill for dinner and insisting, 'This one's on me, Beef!' Even in my dreams, that scenario remains a fantasy. But one dream became a reality in Monaco not long ago when I met, and later had lunch with, the greatest man of my time, Nelson Mandela. When the former South African President came on stage during the awards ceremony, he shook my hand and said,

'I have always wanted to meet you, Ian. You are one of my heroes.' That's when my tongue disappeared. When I finally found it, all I could mutter was a rather pathetic, 'Thank you very much.'

The next day Kath and I were invited on to a yacht to have lunch with Mandela. I was spellbound, as was everyone else around that table. I have never seen one person have such a humbling effect on a group of people. I imagine that is what it would have been like to have been in the presence of Gandhi, or Martin Luther King. I kept looking at this man who had been held captive by a racist regime for 27 years, watching for the slightest hint of hatred or animosity towards those who kept him imprisoned in shocking conditions for almost three decades. I saw none, because there was none. A truly amazing character, full of humility and integrity, whose sole aim was to make things right in the new South Africa.

'I have never seen one person have such a humbling effect on a group of people.'

Later that year, Kath was flying out to South Africa to join me. I was playing in a big charity golf event that Ernie Els organizes each year. Kath recognized one of the Mandela entourage from the Monaco meeting. They talked and Kath was told that Mandela was on the flight. A few minutes later, the man himself appeared and sat down for a chat. That's the man he is, nothing hidden, nothing formal. After an hour in his company, you feel as though you've known him for 20 years. He also has that rare ability to get people to open up, to get the best out of them: you want to aspire to his high standards. Of all the people I've met, such aura and charisma has been unique. I've been lucky to meet some fascinating and influential characters because of my cricketing prowess. As I approach my own half century, I have started to put together my dream dinner party. Can you imagine sitting down with Nelson Mandela, John Arlott, Viv Richards and Elton John around the table? What an evening that would be!

'A truly amazing character, full of humility and integrity, whose sole aim was to make things right in the new South Africa.'

I put down the fact that South Africa still exists to one man: Nelson Mandela. You only have to look at what is happening in most African states, especially one or two very close to South Africa, to know what might have happened here too. It will be a very sad day, not only for South Africa, or Africa, but for the whole world, when he is no longer with us.

He was genuinely interested in all sports when we talked. I believe he boxed in his younger days, but he had a better than working knowledge of cricket and rugby. Mandela always had the right word for every occasion. His presence has always provided a significant boost for South African national teams. The home side were unseeded when he declared the 1995 World Cup open at Newlands. Yet, that day François Pienaar's side beat the holders, Australia, and went all the way to the final, overcoming the huge favourites, New Zealand. President Mandela was there again at Ellis Park, wearing Pienaar's No. 6 jersey. It was a masterstroke, and the picture of Pienaar and Mandela embracing with the World Cup is one of the enduring images of the new South Africa, the Rainbow Country.

Mandela made his presence felt a few months later during England's first cricket tour to South Africa for 30 years. The President was due to meet the tourists before the start of the second day's play against an Invitation XI in the Soweto township. But foreign duties meant a change of plan, and the authorities were given 15 minutes' notice on the first day that the most famous ex-political prisoner was about to make an unscheduled visit. Play had been under way for half an hour, but nobody cared as the cricket came to a halt, and both sets of players lined up to meet Mandela. Even the tired old hacks in the press tent wanted a glimpse of him. He had a special word for Devon Malcolm, who had routed South Africa with his nine for 57 at the Oval the previous year. 'I know you. You're the destroyer!' was Mandela's greeting.

With those words he did more for Devon's self-esteem than the England management team led by Ray Illingworth succeeded in doing all tour! With the series deadlocked going into the final Test in Cape

Town, Mandela visited Hansie Cronje's team and was pictured with his arm around their new cap, youngster Paul Adams. The home side won by 10 wickets in less than three days. The Mandela magic had worked again, as it has done many times in areas much more important than sporting encounters.

The scenes that greeted Mandela's release from Robben Island early in 1990 were remarkable. I'm sure it was a scenario few of us ever anticipated. Because no one had seen a photograph of him for nearly 30 years, most of the newspapers and magazines tried to come up with an artist's impression of what Mandela would look like. But no one came close. I was astonished at how distinguished and statesman-like he was as he took his first few steps of freedom.

For decades in Britain, Mandela and his ANC colleagues were portrayed as terrorists; but they were involved in a struggle for survival. Did he do anything that any of us would not have done in the same unjust situation? The answer to that is 'No'. When you read his closing statement in his 1963 trial, you realized that Nelson Mandela had great dignity, even then. It was not only in South Africa that the real image of this freedom-fighter was distorted. His will to survive and succeed must have been formidable. That it did not spill over into hatred and the desire for revenge when he held the upper hand, to me, says more about this remarkable human being than anything else.

Vic
Marks

As a cricketer, Vic Marks was very much under-rated, not only by the public but also by the selectors, and I felt he should have played far more cricket for England than his six Tests and 34 one-day internationals.

At Somerset we knew his value. Although we had the big names in Viv Richards and Joel Garner he was just as important a part of our team, which dominated the one-day county competitions in the late 1970s and early 1980s.

He was a more than useful off spinner; he would give the ball plenty of flight and he used guile as well. A measure of his ability was the number of batsmen he'd lure into the drive and had caught in the arc between extra cover and mid on.

Vic was no mean batsman either, and as a bowler I could sympathize with opponents who use to be driven up the wall by him. He could be infuriating.

With the bat, Vic could never be accused of orthodoxy. He had an extraordinary ability to work the ball into uncovered areas from obscure angles. I remember during one of his innings for England, Ian Chappell was commentating and told his viewers that Vic could only score runs on the off side. Within seconds Chappell was made to eat his words, for the next ball after he made the observation, Vic promptly carted a ball pitching outside off stump over midwicket for a one-bounce four.

As a bowler, he had the knack of keeping you guessing; guessing whether one of his so-called 'off-breaks' would ever actually turn, and while you waited he would nag you into making unforced errors.

When Vic retired from the game I was not at all surprised that he chose to go into the media and became cricket correspondent of the *Observer*, because he's always had a great sense of humour which infiltrates his copy, plus a good knowledge of the game.

But it was the amount of time Vic thought about the game and the exhausting effort he put into it that always amused me. And you don't need to look any further for the reasons why these days you will see more hair on the skin of a ping-pong ball. I still have this vivid mental picture, drawn from seeing him on so many occasions sitting quietly alone in the Taunton dressing room, of Vic totally lost in his own thoughts. He would sit there with a fag and a beer, gazing at nothing in particular and twiddling and twirling with his hair, occasionally pulling out huge clumps of the stuff.

But with his twirling habit went hand in hand an ability to see the funny side of something when it would be quite lost on anyone

> 'He was a more than useful off spinner; he would give the ball plenty of flight and he used guile as well.'

sitting around him. Some of the cricket writers have their own little golfing society with fictitious names drawn from the various world tours, and it's no coincidence that Vic is known as Van Der Chortle. Often, the rest of the Somerset players would be sitting in the dressing-room almost totally unaware of Vic's presence, when suddenly he would just start giggling, and once he started there was no stopping him.

And it wasn't always in the privacy of the dressing-room. I remember once sitting on the balcony at Taunton trying to conduct a TV interview with Vic when suddenly he collapsed into laughter. I started too, and after 20 minutes of hopeless falling about the whole interview had to be abandoned.

'A measure of his ability was the number of batsmen he'd lured into the drive and had caught in the arc between extra cover and mid on. Vic was no mean batsman either.'

Vic really was so unlike many cricketers who tend to be a bit gung-ho and laddish. Coming from a farming background, he was from the outset a very placid character. Nothing ever really rattled him and he seemed to be able to produce that giggle or find something amusing in even the worst of situations, which is why he was able to survive the Somerset Mutiny of 1986 when Viv Richards, Joel Garner and myself were forced out of the club by the actions of Peter Roebuck, someone we had counted a friend. Vic was a close pal of all of us and I know his loyalties were seriously tested during that sad time.

His equable temperament has also enabled him to retain his sanity while acting as chairman of the club's cricket committee. With his knowledge of the game, he has much to pass on to younger players, and there will always be one or two around that could benefit from his languid, balanced and off-beat view of life in general. Come to think of it, all that would probably have made him an excellent chairman of England selectors. On second thoughts, although he might have the chuckle of the village idiot, he's got more sense than to apply for such a thankless job.

Rod
Marsh

Rod Marsh will always be regarded as one of the all-time great characters of Australian cricket, not just for his ability – which was highly underrated – but also for his skill as a magician. Put a can of beer in front of him and it would disappear before you could say 'Abracadabra'.

'Swampy' was the engine room of that great Australian side of the early 1970s in many ways because, as all good 'keepers should, he kept the side bubbling even when things were not going their way – which it has to said was not all that often.

His uncertain start in Test cricket may have earned him the nickname 'Iron Gloves', but by the time he retired 96 matches later, not only had he placed a large 'keeper's mitt in the mouths of his critics, he had also set an Ashes record that may never be bettered: in Tests between Australia and England, he recorded an amazing 148 dismissals.

For a small, stocky man he was surprisingly athletic, but his low centre of gravity was ideal for a gloveman and enabled him to spring like a salmon for some of the most spectacular leg side catches ever seen. At times, particularly on dodgy wickets, keeping to Jeff Thomson and Dennis Lillee at their peak must have been a nightmare – imagine taking a low or high bouncer from Thommo at his pace – but he gave two of the great fast bowlers of all time a consistently high level of support. The best compliment I can pay him in this respect is that he made it look easy.

'When it came to playing the game I never met a more committed and dedicated professional, which is why Rod was an inspired choice by the ACB to run their academy in Adelaide.'

He was dangerous enough with the bat to score 3,633, which puts him 17th in the list of all-time Australian batsmen, but he was even more dangerous at the end of a day's play, because when he had a thirst on it was like watching a bath drain. He was not particularly adventurous in his choice of tipple – 'beer, mate' – but once he started he would stop for nothing and for no one. Indeed, his record for the number of cans emptied on the 20-odd hour flight from Australia to England at the start of an Ashes tour – more than 50 I believe – lasted for more than a decade until finally overhauled by the dogged David Boon. The only time I saw him unable to drink was at the end of the Headingley Test in 1981; although he'd won a few bob at the mad odds of 500–1 against England, his inability to speak, let alone drink, in the immediate aftermath resulted from pure shock. When he snapped out of that feeling, however, I understand his mission to drown his sorrows was one of the most spectacular of all time.

It is a great sadness to me that fraternizing with the opposition now seems to be regarded as unprofessional. I just cannot understand why it has gone out of fashion. The fact is that I learned as much about the game, particularly when I first went into international cricket, by going into the opposition's dressing-room for a beer as I ever did out on the field of play. And I could sit and listen to Swampy for hours. Call me a fossil but I simply do not agree that mixing with the opposition on a social basis is unprofessional.

Clearly, played at its most intense, Test match cricket is a war made up of several individual battles. But there is no earthly reason why players shouldn't be friends at the end of it. I wish there was more of such behaviour in the modern game. You would still see a lot of intense rivalry on the pitch, but perhaps some of the worst excesses of player behaviour would be curbed by the friendships that would develop in the bar afterwards.

That said, everything has to be done in moderation. I remember on one occasion playing in a Test match at the Adelaide Oval. As usual at the close of play we chatted away and one story led to another. Casually glancing at my watch after an hour or so I was somewhat taken aback to find the time to be a quarter to eleven. Worse, when we tried to leave the ground we discovered that the security men had long since locked up. In the end we decided the only thing for it was to scale a wall. And although the two slavering guard dogs who came to investigate thought that was a brilliant idea, at least their barking alerted a man with a bunch of keys.

All that having been said, when it came to playing the game I never met a more committed and dedicated professional as Rod Marsh, which is why he was an inspired choice by the ACB to run their academy in Adelaide, and later by the ECB when English cricket finally followed suit in 2001.

Malcolm Marshall

Even in the outstanding line-up of West Indian fast bowlers who terrorized batsmen all over the world for 25 years, Malcolm Denzil Marshall was something special.

He was an absolutely awesome cricketer whose speed and hostility were relentless and, in the case of many opponents, ruinous; yet he was incredibly popular among his contemporaries, and his early death at the age of 41 was mourned throughout the cricketing world like a family bereavement.

Of all the quick bowlers I've faced in my career, only Dennis Lillee was Marshall's equal. On the pitch, he was a fearsome, dignified opponent, but away from cricket he was a charming man and great friend. Whenever England toured the West Indies, you could be sure that within 24 hours of touching down in Barbados there would be an invitation from Marshall to sample some of the local hospitality at a little rum shop up Holders Hill.

We would meet in this unassuming little place which served the best jerk chicken in the Caribbean, sit down over a big plate of it and enjoy the view. He would drink rum and Coke, I would order rum and ginger ... but there was only one slight drawback. At this bar, you didn't buy rum by the shot, it was only sold by the bottle. Naturally, we would always do the decent thing and polish off every last drop. Marshall was a fiendishly difficult opponent, but he was a genial host and, somehow, Caribbean tours will never be quite the same again without our sun downers on Holders Hill.

As a bowler, he was sensational: many rate him as the best of all time, and his record of 376 Test wickets at 20.94 each – an average unsurpassed by any bowler who has topped 200 wickets – bears out that argument. At 5ft 11in, Marshall may not have had the height, or have been as physically

BEEFY ON MARSHALL

Born: 18 April 1958, Bridgetown, Barbados
Died: 4 November 1999, Bridgetown, Barbados
Country: West Indies
Tests: 81
Wickets: 376
Average: 20.94
Beefy analysis: Of all the quick bowlers I ever faced in my career, only Dennis Lillee was Marshall's equal. On the pitch he was a fearsome, dignified opponent. Away from cricket, he was a charming man and a great friend.
Beefy moment: His rearrangement of Mike Gatting's facial features.
Do mention: Batting one-handed against England after injury to enable a teammate to reach his century.
Don't mention: A batsman's weakness. He'd exploit it.

intimidating, as, for example, Joel Garner or Colin Croft, but he could generate exceptional pace and formidable bounce. He terrified tail-enders, especially when he came round the wicket and dug the ball in short of a length, and I dare say he frightened a few top-order batsmen, too.

We had some great battles, both at county and Test level, but the match in which I will always remember Marshall at his most lethal, and with a little shudder, was a one-day international in Jamaica in 1986 on the so-called 'Blackwash' tour. Carrying a groin strain, I was stood down to 12th man and I can't say I was all that sorry to miss out on the carnage and bloodshed that followed. On a pitch with geological similarities to a corrugated roof, Marshall bowled at the speed of sound – as poor old Mike Gatting, discovered to his cost.

If you have ever seen the effects of a ripened tomato being splattered across someone's face, you'll have some idea of the damage inflicted by a Malcolm Marshall bouncer which hits you on the nose. Which is precisely what happened to Gatt. England had made 47 for two when Gatting attempted to hook a lifting ball from Marshall – and missed. There was no protective grille on his helmet, and the result was one of the most sickening injuries I have ever witnessed on a cricket field. Not to put too fine a point on it, Gatt's nose basically disintegrated.

'On the pitch, he was a fearsome, dignified opponent, but away from cricket he was a charming man and great friend.'

The incident was no fun for Marshall, either. When play was finally ready to restart, he was thrown the ball and was almost back to his mark when he turned a peculiar shade of green, flung the ball to the ground and nearly vomited.

'I can't bowl with this,' he exclaimed. 'It's still got his nose in it.'

Upon closer inspection, Marshall had a valid complaint. Such was the force of impact between 90mph delivery and Gatting's beak that shards of bone and fragments of cartilage were embedded in the ball.

Despite the gory sideshow of Gatting's nasal makeover, this was the phase of Marshall's career when he was a truly awesome performer. Venom was only a small part of his repertoire, which in later years included a lethal inswinger and a devastating leg-cutter. At Hampshire, he was always willing to produce his best – even on dead pitches or in games meandering towards a meaningless conclusion – and that set him apart from other overseas imports who might have been inclined to go through the motions and bank the pay cheque.

My former England team-mate, Robin Smith, says that, before the end of his playing career, Marshall could spot a batsman's weakness, nominate the delivery that would get him out ... and scatter the skittles next ball. He was that good.

A phenomenal cricketer and an affable guy off the pitch, Marshall was also a good friend to my son Liam when he was on the Hampshire staff. He is sadly missed by a lot of people within the game, not least in the Botham household. It speaks volumes for the esteem in which he was held by his own people that five West Indian captains were among the pallbearers at his funeral.

Glenn
McGrath

I never believed it possible that Australia would produce another fast-bowler to rank alongside Dennis Lillee. Yet Glenn McGrath has earned the right to be mentioned in the same breath; a truly magnificent bowler. When the 2001 Australians arrived in England, captain Steve Waugh remarked, 'He never seems to bowl a bad ball, there is never any sign of a half-volley.' And then added rather ruefully, 'Not even in the nets.' I suppose it might be of slight consolation to England's batsmen that their Ashes counterparts have to live off scraps from McGrath, too.

Glenn is the archetypal fast bowler – mean and horrible on the field. Nobody in the modern game knows how to get into batsmen better than Glenn McGrath. I have no problems with that – he knows how to take it back. Almost every day the Australians spent in England before the 2001 Ashes kicked off, there was some public pronouncement from McGrath about how England were going to get hammered. That's a dangerous game in any sport where you can soon be exposed as all mouth and no trousers. But not Glenn McGrath. Whatever he threatens is usually backed up with the ball. We can blame Allan Border for that. Border was at the crease for Queensland with McGrath running in for New South Wales. AB had seen it all before, another young upstart fast bowler trying to make a name for himself by unsettling the long-serving Australian skipper. McGrath decided on a withering stare at the end of his follow-through rather than a volley of abuse. 'Nice glare,' said AB, 'but can you speak?' Nowadays batsmen all over the world know the answer to that one.

Yet, for all that, I can assure you that Glenn McGrath is one of the nicest blokes I've ever come across. The 6ft 5in lad from Dubbo nicknamed 'Pigeon' is no Jekyll and Hyde figure. McGrath has a job to do on the field and gets on with it to the very best of his ability. Whatever it takes, basically. Off the field, he's a caring husband, doting father and country boy, whose sporting success has allowed him to buy up half of New South Wales's bush. McGrath loves nothing better than heading

BEEFY ON McGRATH

Born: 9 February 1970, Dubbo, New South Wales
Country: Australia
Tests: 81
Wickets: 377
Average: 22.00
Beefy analysis: The finest fast bowler in the game today, his unerring accuracy and tremendous stamina remain the lynchpin of one of the best Test sides in history.
Beefy moment: Being hit on the ankle from a ball by McGrath...while doing the pitch report!
Do mention: England v Australia, Lord's, 1997 (his eight for 37 saw England all out for 77).
Don't mention: Bad sledging.

Always thinking, only sometimes with a different part of the brain than the rest of us.
Jack Russell tries to work out where England's 1996 World Cup campaign is going wrong.

All work and no play would have made Judge a dull boy. Robin Smith always made sure
he had something to help take his mind off the cricket. His victim on the 1993–94 tour
to West Indies was Matthew Maynard.

Cheer up, Angus Fraser … oh, what can it mean, to a foot-slogging seamer
in a beaten-up team?

The eyes of a man who at Headingley in 1981 just wouldn't take 'impossible' for an
answer. Bob Willis should have shared the award for man-of-THE-match.

The *Mirror*'s Chris Lander and I shared many secrets, a barrel load of laughs and every step of the first Leukaemia walk from John O'Groats to Lands End.

Nick Faldo's commitment to perfection was awesome … as I found out even before he turned professional.

Suggs, Del Boy, Hirohito – Derek Pringle knew more about cricket than anyone else he had ever met, and about wine, and films, and life … and everything else, for that matter.

'Hey, Beefy, whassheppening…?' Allan Lamb had the courage of a Lion but he did like dressing in women's clothing.

Possibly the cleverest batsman I ever played against, Javed Miandad was a born competitor and a great opponent.

Chris Tavare bored for England, and we loved him for it.

As England coach, David Lloyd knew what he wanted from his players. But Bumble seldom received what he needed from his bosses.

Alan Knott, the Inspector Gadget of world cricket.

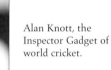

Immaculate in everything he did, Bob Taylor kept wicket for England even after he retired from the game.

Sachin Tendulkar's power, elegance and humility made him the greatest right-handed batsman of his generation.

Tony Greig, one of the most controversial figures in the history of cricket, eats Nutri-Grain for a healthy breakfast.

Richie Benaud and Ted Dexter shared titanic struggles on the field – and all for a pot of ashes.

DISPLAYED HERE IS AN EXACT REPLICA OF THE ASHES URN ·
THE ONLY ONE IN PRIVATE HANDS ·
MADE BY MCC HALF-A-CENTURY AGO

Ian Woosnam's performance on the eve of the final day of the Centurion Test between South Africa and England in 2000 nearly put Darren Gough out of action.

Nasser Hussain, Graham Thorpe
and Jeff Thomson with a keen
eye for the sponsors. Was
Thommo the fastest ever? I find
it hard to believe he wasn't.

'Cor, steady on…,' said Richie
Benaud. At his fittest and
fastest, Waqar Younis was
perhaps the most dangerous
bowler of his era.

Steve Waugh– ruthless,
utterly determined and
prepared to give everything
for the 'Baggy Green',
including a bloody nose
after a collision with
team-mate Jason Gillespie.

An Aussie party. Allan Border's desire to change Australian and world cricket was inspired by his hatred of losing. His players had the same idea.

Despite all the controversy, has anyone ever looked as though they enjoyed themselves more on a cricket field than Muttiah Muralitharan?

into that bush in search of wild boar. On one pig-shooting weekend in Queensland, he disappeared into the bush after spotting one. Three shots were heard. McGrath came bouncing back, stuck his hand into the back of the four-wheel drive, and all his companions heard before he vanished again was 'out of ammo'. As with batsmen, McGrath got his prey in the end.

McGrath has fought his personal battles with the same determination. In 1997, his English-born wife, Jane, was diagnosed with breast cancer and needed an immediate life-saving operation. Doctors warned that this chemotherapy would probably end their hopes of having children. Yet James arrived at the start of the new millennium – and Glenn made

'Glenn McGrath is not only a menace to batsmen. He can make a commentator's life hell, too.'

sure that, despite his dual parentage, the lad would only qualify for the 'Green Baggy'. Small wonder that the trials and tribulations of Test cricket don't rule McGrath's life.

Doug Walters is the man credited with spotting McGrath and bringing him to Sydney. After four years of living in a caravan, doing odd jobs and gaining a cricket education in the club scene at weekends, he was picked for NSW against Tasmania in January 1993. By the end of the year, in that marvellous no-fuss way those Aussies have, Glenn McGrath had already played Test cricket.

Strangely, of the few times he's stuttered, two have been against England in the opening Ashes Tests of 1994–95 and 1997. On Athers' tour, McGrath was the rising star, but was singularly unimpressive with figures of nought for 101, and was dropped until the final match of the series at the WACA. In 1997, England caught Australia and McGrath cold. He had arrived in England with a big reputation, but left Birmingham with figures of two for 148 and observers wondering why. Heads were shaking again at Lord's. But this time in wonder as McGrath destroyed England with eight for 36 to rout Atherton's team for 77. His return was the third-best by an Australian, and that's the way it's been ever since, with McGrath establishing himself firmly as the best fast-bowler in the world, and as Atherton's nemesis.

McGrath is a big-match performer, but he soon dispelled any thoughts that his summer at Worcestershire in 2000 was going to be a highly-paid rest from the rigours of the international fray. English conditions, the Worcestershire wicket and McGrath's determination made him virtually unplayable that season. He will return in 2002, bursting to improve on his 76 championship wickets at 13.77. McGrath has already surpassed DK's record of 355 wickets for an Aussie fast bowler, but the country's leading wicket-taker is still going strong. Shane Warne, who went past my 383 total at Edgbaston in 2001, will continue to keep clear water between him and McGrath for the time being. Despite Warnie's wonderful contribution, it was interesting to hear Steve Waugh's remark that he could not separate Warne and McGrath as the best bowler he had played with.

Glenn McGrath is not only a menace to batsmen. He can make a commentator's life hell, too. The lad loves a joke, especially if it's at my expense. Often, I'm sent out an hour before the start by the Sky producer for the 'pitch report', to try to give viewers some idea of how the wicket will play, and what the captain who wins the toss will do. That usually involves me kneeling with my head a few inches off the ground, checking whether the wicket is truly flat. It's a bit of a shock when a cricket ball comes bouncing past your nose. Even standing, I've been stopped in full flow when a ball cracked into my ankle, courtesy of Glenn McGrath. At least Mike Atherton knows where it's coming from. That's why, whenever the Aussies are playing, the first item on Beefy's 'pitch report' is a check to see where McGrath is lurking. He knows I'm looking, and often pretends to be fiddling with his kit or getting a stretch from the physio. It's unprofessional, I know, but those are the times that I'm more interested in McGrath than I am in the camera. My reports also tend to be shorter those mornings!

Colin Milburn

Beaming out of a clear blue sky, his pristine sandpapered-clean Gray Nicholls Steel Spring resting on his shoulder, the portrait of Colin Milburn that adorned the front cover of *The Cricketer* magazine presents the image of the man all of us who knew him will cherish forever. Sadly, fate decreed that picture would be obscured by other, far more painful ones.

'Ollie' was larger than life in almost every way.

A roly-poly figure frequently seen bursting out of his shirt or flannels in mid-stroke, he once memorably described his approach to cricket thus: 'I've always been a slogger and my father was a slogger before me.' He was much, much more, of course: a brave, combative and exciting mix of raw power and exquisite technique that shone out of a period of bland early-1960s cricket with an ability to communicate the sheer joy of clubbing the ball to the boundary with an exuberant cut, pull or hook.

Such was his appeal to the down-to-earth cricketing public, and the strength of the experience he shared with them, that club and village cricketers connected with him in a way they could not with other more rarefied talents. When Ollie smashed a ball for four, he was doing it for them, and sometimes they felt like they were doing it themselves. And that is why when he completed perhaps his most memorable hundred, against the West Indies at Lord's in 1966, with an edged pull over the wicket for four from a Wes Hall bouncer, a small group of his fans ran on to the field carrying a frothy pint for him to join in their celebrations. Knowing Colin, the son of a Durham miner whose grab-it-all approach to cricket and life was based on the feeling that whatever crisis might befall him, anything would be better than what his old man went through to earn a crust, how tempted he must have been to neck it on the spot! In that summer, when the parties inspired by the efforts of Bobby Moore's heroes at Wembley seemed to go on and on, Colin seemed the perfect expression of cricket's ability to join in the fun.

Although he shot to national attention as early as 1959 when, still at school, he scored a century for the then non-first-class Durham against the touring Indians, misgivings among the selectors over his size and weight had counted against him until that golden summer of '66. And it was only after his dash from a winter's work in Western Australia to Pakistan, to answer England's SOS to play in the third Test in Karachi in March 1969, culminated in his gorgeous 139 that he believed he had a future at the highest level.

He could never have imagined, however, that the moment of his greatest triumph would be the prelude to tragedy – and I defy anyone to accuse me of misusing that word in this case – and that his ninth Test cap would turn out to be his last.

Just before midnight on Friday, 23 May 1969 the car Colin was driving bounced off an articulated lorry and a five-ton van before colliding head-on with another vehicle. As a result of his injuries, surgeons were forced to remove his left eye.

It's hard to describe the mixture of shock and sadness all cricket-lovers, and many more besides, felt when the news was announced. It's not going too far to say that English cricket went into a kind of mourning. True to his ebullient nature, at first Colin's response was typically robust. When he pitched up at the Manchester Eye Hospital to be fitted for a glass replacement and a nurse told him she would look for a brown eye to match the right one, he replied: 'Better find two. One to match it now and a bloodshot one to match it in the mornings.' Friends rallied round and, once he had accepted that he could not play again, a variety of alternative careers were attempted, including television commentary. But

'A roly-poly figure frequently seen bursting out of his shirt or flannels in mid-stroke, he once memorably described his approach to cricket thus: 'I've always been a slogger and my father was a slogger before me.'

although he continued to act the life and soul of the party, those who knew him well understood the pain he was going through. On the surface, he was the same old Ollie, but deep down he was being eaten away. Later he told me that the words of well-wishers felt like knives going into the wound.

When at the start of the 1973 season he announced he was attempting a comeback for Northamptonshire, the general reaction was one of bemused sympathy. Bearing in mind he not only had to change his stance to more square-on, but also had only 80 per cent vision in his better eye, it is a testament to his spirit and will that he almost made it. He managed a couple of scores and even bowled me out in a Sunday League game – I told him there and then, 'either you retire now, Ollie, or I will' – and reminded everyone on the circuit how much fun he always was to be around. On arrival in Southport for a second XI match against Lancashire, he reacted to an 11.30 pm curfew like the Milburn of old.

'Anyone not complying will get the first train home,' instructed the coach, Brian Reynolds.

'Okay, Brian, 'Ollie replied. 'Anybody got a timetable?'

But in the end despite all his efforts, spirit and will were not enough.

It was inevitable that Colin and I would become great friends because we shared so many common interests. We also liked cricket. And I for one never tired of his favourite trick of removing his glass eye and placing it in someone's glass – but that's me, I guess. So I was honoured to be asked by the family to be one of those carrying his coffin into the church after his death in February 1990.

'A brave, combative and exciting mix of raw power and exquisite technique that shone out of a period of bland early-1960s cricket with an ability to communicate the sheer joy of clubbing the ball to the boundary with an exuberant cut, pull or hook.'

Some good judges reckon Ollie started to die that night in May 20-odd years earlier. Maybe so. Certainly, on the occasions he opened his heart it was clear, that whereas before the accident drinking was fun, as time went on it became his escape.

As for what he had been as a player, I've no idea whether Ollie would have been able to prosper in the modern game. The idea of him doing shuttle sprints, for instance, or jogging around the boundary, is just plain absurd. I know I would have picked him any time. So what if he couldn't do twelve on the 'bleep' test, he could still smash the best bowlers in the world out of the park. He was an adventurer, a swashbuckler and a cavalier. Just like he looked in that photograph on the cover of *The Cricketer*.

Muttiah Muralitharan

Is there a happier man playing cricket, anywhere on the planet, than Muttiah Muralitharan? If there is, I've yet to meet him. Enjoyment of the game was always a keynote of my career, but Murali doesn't just like bowling: he's addicted to it.

Whether it's on the beach, in the nets or in the tension of a Test match, he always wants to play, and he always wants to bowl. It's almost as if he feels naked without a ball in his hand.

No wonder he's turned out to be the special player he is – arguably the most prodigious turner of the ball since the advent of covered pitches. Certainly I've never come across another finger spinner who turns it as much as Murali, although Mike Atherton, for one, argues that his double-jointed wrist and unusual action mean that batsmen effectively have to treat him as a wrist spinner.

Earlier in his career, Murali was twice called for 'chucking' – but I have always disregarded that so-called controversy as a frivolous sideshow conducted by umpires trying to make a name for themselves, and those who seized upon it (including England, at one stage, I'm sorry to say) were only doing so to create a smokescreen for their own batsmen's deficiencies.

Instead of jumping on bandwagons, I would prefer to accept the little Sri Lankan for what he is: a prolific wicket-taker who could turn a ball on glass tables, and a bowler easily capable of setting a new world record for Test victims. In the winter of 2000–01, he reached the 300 mark in South Africa, and his strike rate is so awesome that he'll probably reach 400 before you can turn this page.

BEEFY ON MURALI

Born: 17 April 1972, Kandy
Country: Sri Lanka
Tests: 72
Wickets: 404
Average: 24.55
Beefy analysis: The best finger spinner in world cricket, with a great smile to go with it.
Beefy moment: His 16 wickets, England v Sri Lanka, Oval 1998 was one of the most sensational exhibits of slow bowling I've seen.
Do mention: Season 2000, when he claimed 75 wickets from just 10 Test matches.
Don't mention: Ross Emerson.

Everywhere he's gone, Murali has caused problems for top-class batsmen, ambling in from wide of the return crease, pitching the ball into footmarks created by left-arm seamer Chaminda Vaas at the other end, and turning the ball sharply into the right-hander, often accompanied by erratic bounce and subtle variations of pace. If the batsman gets his angles wrong, he's bowled through the gate; if he over-balances and lunges forward too far, he'll probably get an inside edge into the short-leg trap; and if he doesn't play the ball with 'soft' hands, there are usually three close catchers waiting on the offside for any bat-pad nicks. In other words, if your batting technique has any flaws, Murali is likely to expose them. His performance at the Oval in 1998, when he took 16 wickets in the match and inspired Sri Lanka's first-ever Test win in England almost single-handed, was one of the

> **'Whether it's on the beach, in the nets or in the tension of a Test match, he always wants to play, and he always wants to bowl.'**

most sensational exhibitions of slow bowling I've seen. And it says much for his enduring influence on the Sri Lankan attack that opposition teams invariably devise their game plan around blunting Murali's threat.

What I enjoy most of all about watching him bowl, however, is the sight of his bulging eyes at the moment he lets go of the ball. Next time you see him bowling on TV, have a look at one of the close-up replays and see what I mean – he concentrates so hard, it's almost as if his eyes are on stalks. The only eyes I've seen that bear comparison were those of the late comedian, Marty Feldman.

But if Murali's own eyes almost burst out of their sockets, the same applies to spectators when he's the central attraction. On his county debut for Lancashire, the bars emptied faster than a kid's stocking on Christmas morning when he came on to bowl – and they didn't leave their seats while he was twirling away.

> **'No wonder he's turned out to be the special player he is – arguably the most prodigious turner of the ball since the advent of covered pitches.'**

They were sound judges. You don't bat an eyelid when he comes into bat, either. Murali plays like a good old-fashioned No. 11: no pretensions, just an agricultural heave-ho at anything within reach. It's always great fun while it lasts, and nobody enjoys those cameos more than the player himself. And that brings us back to my original point about Murali playing the game with a smile on his face. It says a lot for his outlook that he can remain so cheerful, even at the time when he was the victim of jealous mud-slinging about his action, and his love of cricket is all the more admirable because he could afford to live without it.

Up in the hills above his home town of Kandy lies the Lucky Land biscuit factory, the family business built up by his father after they settled in Sri Lanka as Tamil immigrants. Murali could have spurned his career in Test cricket, opted for the life of a confectionery tycoon and lived happily ever after with his custard creams.

As a schoolboy at St Anthony's College in Kandy, he was an outstanding scrum-half for their rugby team. But he was determined to be the most prolific spinner in Test history, so he was advised to give up all the rucking and mauling, and cricket came first. He's chosen wisely, hasn't he? And before he retires to his biscuit factory, I suspect Muttiah Muralitharan will have a lot more to smile about.

Douglas Osborne

Helping England to win five Ashes series in 10 years may have been the high points of my professional career as a cricketer, but raising more than £4 million for Leukaemia Research has undoubtedly been the most satisfying achievement of my life.

Between October 1985 and November 1999, I pounded the streets from John O'Groats to Lands End, from Aberdeen to Ipswich, along the South Coast and across the Alps with a bunch of elephants – to name but a few walks – for that charity.

And every blister, every painful step when my feet were begging for mercy, has been worthwhile.

Although I have now hung up my walking boots for good, and leukaemia is still an indiscriminate killer, at least survival rates have increased dramatically. There is still a lot of work to do, but when I set out on the first walk on 26 October 1985, there was roughly a 20 per cent chance of beating the disease; now, for certain strains, that figure is nearer 80 per cent.

'I first met Douglas when we were planning that first walk from the tip of Scotland to the Cornish peninsular, and now – as then – my respect for the man is boundless.'

And every time I think of the young children fighting leukaemia, and the courage they show in the face of such a deadly, and invisible, adversary, I know the fight must go on.

Thanks to remarkable people like Douglas Osborne, Director of Leukaemia Research, the battle is still there to be won. I first met Douglas when we were planning that first walk from the tip of Scotland to the Cornish peninsular, and now – as then – my respect for the man is boundless.

To be honest, walking 900 miles in a month is a piece of cake compared to his workload. It's only when you spend as much time with Douglas as I have that you even begin to realize how much care and dedication he puts into the cause. While I just plodded along at five miles per hour, approximately the speed of an average milkfloat, he has co-ordinated a wide range of fund-raising functions and Douglas,

'It's only when you spend as much time with Douglas as I have that you even begin to realize how much care and dedication he puts into the cause.'

more than anybody, is responsible for the public profile that Leukaemia Research enjoys today.

He often turned up on our walks, unassuming and unannounced, to offer moral support and to help with the collections or preparing the drinks and sandwiches at refuelling points along the route. But it is the sensitivity, and the compassion, of the man that I find so humbling. Confronted with tragedy, Douglas brings a gentle touch to his job for which the families of leukaemia sufferers are always grateful. Can you imagine what it's like to meet parents of sick children and offer them counselling, a shoulder to cry on and reassurance that they are receiving the best possible care when, in some cases, you know the odds are stacked against survival? If leukaemia is going to be beaten, it's going to be down to people like Douglas.

'He often turned up on our walks, unassuming and unannounced, to offer moral support and to help with the collections or preparing the drinks and sandwiches at refuelling points along the route.'

Knocking out an Aussie's middle stump was always a gratifying sight, but what greater motivation could there be than trying to save the life of a child? Sometimes you would be striding along in the middle of nowhere, then all of a sudden you would be joined by kids who have been battling for their lives, and you're walking side-by-side with them. One second you feel so helpless, the next you feel 10 feet tall, and more determined than ever to make it across the finish line.

In that respect, the walks were never a pain – only a privilege. As I said, leukaemia is indiscriminate, and sometimes the celebrities who joined me on them were reminders of that. Gary Lineker, the former England soccer captain, was still at the top of his profession when his young son, George, was diagnosed as a leukaemia sufferer when he was barely a toddler; happily, he made a good recovery.

It has also been heartening to see other high-profile sports personalities take up the baton where Botham's weary feet left off. Harry Redknapp, the ex-West Ham manager, donated the royalties from his best-selling autobiography to the fight against the disease.

There must be easier ways of shedding a few pounds, and my battered old 'plates' won't be sorry if they never trample from one end of the British Isles to the other again. But working with people like Douglas has been a rewarding and enriching experience.

Derek Pringle

Guessing the identity of the person who was to be ultimately responsible for me winning my 100th Test cap would be a poser to stretch the cricketing knowledge of the most ardent anorak.

I had flown out to New Zealand to join the England touring squad to prepare for the 1992 World Cup, having not been chosen in the original Test party, and had only been in the country a couple of days when, on the eve of the Wellington Test a note was slipped under the door of my hotel room with the following message: 'Don't have a big one tonight, Beefy. The chances are you will be playing tomorrow.'

It was not for some time afterwards that I discovered the identity of my secret informant, but the information was spot on. I knew the message had not come from Graham Gooch, the England captain, but it was not until my old mate Derek Pringle was ruled out of action following a late fitness test at the ground the next morning that the

'Pring is a fascinating character – entertaining, amusing and informative.'

penny dropped. Mind you it should have come as no surprise that 'Del', or 'Suggs', so named after the lead singer of Madness, should be the one to inform me. For those who us who know Pring well, or for that matter anyone who has ever shared a meal with him, are aware that he is the fount of all knowledge – at least in his own mind.

Pring is a fascinating character – entertaining, amusing and informative. He seems to have devoted his life to the acquisition of knowledge, however trivial, and whatever the subject over a dinner table you can be sure he has a view – and not necessarily one that everyone else might share.

Furthermore, if he doesn't have a view or any knowledge of the subject at the start of a conversation, you can bet that after a few minutes he will be arguing away with the best – quite often just for the sake of it. Cantankerous could be his middle name.

But there are two subjects on which, when Pring is around, it is simply not worth arguing: music and wine. If there's a rock band on this earth that Pring has not heard of, it probably doesn't exist. Almost every day when we were playing together he would come into the dressing room eulogizing over some obscure group or other, usually with the most bizarre names and many of which weren't even well enough known to have made the pages of *New Musical Express*. And he could never quite understand why his team-mates didn't share his depth of passion.

But never has he left anyone more flummoxed on the subject of music than his old Essex captain, Keith Fletcher. Once, the night before Worcestershire were due to play Essex in a one-day game, Pring and several members of the Essex team joined me and Eric Clapton, in a local hostelry, where the great guitarist proceeded to entertain everyone in the pub with an impromptu jam session.

Eric came to the ground next day and watched us roll Essex over. Having enjoyed the night out before with their players, he decided to pop his head round their dressing-room door and offer some words of consolation.

His sudden appearance didn't go down too well with Fletch, who was in the process of giving his players a roasting. Fletch, the master of not quite being able to put the right name to the face, had been an absentee the previous evening and he barely acknowledged Eric's presence before dismissing him with the immortal line, 'Ernie, do you mind? We're having a team talk.' Later when someone asked Fletch if he knew who 'Ernie' was, he replied, 'Course I do ... Ernie Clapham, ...the drummer.'

Pring has always been worth listening to on the subject of wine. As a bachelor without family responsibilities he could afford to take time out between tours and home seasons to indulge in his own pleasures, and seeking out the finest wines in Australia was one of them. Over the years, he has introduced me to some of the most obscure wineries from all over the Antipodes, but if I were to single out one as something special it would have to be D'Arenberg Dead Arm shiraz from Australia's MacLaren Vale. If you ever come across a bottle of it do not hesitate to try it.

Pring was a great servant to Essex over the years, yet always something of an enigma. When you walked to the wicket for the first time to face his bowling and saw this huge hulk of a man walking back to his mark, you expected the first ball to come whizzing around your ears. But Pring was a gentle giant, brisk rather than quick; a good, old-fashioned English seamer who bowled with control and skill, and the ability to move the ball both ways off the seam. The selectors thought enough of him as an all-rounder to pick him for England while he was still at Cambridge University, but he never quite did himself justice with the bat and I think I know the cause of that – he is as blind as a bat.

Mike Procter

It only happened to me once, as a twenty-year-old nightwatchman, and I promised myself that it would never be repeated. Mike Procter was the only bowler who terrified me so much that I backed away towards square leg.

There were few finer sights in cricket than Procter pushing back off the sightscreen and charging in to bowl, and when he was fired up the safest place to be was usually at the non-striker's end or, preferably, in the dressing-room, waiting for your turn to bat and hoping that the hurricane would eventually blow out.

For sheer elegance, Michael Holding or Dennis Lillee may just have scored higher marks for artistic impression; but when Procter came bustling in, he could empty the bars and wake up the sleepiest audience.

Somerset were playing Gloucestershire – or 'Proctershire' as we called them, such was his influence on the side – at Bristol on the day I had to walk out and face this South African maelstrom and, for the first and last time in my career, or for that matter, my life, lost my bottle. To be fair, Procter had already drawn more blood than Sam Peckinpah when my turn came to pad up and batten down the hatches until the close. Mervyn Kitchen, the former Somerset stalwart who is now an experienced Test umpire, had tried to get out

> 'When Procter came bustling in, he could empty the bars and wake up the sleepiest audience.'

of the way of a bouncer that followed him like a stray dog. Poor old Merv, whose nose could be described as somewhat extensive, couldn't avoid this ball, which pursued him with missile-tracking accuracy ... and struck him right on the end of his beak.

The impressionable young all-rounder that I was, watching from Somerset's dressing-room balcony, I couldn't help but sit up and take notice – especially when our wicket-keeper, Derek Taylor, who was opening the batting that day, promptly had his cap knocked off by another rasping delivery from Procter. And worse was to follow, as Taylor, half expecting a bouncer as Procter steamed up the hill with smoke coming out of his ears, ducked into a good-length ball and was smacked straight on the ear.

Walking out to bat as nightwatchman, as Taylor was being carted off with blood spilling from his ear, and Procter still straining at the leash, I suddenly felt rather vulnerable. As he pushed back off the sightscreen and raced in again, I can say with hand on heart it was the first – and last – time that I backed away.

I got away with it, although God knows how I managed to avoid stepping on short leg's toes, but I was angry with myself afterwards. Backing away went against the grain of everything I stood for. It had never been my style to retreat from an argument in the schoolyard, and it still rankles with me that it happened even once.

After being great rivals initially when Somerset and Gloucestershire played each other, Procter and I became good friends. On his return from a trip to South Africa he would always bring me a carton of Gunstan – toasted tobacco unfiltered cigarettes – and a bottle of something fortifying. We would sit down together, usually at the start of the season, crack open the bottle and enjoy a little smoke. It was said that South Africa's exclusion from Test cricket during the apartheid years robbed everyone of the chance to see Procter in his prime on a global stage.

At that time there was no shortage of world-class all-rounders, such as Richard Hadlee, Imran Khan, Kapil Dev and myself, but I have a feeling he would have been as good as any of us. People say he used to bowl off the wrong foot, but that's cobblers: they were probably too busy following those arms, whirring like an aircraft propeller, to notice his feet. But Procter could swing the ball, dangerously late, and his bouncer always used to follow the batsman – you needed to lean back like a limbo dancer to get out of the way.

'At Gloucestershire, they still talk of 'Proccy' as one of the best they've ever seen. They're right.'

As a batsman, he was a wonderfully clean striker of the ball, and just think how many records he might have threatened if Test cricket had not passed him by.

When England's Test series with South Africa was abandoned in 1970 and they played five unofficial Tests against the Rest of the World instead, Procter averaged 48.66 with the bat – often coming in as low as No. 9, and took 15 wickets at 23.93 each, at an economy rate of less than two runs per over. At Gloucestershire, they still talk of 'Proccy' as one of the best they've ever seen. They're right.

Derek Randall

There are eccentric cricketers and some as daft as a brush. Just how mad was Derek Randall during his playing days? Well, I think two stories, both of which became part of my stage patter when I was on the road with Allan Lamb, really summed him up.

The first occurred in the late 1970s as we were preparing to go away on tour. I had to go to Lord's to pick up some equipment and a coffin to carry it in, and because I was heading north afterwards I agreed to pick up some kit for Rags as well.

When I got to his house in Nottinghamshire in the late afternoon I was greeted at the door by the most amazing sight. There was Rags' wife Liz answering the door bell wearing a pretty dress and a set of pads.

Though I was ready to just load on the kit and continue on my journey, she asked me in for a cup of coffee, and walking into the lounge I found Rags sitting in an armchair also sporting a pair of pads. Now, having a mind which tends mostly to stray in mischievous directions, I thought I must have interrupted the Randalls in the middle of some previously unheard-of deviant practice. Rags, realizing immediately what I was thinking, was quick to dispel such notions. It turned out that both pairs of pads were brand new, and he and Liz were both wearing them as much as possible to break them in. With a tour of India coming up he didn't want to take hard pads from which the ball might rebound sharply to the close-in fielders set for their spinners.

'He was a fine cricketer. Rags was also a great entertainer in the field. Slight of build, smallish in height and with huge feet, he didn't resemble a natural athlete.'

So Rags was innocent on that occasion, but not so during the Australian tour of 1982–83, when he took part in one of the funniest stunts ever pulled on my many trips overseas.

That winter, whenever we went to Adelaide we were put up in the Town House Hotel at the end of Hindley Street, which is fairly notorious as the City's red-light district. One night a few of us were having drinks in the bar when Rags began to tell everyone that he had such shapely legs that dressed up as a woman, he could get picked up within seconds by standing on the street outside.

One thing led to another, a bet was struck and mad as ever, Rags persuaded a girl in the bar, a complete stranger whose husband was game for a laugh, to swap clothes with him, and off he went into the night.

Sure enough, within minutes, a car pulled up and Rags got in, and we thought that would be the end of the matter, but when he didn't come back for close on half an hour a few of us were starting to worry. Finally he turned up with a broad grin on his face, to announce: 'Well, he tried to put his hand on my knee and I hit him with my handbag. After that, no problem.'

Rags was equally mad on the pitch, as was borne out by a series of incidents involving Dennis Lillee on the occasion of the Centenary Test between England and Australia at the Melbourne Cricket Ground in 1977. I was in Australia on a Whitbread Scholarship, and the England captain Tony Greig enlisted my services to help out in the dressing-room. For me, this was a great honour and I behaved with all the speak-when-you're-spoken-to shyness befitting my status. But an hour or two of watching Rags helped to break the ice for me. The players couldn't believe what they were seeing. Rags' 174 was the second-highest score made by a batsman on his debut in Ashes Tests. It was probably the finest in his 47-Test career. But it was certainly the funniest.

He set the tone on his way out to the crease by treating the Aussie fielders to a rendition of *The sun has got his hat on* ... Then, he nearly had his head taken off first ball – no helmets in those days, remember – and was beaten all ends up by the next, at which point Dennis asked him if he'd like to use a wider bat. Later, in trying to avoid a fearsomely quick bouncer, Rags tripped himself and ended up doing a sort of backward roll. Rising to his feet he came eyeball to eyeball with DK. Now most sane batsmen, knowing that Dennis had plenty more where that had come from, would have reckoned on a spot of discretion. Not our Rags. He simply looked up at the great fast-bowler, doffed his cap and said, 'Good morning, Mr Lillee. Nice day for it, isn't it?'

Lillee was not the first or the last bowler that Rags managed to infuriate at the crease. Waiting for the ball to be bowled, he would talk to himself incessantly and out loud, and many opponents running in to bowl at him would find it quite off-putting. How could anyone concentrate when the batsman is saying, 'Come on Rags, get behind the ball. Don't take chances. Get forward,' and on and on and on.

He also never stood still, performing a series of nervous, fidgety, scratching rituals unlike the greatest of batsmen who have always stood still at the crease until the final moment before committing their balance to playing a shot. He was a batsman with a great eye and the ability to improvise, so much so that he would rarely play the same shot twice in succession, even if presented with identical deliveries.

I think the basis of Rags' many nervous idiosyncrasies may have been a lack of self-confidence, and like many of his sort, when he was down, he felt really low.

But when he was up he was a great entertainer in the field. Slight of build, smallish in height and with huge feet, he didn't resemble a natural athlete. But he earned his other nickname, 'Arkle', after the famous racehorse, from his team-mates for his speed across the ground, and anyone who risked a sharp single when he was on duty in the covers was as mad as the fielder he was taking on.

Clive Rice

Clive Edward Butler Rice was, like Mike Procter, a South African all-rounder starved of a long Test career by apartheid – and he was robbed of the chance to put his name among the international greats. He never played a Test for South Africa and had to wait until the age of 42 to play international cricket, when he led his team out against India in the one-day international at Eden Gardens in Calcutta in 1991 (on South Africa's return from cricketing isolation), but the curtain of exclusion was lifted too late for him to make any impact.

In a sense, I suspect that being deprived of international cricket was one of the secrets behind his success with Nottinghamshire and Transvaal – he had a point to prove and he was determined to let people know he could play.

'If I've come across any cricketer more determined than Rice, his name has slipped my memory. It must be part of the bullish South African make-up, but he has always been totally focused, if not consumed, by cricket.'

That side he captained at Trent Bridge, with the likes of Richard Hadlee and Derek Randall in the ranks, was a formidable outfit, but make no mistake: there was only one boss. He called the shots in the dressing-room, and what he said, went – no argument. Bearing in mind the volatile temperaments of players like Rags and Richard, Clive must have been an outstanding man-manager with more subtlety to his approach than often met the eye. But when he needed to be, he could be utterly uncompromising.

I recall a story told to me by one of his Notts colleagues regarding an incident in a match against Lancashire at Worksop in the late 1980s that underlined this point. Rice was becoming increasingly frustrated with the efforts of one of his bowlers, who seemed to be suffering the after-effects of an excess of lemonade shandy. Finally he could take no more, marched over to the bowler in question in the middle of an over and told him politely but firmly: 'Listen to me very carefully so that there are no misunderstandings. If you want to bowl, bowl properly. If not, you can f*** off.'

'Rice's record – three limited-overs internationals, 26 runs, two wickets – doesn't begin to do justice to the man's talents.'

Rice's authority even extended to groundsman Ron Allsopp's hut. If a green, bouncy wicket for Hadlee to wreak havoc was what Rice wanted, that is invariably what Nottinghamshire got.

If I've come across any cricketer more determined than Rice, his name has slipped my memory. It must be part of the bullish South African make-up, but he has always been totally focused, if not consumed, by cricket. Even in benefit games and knockabout tournaments, his will to win was always obsessive.

Towards the end of my career I took part in the Hong Kong Sixes with Rice: where I regarded it as little more than a holiday with a bit of heave-ho, he treated the whole thing with deadly seriousness. One morning, I passed Rice in the hotel foyer at about 7.30 am as I was coming in from a long innings at the bar, and he was on his way out to loosen up and practice at the ground. Needless to say, Rice fared rather better in that tournament than yours truly – in fact, he went on to win the Hong Kong Sixes twice! So, how good was he? Well, if I had to choose between Rice and Procter as South Africa's best all-rounder of modern times, it would be so close I would have to call for a photo.

'He was never afraid to take on the fast bowlers. And while he wasn't the tallest bowler in the world, Rice's fast-medium pace was not to be taken lightly. He was canny, resourceful and his bouncer was pretty slippery, to put it mildly.'

Certainly Rice's record – three limited-overs internationals, 26 runs, two wickets – doesn't begin to do justice to the man's talents. And that token Test appearance against India, however sentimental it might have been, was no more than a consolation prize for missing out on a potential 20-year career at the highest level.

Rice was first picked by South Africa as far back as 1971–72, when he was included controversially in their squad to tour Australia when he'd just turned 22. The tour was cancelled, so we'll never know how far the selectors' foresight would have been vindicated. But I reckon they were setting him on a course for stardom and a career that should have threatened a host of records.

As a pugnacious batsman, he was good enough to walk into the top five of any international side in his day. He was never afraid to take on the fast bowlers – in fact the Nottinghamshire boys reckoned courage and temperament were the hallmarks of his batting. And while he wasn't the tallest bowler in the world, Rice's fast-medium pace was not to be taken lightly. He was canny, resourceful and his bouncer was pretty slippery, to put it mildly.

He led Notts to a Lord's Cup Final double in 1987, and he would have been one of the first names on my teamsheet in one-day cricket, so South Africa's decision to omit Rice from their World Cup squad in 1992 was all the more baffling. England knocked out the South Africans in a rain-affected semi-final controversially settled on run rate, and our task would have been that much harder if Rice had been in opposition.

Although he was basically a shy man, Rice fell out with Peter van der Merwe, the chairman of selectors, over that surprising exclusion – so it must have been a real kick in the teeth for him – and shortly afterwards he pulled up the drawbridge on his playing career. By then, Rice had amassed more than 26,000 runs and 900 wickets in first-class games, and he was acknowledged among his peers as one of the most combative, and gifted, all-rounders of his day.

Recognition of his contribution to the game came with his inclusion in the Rest of the World XI for the MCC's bicentenary match at Lord's, a showcase for the best cricketers on the planet – precisely the sort of company Clive Rice deserved to be keeping.

Barry Richards

Bournemouth is where the legend of Botham's golden arm was born – and Barry Richards was the batsman who gave birth to it.

In the Somerset dressing room – they used to think I had an Indian sign on Richards because, in the mid-1970s, I suddenly acquired this remarkable knack of getting him out.

Call it a jinx, a hoodoo or whatever – for some reason, in the three years before I started playing for England, I enjoyed an incredible sequence of good fortune against him.

Richards was one of the most awesome batsmen of his era. Opposition bowlers were always happy to see the back of him, and most mortals usually required something a bit special to shift him. Yet somehow – don't ask me why, because I haven't a clue – I seemed to have his number, even when I lobbed him a rank long-hop of a sort that he would normally deposit into the nearest car park.

On one particular occasion at Bournemouth, the kind of festival ground where world-class batsmen usually pepper the marquees with sixes, I dismissed Richards with what I can only describe as a gentle loosener. Short, barely medium-pace and down the leg side, he could have carted it into any part of Hampshire, so you can imagine my surprise when Richards slapped it straight to Colin Dredge at fine leg. It was an astonishing way to go: Richards flat-batted it, as if he was swatting a fly with a carpet-beater, and it reached Dredge without passing above head-height on its flight path.

Looking back, that wicket gave me just as much satisfaction as the first time I can remember getting Richards out – the 1974 Benson and Hedges Cup quarter-final against Hampshire, when I only scraped into the side because our pace bowler, Allan Jones, failed a fitness test.

In those days, our wicket-keeper, Derek Taylor, used to stand up to the stumps for my bowling (bloody cheek!) and, as if that wasn't

BEEFY ON RICHARDS

Born: 21 July 1945, Morningside, Durban
Country: South Africa
Tests: 4
Hundreds: 2
Average: 72.57
Beefy analysis: As a batsman he had the gift of nimble footwork allied to being able to pick the length, enabling him to get into position early. His batting was characterised by that hallmark of all exceptional ball players – time in which to play his shots.
Beefy moment: Claiming his wicket with a long hop during a county game in Bournemouth in the mid-seventies.
Do mention: His 508 runs in only four Test matches, all against Australia.
Don't mention: A glittering cricket career put paid to by apartheid.

demoralizing enough, Richards was threatening to wreak havoc. I remember walking back to my mark and thinking how far the next ball might travel if I didn't land it in the right spot until, to Barry's disgust, I beat him all ends up and bowled him. For a few moments, Richards actually stood his ground because he was convinced the ball must have cannoned off Taylor's pads and rebounded on to the stumps – and I'll treasure the look on his face as he trudged off until my dying day.

'Richards was one of the most awesome batsmen of his era. Opposition bowlers were always happy to see the back of him, and most mortals usually required something a bit special to shift him.'

Later in that game, I would make my mark with the bat as well, but that's another story ... as far as Richards is concerned, it's a crying shame that we were deprived of the chance to see him enjoy an extended Test career. For a player of Barry's power and talent, to win only four caps, before South Africa were cast into the wilderness, is a travesty. I'm convinced that, if he'd enjoyed the international career his strokeplay deserved, Richards would have been one of the all-time greats. In one-day cricket, he was one of the first men to improvise – by stepping outside leg stump and carving the ball over extra cover, for example.

'I'm convinced that, if he'd enjoyed the international career his strokeplay deserved, Richards would have been one of the all-time greats.'

Just imagine being captain of Hampshire's opposition when Richards was in full cry at one end – and his opening partner, Gordon Greenidge, was on the warpath at the other. Now that's what I call carnage.

When South Africa's tour of England in 1970 was called off, for political reasons, Richards appeared for the Rest of the World XI which was cobbled together to provide Ray Illingworth's side with alternative Test action that summer. He only scored one half-century, but Tony Greig – by no means a timid striker of the ball himself –

says Barry gave it a fearful whack to remove the shine from the new ball. That's why I'll always be grateful that, as an aspiring young swing bowler, I never had to suffer too much at Richards' hands ... and that the 'golden arm' found its range that afternoon at Bournemouth.

In recent years, I've got to know Barry better than most through our commitments in the commentary box, and he's a guy who lives and breathes cricket. I guess he's trying to make up for all those years when he was denied a glittering Test career in the middle by talking a good one now, but I wish the world had seen more of Barry Richards' talent when he was at his peak. We wuz robbed.

Viv Richards

I find it hard to believe there was ever a better batsman than Isaac Vivian Alexander Richards. I had the great pleasure of sharing a flat with him in Taunton, and the greater privilege of occupying the same dressing-room at Somerset for many summers. It's impossible to argue with the late Sir Don Bradman's amazing record, but I have only seen black-and-white footage of him in action. After we had been brought together at Somerset by Brian Close, I was lucky enough, and sometimes unlucky

enough, to grow up with Viv and witness some of his most memorable innings from the length of a cricket pitch. Batting with him was a joy, bowling at him was a nightmare, although even when Viv was dispatching me to all parts, I could console myself with the thought that I was assisting, however unintentionally, in something very special.

We first met at Lansdowne Cricket Club, near Bath, as members of the same Somerset Under-25 side. Viv introduced himself and, in that matter-of-fact way of his, declared, 'From what I hear, you are going to get all the wickets for Somerset in the years ahead, and I'm going to get all the runs.' History proved that a fair assessment. Not in that debut match, though. Viv got out first ball and I didn't take a wicket. We both made an impact, though. I scored a hundred, while Viv took five for 20!

> 'Batting with him was a joy, bowling at him was a nightmare, although even when Viv was dispatching me to all parts, I could console myself with the thought that I was assisting, however unintentionally, in something very special.'

Once he started to make them, however, the runs were not slow in coming. I remember driving back from Bristol to Taunton with him one night early in our careers. Viv was 30-odd not out and, out of nowhere, suddenly announced that he was going to score 200 the following day. For all Viv's undoubted confidence, he was not a bragger. I'd never heard him make a prediction like that before. The next day he reached that double century with the biggest six I've ever seen.

Of all the great players I batted with and against, Viv is the man I would pick to bat for my life. Yet it's our personal friendship that I value most of all. Our playing days are over, but there's a bond that will last for ever. Viv is not my friend, he's my brother. He's godfather to my son, Liam, and very much part of my family. I'm delighted that his immense contribution to cricket has been recognized; Viv is a cricketing knight and was named as one of *Wisden's* Five Cricketers of the twentieth century.

As vivid as his on-the-field exploits remain, I treasure all the fun we had together after stumps. I first came across his wicked sense of humour very early in our time together at Taunton. Viv was very close to his fellow Antiguan, Andy Roberts, who was making a name for himself at the time by regularly hitting county batsman with one of the two different bouncers he had perfected. The grapevine was buzzing with tales of his exploits, and Viv revelled in his friend's growing reputation. One day, after close of play, we were sharing a beer with some of the Glamorgan batsmen. As they were due to play Hampshire in their next championship match, naturally the subject of Roberts cropped up. Viv was asked what he thought of his mate, and he replied very solemnly, with his best impression of a BBC newsreader: 'Here is the news ... another ambulance has been sent for in Southampton ...' From then on, whenever an opposing batsman asked him about the menace he was about to face, Viv would repeat the bulletin. And what a singing voice! His huge chest cavity housed lungs so powerful that his *basso profundo* could blow the windows from the new NatWest media centre at Lord's without the aid of a microphone!

The insensitive dismissal of Viv and Joel was the reason I left Somerset. I still cannot believe that these two great servants of the

---

BEEFY ON RICHARDS

Born: 7 March 1952, St John's, Antigua
Country: West Indies
Tests: 121
Hundreds: 24
Average: 50.23
Beefy analysis: A man I would pick to bat for my life. Viv would strike fear into the heart of opposition bowlers just from his swagger to the wicket. He played shots all round the wicket, and would set out to dominate the bowling from the moment he reached the crease.
Beefy moment: Batting with Viv for Somerset.
Do mention: West Indies v England, Antigua, 1986 (his second innings century off only 56 balls, with seven sixes).
Don't mention: Peter Roebuck, diesel cars.

---

county were treated so shabbily. The fact that the Somerset trophy cabinet was regularly restocked during our years together was largely down to those two, and the intense rivalry between them, as were the almost annual trips to Lord's for cup finals. Viv loved the place. His first big game there was the 1975 World Cup. Viv made only five runs, but still left his mark with three magnificent run-outs that helped West Indies to lift the inaugural trophy.

Viv always rose to the occasion when Somerset reached Lord's and sometimes, win, lose or draw, the results would leave Joel grumbling about the lot of the fast bowler. Joel often produced some remarkable bowling figures in these final – four or five wickets for around 20 runs, but the Man of the Match or Gold Award would invariably go to Viv for a dazzling century or crucial innings. The adjudicator would pay tribute to Joel, but them nominate Viv, which would make Joel even more cross! Joel would sit growling at the back of the dressing-room, mumbling about cricket being a batsman's game. He had a point. Lord's turned Viv on. He loved the big crowds, the big occasion, the atmosphere. Even his walk to the wicket was special. As Lancashire's Jack Simmons said: 'When Viv comes out to bat he doesn't walk, he swaggers, moving his hips and shoulders with an air of authority that is saying he is better than any bowler he is going to face.'

'Of all the great players I batted with and against, Viv is the man I would pick to bat for my life.'

I loved Phil Tufnell's description of the first time he had to bowl at Viv in a Test match, the masterblaster's 122nd and final appearance for West Indies in the Oval Test of 1991, and our final confrontation at international level. Explaining the sheer terror he felt at having to bowl at Viv on a flat wicket, Phil wrote in his autobiography: 'There was nothing for it. I simply had to bowl the ball, so I did. I gave him my best looping, spinning, ball-on-a-string. It was cleverly-flighted and dropped on a perfect length ... and Viv played it with his dark eyes closed. Then he looked at me from under that peaked West Indies cap, a strange, piercing look of contempt. 'Is that the best you have, Philip?' said the look. 'Is that it?

Is that what I walked all the way out here to bat against?' And I thought to myself: 'Jesus Christ Almighty. This bloke is going to whack me f****ing everywhere.'

How well I recall that feeling of helplessness, nowhere more than on Viv's home island of Antigua at the end of our 1986 tour. The St John's Recreation Ground had become a new Test venue during our previous tour, when I was captain. Viv, with the perfect sense of occasion, hit 114 (90 in boundaries) three days after his wedding to Miriam. David Gower was skipper in 1986, and we travelled to Antigua attempting to prevent a humiliating whitewash. We lost by 240 runs, and on the fourth afternoon Viv created history by going on to complete an undefeated 110 in 83 minutes. His century came off only 56 balls. I had got Viv out in the first innings, but there was no way to bowl second time around. His knock included seven sixes, a record for a Test innings.

I'm often asked how you bowled at Viv in that mood. You didn't. You prayed. The main strategy was to try and bowl dot balls, stop him scoring and hope that, with the crowd on his back, he might get frustrated. That was Plan A. There was no Plan B. If Plan A didn't work, you just had to do your best, swallow the medicine and hope that, if he kept hitting the balls out of the ground, the supply would eventually run out. He was the complete player. I remember taking the new ball in Barbados about eight overs before the end of play in 1981. Viv had just reached 50. The crowd were cheering his century before the close. He was awesome. He kept smashing it – hooking, cutting, pulling, driving, everything – and there was nothing we could do about it. It didn't matter where or how we bowled.

Cars were a different story. Viv had one or two problems there. After one Lord's final, Viv was following me back to the motorway, and said he needed petrol as we got into our cars. We pulled in the services just past Heathrow and I waited just beyond the pumps. There was quite a queue and I was surprised when he emerged quite fast. I soon found out why, as thick, black smoke started pouring out of his car a few hundred yards up the road. Viv had ignored the queue and spotted a vacant pump. The two Indian attendants in the shop had started waving at him, but Viv just gave them the thumbs up. Of course, Viv had filled up his sponsor's brand new car with diesel, and the attendants had been trying to warn him. Less than a week in his possession, it was towed to a garage and had to be flushed out. A few years earlier, Viv had smashed into a gatepost when leaving a benefit game in Devon after bending down to flick off some ash that had blown on to his trousers. Viv was always immaculately turned out, and hated any blemish or crease on his clothes.

I've been quoted as saying I could never have looked Viv in the face again if I'd gone to play cricket in South Africa. Later, as the political situation there started to change, there were serious discussions about Viv and me going there as part of a multiracial side. I've always felt that sportsplayers can break down more barriers than politicians. I told Viv I'd been approached. He told me to go and see what they had to say, then report back. The meeting went well until I asked what would happen when Viv and I wanted to go into a Johannesburg restaurant for dinner: 'No problem. We'll make Viv an honorary white!' End of discussion. When I told Viv, we both collapsed laughing. Even South Africa's apartheid regime was not going to split us two up.

Andy
Roberts

First of the modern West Indian fast-bowling greats – and a man who could reduce cowering tail-enders to tears – Anderson Roberts was one of the most intelligent bowlers I've ever seen ... and the only one who's ever attempted dental surgery on me without a local anaesthetic, drill or any recognized tools of the trade.

In the same Benson and Hedges Cup quarter-final against Hampshire in 1974, where I had felt so pleased with myself for dismissing Barry Richards,

Roberts was later to rearrange my teeth with the quickest ball I had ever seen – or, to be precise, not seen.

When I marched out to bat at No. 9, Somerset appeared to be chasing a lost cause, with 70 needed off the last 15 overs and only three wickets in hand. Shortly afterwards, Tom Cartwright, the man more responsible than anyone for turning me into a top-class bowler, was out, and our position looked hopeless. With 38 still needed, I hooked Roberts – who had been leaving a trail of broken bones and a small regiment of distinguished batsmen, including Colin Cowdrey, in Casualty that summer – for six. It seemed like a worthy piece of bravado at the time but, with hindsight, it was probably an act of misadventure.

One of Roberts' great secrets was to bowl bouncers at a pace which duped the batsman into thinking you could hook him without being hurried into the stroke ... and the very next ball would be another one, two yards quicker, which cleaned you up. Yours truly fell into the trap – if you'll pardon the pun – hook, line and sinker. From the next delivery after I had tonked him for six, Roberts let go of this red blur and my instinct was to repeat the stroke. Halfway through executing the shot, self-preservation must have taken over from brashness, because I instinctively raised a gloved hand in front of my face, and it probably saved me from serious injury.

In the event, the impact of the ball smacking into my glove forced my own fist into my jaw, knocking out one tooth on the left-hand side and shattering two others clean in half on the right. I was also grazed around the left eye. Most of the following day I was manacled to the dentist's chair, having the remnants of my mouth sorted – not, I might add, before I had spat out the loose chips of tooth and scored the winning runs to secure an unlikely semi-final place for Somerset.

But to this day, I regard myself as one of the lucky ones. No matter how accomplished a batsman you were, Roberts was not a man with whom to take liberties: yet I had dared to hook him for six, and lived. Just.

In those days, of course, there were no helmets to absorb the impact of a bouncer speeding towards your temple, and nobody bowled a sharper one than Roberts. Yet there was much more to 'Fruity', as his West Indian team-mates called him, than chin music. He had a terrific action, moved the ball away from the right-hander and was a wonderfully resourceful bowler. From the mid-1970s, he was to establish himself as the West Indies' main strike bowler. He blazed the trail that so many others, including Holding, Garner, Marshall, Walsh and Ambrose were to follow over the next quarter of a century. It's incredible to think that, when he came over to England for a week's trial at Surrey with his fellow Antiguan, Viv Richards, as twenty-year-old hopefuls, that they were basically written off as also-rans.

Without quoting verbatim, their assessments at the end of that week in the nets read something like this:

RICHARDS: Good eye, but he can only hit across the line. Will struggle to score runs in English conditions.

ROBERTS: He has pace, but no control. Would be too expensive in English conditions.

Oops. There's another shining example of England's blinkered coaching system for you. Roberts, for the record, went on to take 202 wickets at 25.61 each in just 47 Tests.

He was right up there with the very best, not least because he never let sentiment get in the way of business. When England recalled Brian Close to face the West Indies at Old Trafford in 1976, at the age of 45, it was Roberts who decided to go after the old boy and pepper his ribcage with short stuff.

In any other walk of life, Roberts might have been reported to Age Concern, but as a tactic it was as masterful as it was brutal. Close stood there and took his punishment like a man, but the onslaught undermined England's resolve.

That was the summer when Tony Greig promised to make the West Indies 'grovel.' England lost the series 3–0, due in no small part to the fact that Andy Roberts grovelled to no one.

Dave Roberts

Magic sponges, healing hands, top bloke. Dave Roberts, known to everyone in cricket as 'Rooster', was much more to me than just a physio with Worcestershire and England. He was like a second dad.

When I suffered my career-threatening back injury in 1988, Rooster was the guy who spent countless hours nursing me, bullying me and encouraging me to stay positive on the long road to recovery.

He came to see me nearly every day in hospital, when I was like a bear with a sore head, and in those long months of rehabilitation he probably saved me from being carted off to the cuckoo's nest.

Even now, I still shudder at the memory of the day my back finally 'went' during an early-season championship match against Somerset. I fell awkwardly attempting to stop a ball at second slip, and by the time we were back in the dressing-room minutes later during a break for rain, I knew my discomfort was not just run-of-the-mill stiffness. When the umpires told us it was time to get back out on the field, I was paralyzed and had to be winched to my feet by two team-mates.

'As for my debt to him I'm not sure I'll ever be able to repay him.' After the operation performed by the surgeon, John Davies, I could hardly move for about six months and I was depressed, not to mention terrified, that my playing career might be over at the age of 32. For two weeks all I could do was to lie in a hospital bed, occasionally being turned over like a joint of Sunday roast, before taking a few apprehensive steps around the ward. God, that was hard work: it was like wading through half-set concrete.

But once I was well enough to start walking and do some light exercise, Rooster was a terrific man to have on my side. Although my chances of playing international cricket again were probably no better than 20 per cent, he made me believe that I could defy the odds, and I owe him a big vote of thanks for that. In hindsight, he had to take his fair share of flak from me in the process, because his cajoling and bullying would often be met with a mouthful of Anglo-Saxon vernacular, but during those months especially, we formed a close bond of friendship. When I was recalled by England during the Ashes series in 1989, it was as much down to Rooster's care and patience, and the attention he devoted to my recovery as much as any physical effort on my part. Typically, unselfishly, he was as pleased for me as I was for myself.

Later in my career, when I needed keyhole surgery on a knee injury, Rooster finally got his own back when I was wheeled into the operating theatre under general anaesthetic. With the surgeon, consultant and anaesthetist all gathered around the operating table in their gowns, Rooster suddenly began pulling faces at me and making a bizarre assortment of farmyard noises. The medical people thought he had been at the laughing gas, but when his cabaret was over Roberts said, very matter-of-factly, 'That's for all the years you've traumatized me, Beef.' And how do I know all this went on while I was spark-out? My knee specialist, Jonathan Noble, told me when I came round an hour later!

Mind you, that wasn't the only occasion when Rooster got his own back on me. He used to love it when I was suffering from niggling injuries like hamstrings, or thighs – anything requiring massage treatment where he could dig his fingers into the offending muscle.

Roberts also gave up a huge amount of time to become the resident physio on my charity walks for Leukaemia Research. At the end of each day's footslog, he would conjure up a bowl of hot water to soak my feet, and make running repairs to any blisters I had acquired over the previous 30 miles. Once, near the end of our East Coast walk from Aberdeen to Ipswich, he had to cut two holes the size of 50p pieces in my heels, when a lad on his mountain bike accidentally ran into me. The pronounced tread on his tyres lacerated two blisters, and when the wounds became infected it was Rooster who administered the emergency first aid. The pain was excruciating, and every step to the finish line was like treading on hot coals. Thanks to Rooster, I managed to complete the course.

Along the route, Rooster often helped to rattle the collection tins and he always took it personally when punters were slow to dip their hands in their pockets.

As for my debt to him I'm not sure I'll ever be able to repay it.

Ricky Roberts

There are very few sportsmen who have known the joy of an Ashes-winning dressing-room as well as the euphoria of claiming a couple of golfing majors. Ricky Roberts is probably unique in that regard. Ricky who? Well, for starters, Ricky is the man who caddied Ernie Els to his two US Open triumphs in 1994 and 1997. Yet I remember him as providing one of the most memorable moments of that most memorable Headingley Test in 1981.

Ricky was only sixteen when he was appointed dressing-room attendant for that match. He was over from South Africa and was on the Yorkshire groundstaff. Most 'gophers' are keen to help, but there are a few who just do the minimum and tend always to be missing when there's running around to be done. Ricky was great, nothing was too much trouble. For the first three days of that Ashes Test, our dressing-room was not the happiest of places after we followed on 227 behind, but Ricky kept smiling and out of the way when it was necessary.

The events of that Monday and Tuesday are now part of cricket history. Even after my undefeated 149, the Australians still needed only 130 runs for victory. Bob Willis's eight for 43 ensured utter pandemonium in our dressing-room. But there was something missing. Champagne. We were struggling to find any at the ground. I knew where there was a ready supply, though – the Australian dressing-room. Bottles and bottles of it had been sitting in a bath chilling for the best part of two days in anticipation.

As you might imagine, I was on quite a high. In the previous Test, I'd resigned after a dozen matches in charge, mainly against the West Indies, following a pair at Lord's. My own form had dipped dramatically, although I never blamed that on the pressures of captaincy. I always thought I might get the job back one day, but I was delighted to be at Headingley as just an ordinary member of the team, under the leadership of the inspirational Mike Brearley. Even by the follow-on, I felt like my old self, taking six for 95 and scoring a half century. Then came that marvellous Monday and tumultuous Tuesday. I was fully back to my old self again, and young Ricky Roberts was about to be the next to suffer.

I called him over and told him we needed champagne. The Aussies, I added, obviously didn't want their supply, so the simplest thing would be to buy theirs at half-price. Such is the innocence of youth that when I reassured him that this was normal practice, and the likes of DK (Dennis Lillee) and Rod (Marsh) would accept this defeat as part and parcel of the normal ups and down in sport he believed every word.

After lighting the blue touch paper, I stood back. As Ricky strode confidently towards the Aussie dressing-room, I wondered whether we'd ever see him again – dead or alive!

Ricky had everything hurled at him – boots, pads, gloves, and even the odd bat, all came his way, as well as a volley of Australian expletives of the most basic sort. And the next time I saw him he was almost horizontal as he was propelled through our dressing-room doorway and across the room. I almost had to prise him out of the far wall. We were in hysterics, and delighted that we had managed to wind the Aussies up ever more on their day of disaster. I'm not sure who took longer to recover from Headingley – the Aussies or Ricky.

The next time I met Ricky, he was caddying for Ernie Els, and helping him to success in two US Opens. As we chatted, it was clear that his champagne experience at Headingley had been one of the defining moments of his life. A decade or so on, he was at last able to laugh about it. Ricky kept shaking his head, still unable to come to terms with how naïve he'd been.

He split from Ernie for a time and went to carry Nick Price's clubs, but Ernie and Ricky were back together for the 2001 Open at Royal Lytham and St Anne's. Ricky plays a bit of golf himself, but isn't as good as the man he caddies for, so I'm able to beat him occasionally. He's settled in England with his family, but life with Ernie means that he's permanently globe-trotting. But, he confesses, however far he travels and how many times he and Ernie get into contention, Ricky Roberts has never managed to forget those few nerve-wracking, life-threatening seconds in Australia's dressing-room all those years ago.

Jack
Russell

A wonderful wicket-keeper, a great team man, but I have to say, totally eccentric. Of course, dressing-rooms in any sport would be deadly dull places without a fair spread of characters, but Jack was one of the more bizarre individuals whose paths crossed with mine during my career. Furthermore I know exactly where he got it from. Jack always idolized Alan Knott, and to be fair, as wicket-keeper/batsmen go, there could be few better role models. But as a man of strange habits, Knotty had few equals until Jack came along...

The extent to which Jack was prepared to go to emulate Knotty even extended to the modus operandum he employed to drive his car the length and breadth of the country on the county circuit. In order to avoid the risk of over-stretching his hamstrings, Knotty attached a wooden block to the top of his accelerator pedal. So what did Jack do? He had a wooden block put on his. And, like Knotty, he also carried a blanket in his car, which like Knotty, he would put over his lap just in case it got cold.

Heard the one about Jack wanting his hands pickled and donated to the British Museum? Or hating anyone calling him by his real name 'Robert'? What about the time he commissioned local builders to erect an extension at his home? The builders were delighted but somewhat puzzled at the following conditions: at the appointed hour every morning Jack would rendezvous with the chaps in a village close to where he lived. He would climb into the driver's seat of their van, hand around the blindfolds, then take them on a magical mystery tour to his castle. At close of play every day he reversed the process, thus maintaining his privacy and his reputation as someone who needs putting away.

But if that seemed eccentric then it was nothing compared to Jack's diet. Most people use their coffins to carry their basic cricket kit and spares. Now I used to wonder why

BEEFY ON RUSSELL

Born: 15 August 1963, Stroud, Gloucestershire
Country: England
Tests: 54
Hundreds: 2
Average: 27.10
Caught: 153
Stumped: 12
Beefy analysis: Completely bonkers – but what a great keeper! Always coaxing and cajoling his teammates on the field, while driving his opponents to distraction with his eccentric batting.
Beefy moment: Jack repeatedly using a single teabag over five days of an Oval Test.
Do mention: South Africa v England, Johannesburg, 1995 (a world record 11 catches in the match).
Don't mention: Batsmen/wicketkeepers.

Jack always wore the same scruffy, floppy white hat and antique gloves, and pads stuck together with sticky tape to prevent them falling apart. Most people felt, and many writers wrote, that it was all down to superstition, but I have an alternative theory. Jack carried the minimum of kit so that he could keep as much room free for tins of baked beans –

'A loner off the field, Jack was very much an important cog on it. Though he, like Knotty, never stood still, he was always coaxing and cajoling his team-mates to keep them lively in the field.'

just in case there were none available at a particular ground where he might be playing. In fact, on tours to India all he seemed to be carrying was rations. If he wasn't eating baked beans, Jack would have a plain piece of boiled chicken, with the skin taken off, a couple of boiled potatoes, with the skin taken off, and some fresh vegetables. His diet never varied.

Neither too, did his tea-drinking habit, which involved downing upwards of 15 cups a day. In fact, when I say 'tea' it would be more accurate to talk about him drinking hot water, flavoured with milk. It was one year in the England dressing room at the Oval that we discovered just how weak Jack liked his tea. On the first day, for his first cuppa he used a new teabag, but it was not thrown away. It was hung meticulously on a hook, and then reused repeatedly throughout the five days, though simply dipped briefly into the water, never left long enough to provide a proper brew.

'Through Jack's sheer professionalism and dedication to the game he has been able to contribute a lot to the development of Gloucestershire's younger players.'

For most of his England career, Jack didn't drink alcohol at all, and he was never seen with us in the bar or having dinner after play was over. He just used to go off and do his own thing. But over the years the disappearing act was to provide him with a secondary career, one

that will keep him going for the rest of his life. Jack developed an interest in art, using his training as a draughtsman, and his sketches and paintings are now much sought after. His original oils are worth several thousand pounds, and prices are still rising. While his team-mates were relaxing, Jack would head off, artbox tucked under his arm, looking for a likely subject to draw or paint. In India, he would capture the chaotic street scenes, scrawny children and beggars. My favourite works of his were a series of charcoal drawings depicting historic parts of Bristol.

A loner off the field, Jack was very much an important cog on it. Though he, like Knotty, never stood still, he was always coaxing and cajoling his team-mates to keep them lively in the field. His wicket-keeping was always of a high standard, but his England career was restricted to 54 Tests once the selectors decided that Alec Stewart could fill the important all-rounder's spot with bat and gloves.

When his Test career ended I fully expected Jack to retire immediately and concentrate on his art, but that didn't happen, because of the astonishing one-day revolution that occurred at Bristol, where the sideboard in the Gloucestershire committee room is now groaning from the weight of trophies.

The county's coach John Bracewell has given Jack responsibility for handling the team's fielding, and under him they have now become the one-day aces when it comes to preventing the opposition scoring runs. Through Jack's sheer professionalism and dedication to the game he has been able to contribute a lot to the development of their younger players. For their sake, I just hope he hasn't passed on some of his wackier ideas.

AC
Smith

Alan Christopher Smith – AC to everyone in cricket – became a firm friend and trusted ally on my only tour as England captain. The trip to the West Indies in 1980–81 was dogged by political problems and the tragically early death of Ken Barrington, but, as tour manager, AC steered us through the diplomatic and emotional minefield with great skill.

It might surprise some people that I rated AC so highly. After all, he was an Oxbridge type who reached the higher echelons of the TCCB (now the

ECB) – the very sort to whom I usually take a instant, unnatural and totally unjustifiable dislike.

But he was not one of the gin-swilling dodderers to whom I once referred so infamously. On the contrary, AC always saw the players' point of view and, whenever he could, he backed us to the hilt. Crucially, he certainly was not an administrator who thought he was more important than the players under his charge.

The problems on that Caribbean tour blew up when the Guyanan government objected to Robin Jackman's South African connections (his wife is from that country). The Georgetown Test was cancelled, and for a time it looked as though we might be going home early.

Without AC's patience and tolerance, the tour could have fallen apart. He did a remarkable job. There were people trying to manipulate us for political gain. The situation became quite unpleasant, as hostilities were aroused by outsiders with no interest in bats or balls. At times, we were effectively prisoners in our hotel. AC and I spent many evenings chatting in the room, trying to work out what to do next, although his first thought was always to try to shield me and the team from the distractions. He had the patience of Job and the knack of keeping people talking to each other, no matter what their differences.

'He is a very pleasant bloke to spend time with, and he can laugh at himself, which is a quality I admire. Although he is one of the best diplomats I've come across, I'm afraid I have to say he was one of the worst wicket-keepers.'

As if the Jackman Affair were not enough, we also had to deal with the mighty shock of Kenny's death. I will always remain convinced that the political problems contributed to his fatal heart attack – he looked so tired, tense and short of sleep, worrying himself silly about how all the nonsense would be affecting his players. We all loved Kenny, and AC was very tactful and sympathetic during a time when we were extremely upset.

AC was equally supportive on the 'sex, drugs and rock 'n' roll' tour of New Zealand in 1983–84. There were some amazing stories flying around which surprised even me – and I have a pretty active imagination. But, once again, AC was unflappable. Over the years, there has often been flak flying in my direction from Lord's, and AC felt like my ally behind enemy lines. What's more, he is a very pleasant bloke to spend time with, and he can laugh at himself, which is a quality I admire.

Although he is one of the best diplomats I've come across, I'm afraid I have to say he was one of the worst wicket-keepers. We began to call him 'Teflon', when the non-stick coating for frying pans first came out and the nickname was quite original. I have this image of AC turning up at somewhere like Bath and keeping wicket wearing a cravat. He looked like one of the last of the great amateurs. Unfortunately, he kept like one too.

'He could also bowl seamers off the wrong foot with a windmill action and, against Essex at Clacton in 1965, actually removed his pads, went on to bowl and performed a hat-trick.'

He could also bowl seamers off the wrong foot with a windmill action and, against Essex at Clacton in 1965, actually removed his pads, went on to bowl and performed a hat-trick.

Somehow AC played half-a-dozen Tests for England as a wicketkeeper/batsman and was a successful captain of Warwickshire from 1968 to 1974. Under his leadership, the county won the old Gillette Cup in 1968 and the Championship in 1972. He was one of the first to see the value of bringing star quality overseas players into county cricket, and their magnificent sides contained such great talents as Rohan Kanhai, Alvin Kallicharran and Lance Gibbs from the West Indies as well as some top home-grown players such as M. J. K. Smith, Dennis Amiss, John Jameson and Bob Willis. A decent soccer player, AC won a blue at Oxford and later served for a time as director of Aston Villa Football Club.

He had two spells as a Test selector as well as managing England tours, and it was in this capacity that he honed his legendary skills at stonewalling in the face of tricky questions. This came in so handy later when he graduated from being Secretary of Warwickshire to Chief Executive of the Test and County Cricket Board.

Some of the classics from the AC Smith book of straight-talking include: 'No comment, but that's off the record'; 'I've nothing to say, but don't quote me on that.' And he would often respond to the tamest of enquiries, as in 'How disappointed are you that England have lost 5–0 to West Indies again?' with a sharp intake of breath through his teeth and the answer '...ish'. To me, though, there was nothing 'ish' about AC. He helped me a great deal during some very difficult times.

Robin
Smith

The way Robin Smith was discarded by England was nothing short of scandalous. He was dropped after top-scoring in six of his previous 13 Test innings and never reappeared.

The last time we saw Robin batting on the international stage was in Cape Town in January 1996. He was just 32 at the time and had a Test-career batting average of 43.67, with nine centuries and 28 half-centuries.

When you consider some of the batsmen who have been chosen since, you could say that there was no justice for the man we called 'The Judge'. Ray Illingworth was England's chairman of selectors, and it was he who apparently decided that Robin's day was done. It was not the only example of Illy's poor judgement, but it was perhaps one of the clearest.

'Robin was a tremendous Test match batsman. He was brave as a lion and hit the ball with brutal power. He had all the weapons, but his absolute killer was the square cut off front or back foot.'

Of England batsmen who made their debuts after 1970 and have scored a worthwhile number of runs, only David Gower had a higher Test average – by 0.58 of a run. And The Judge, so called because the crinkly haircut he favoured made him look like one, cared so much about playing for England that it hurt. After our 1992 World Cup Final defeat against Pakistan, nobody in the dressing-room was more shattered than Robin, and he hadn't even played in the match.

Robin was a tremendous Test match batsman. He was brave as a lion and hit the ball with brutal power. He had all the weapons, but his absolute killer was the square cut off front or back foot – of the players I have seen over the past 35 years, perhaps only Gordon Greenidge struck that shot as hard as Judgey.

There was a perception, justified at times, that he was vulnerable to spin, because he didn't play the ball with 'soft' or giving hands. But he was written off far too early against slow bowling. There is no question that he could have learned and adapted, as indeed he was managing to do. He just needed more help to learn the art of facing spinners, which shouldn't have been too difficult to arrange. I didn't see too many others playing Warne, Kumble & Co. with the proverbial stick of rhubarb, by the way.

Smith will best be remembered for his brilliant counter-attacking against fast bowling. Over the years, he had some epic duels with the likes of Curtly Ambrose and Courtney Walsh and, in particular, Merv Hughes. A confrontation with Big Merv always got Robin's juices flowing. It was a compelling spectacle to watch this huge, moustachioed Aussie bouncing and sledging the powerful, hyperactive South-African-born batsman. Smith never kept still between deliveries, dancing on the spot and swaying out of the way of imaginary bouncers. But he never ever took a backward step against fast bowling for the simple reason that he absolutely loved the physical nature of the challenge. In fact, the faster the bowling, the more Judgey seemed to relish it.

Robin was helped in pursuit of his sporting ambition by having sports-mad parents. His brother, Chris, who also represented England and Hampshire as an opening batsman, also benefited. Robin's old man, John, was driven by the desire to see his lads play top-level sport, whether cricket, athletics, at which Robin broke all records at his school, or his other great love, rugby.

'Smith will best be remembered for his brilliant counter-attacking against fast bowling.'

John's obsession would often have hilarious results. When he felt that Robin needed to practise his goal-kicking after school, John would persuade the local club to switch the floodlights on so that his son could stay out long after dark. Then, when the club finally told him they couldn't afford to do so any longer, John would position himself behind and between the posts and guide Robin through the darkness. Neither man could see the ball once it had left Robin's boot, so after each kick had landed, John would shout out 'two metres right, my boy,' or 'one metre to the left'. Often, Judge told me, all he heard was a dull thud as the ball landed on the top of John's nut.

John used to get carried away watching Robin playing school rugby, and lived every pass and tackle with him. On one occasion when Robin set off for a 20-yard sprint for the line to score, he suddenly became aware of the presence of a man on the other side of the sideline running with him every step of the way, and he was even more surprised when the guy leapt over the line with him. He was not at all surprised to find out, however, that the man in question was his dad.

Judge is a trusting and loving guy who takes people at face value. He is refreshingly free of cynicism but, if anything, a touch naïve and this has led him into trouble, particularly with money, when he was fleeced for virtually everything he possessed – several hundred thousand pounds – by a man he thought he could trust.

Some people had been telling Judgey to sever his connection with the man but, typical of him, he wanted to remain loyal. Well, this bloke ripped off Judgey so badly that he and his wife Kath had to sell their lovely house in Hampshire. He should have enjoyed the bumper benefit he enjoyed in 1996, but ended up with virtually nothing. I remember Judgey telling me about the time he went to a meeting with other people who had suffered from this person's dishonesty. And, instead of feeling sorry for himself, his heart went out to pensioners he met who'd lost their life savings.

Fortunately, Judge is the sort of person who might be able to recoup his losses. He has unquenchable enthusiasm and loves wheeling and dealing. In fact, during the West Indies tour of 1993–94, coach Keith Fletcher hinted that Smith was too interested in making money when he should have been paying more attention to making runs.

That was unfair, because there have been few batsmen who spend more time in the nets than Smith. His business ventures have included up-market tours for cricket supporters – Judge's Tours – and a bat-making company called Chase. I'm always telling him he should use his name and call them Judge bats.

Despite having his international career curtailed prematurely, Judgey kept playing for and captaining Hampshire. Shane Warne will tell you that one of the main reasons he signed for the county in 2000 was the presence of Robin Smith. It has taken both mental strength and a love of cricket for Judgey to keep his pecker up after so much disappointment. It has also taken massive amounts of courage, and that is the nature of the man I am proud to call a friend.

Garfield Sobers

Perhaps the greatest compliment anyone ever paid me was to mention my name in the same breath as that of Gary Sobers. He was, without doubt, the finest all-round cricketer in history. There was nothing this man could not do with a bat or ball.

Along with Ken Barrington, Sobers was my childhood cricketing hero, and it is one of my great joys that I have got to know him well in recent years. We've played many rounds of golf together – usually at the Royal Westmoreland in Barbados. He plays off a handicap of around eight, and as with all the great competitors he hadn't got it in him to try anything less than 100 per cent. Whenever you hear his complaint of some ailment or other, normally 'my eyes are not so good, man' or 'the knee is playing up again', beware.

I cannot think of a facet of the game of cricket in which Sobers was anything other than brilliant. He was a dazzling left-handed batsman, who could bowl left-arm fast, swing, seam, orthodox spin and wrist-spin. And not merely adequately. He did all of them as well as, if not better than, the specialists in all of those fields. He was an outstanding close-to-the-wicket catcher and fielder in the deep, and even kept wicket at times. He was also an enterprising and attacking captain who, if his team was struggling, would take it upon himself to try dig them out of trouble with his individual genius. His reasoning was simple. He was their best player, so he owed it to his team to take the major responsibility.

'Gary, of course, became the first player to strike six sixes in one over in first-class cricket.'

For almost 20 years, Gary maintained a remarkably high standard considering his workload and the sense of expectation resting on his shoulders every time he took the field. He moved with the grace of a cat and played the game with great style and dignity. A smile was rarely far from his face and, as far as I know, he made no enemies. Perhaps he would have been a lousy umpire or not very good at baking cakes for tea – he must have been hopeless at something to do with cricket!

Some of his exploits have taken a permanent place in the game's folklore. When Gary scored his first Test century against Pakistan at Sabina Park, Jamaica, he went on to reach 365 not out, a score that stood as the highest Test innings in history until Brian Lara surpassed it some 36 years later. Gary was there in Antigua to congratulate Lara in person on his achievement. The match came to a standstill for about 15 minutes as Gary strolled out to the middle to embrace the successor to his crown.

Gary, of course, became the first player to strike six sixes in one over in first-class cricket. I remember as a child watching the black-and-white TV pictures of the balls delivered by Glamorgan's left-armer Malcolm Nash disappearing over the boundary ... and yes, watching him smite those mighty blows definitely had an influence on the way I played my game. Many years later, I played on the ground in Swansea and it is not until you walk out to the middle that you realize how huge some of those hits must have been. The last one travelled halfway down the street outside the ground towards the sea – or that's what the locals tell you, anyway.

Gary was born with five fingers instead of four on each hand – the extra two were removed when he was a boy. He was one of seven children, and, after his merchant seaman father died at sea, was brought up by his mother. Gary excelled at all sports and played both soccer and basketball for Barbados. By 16, he was representing the island at cricket, and a year later, he played his first Test match.

After he scored his 365 not out at the age of 21, Sobers was on his way to becoming a household name across the cricket-playing world. People talk about all-rounders such as Keith Miller, or even great entertainers like Denis Compton, but to me Sobers was the first superstar of the modern game. He attracted people to the ground and put bums on seats, simply because of his enormous talent and charisma.

Perhaps his greatest series was in England in 1966. Leading the West Indies, he scored 722 in five Tests, at an average of 103, took 20 wickets at 27.25, and held ten catches. The Windies won the series, of course. He was a legend in Australia, where he played with great success for South Australia, and Sir Donald Bradman described his innings of 254 for the Rest of the World against Australia at Melbourne in 1971–72 as perhaps the best he ever saw. Sobers also played county cricket for Nottinghamshire with great distinction.

As I have indicated, Gary is one of those guys who has to be competitive, no matter what he's doing, and I'm sure that's why we get on so well. People often ask me how I would have managed if I had been just a batsman. Would I have become bored if I hadn't been a bowler as well? My answer has always been 'yes', because I was born without the patience to stand around in the field all day.

It is a question I must ask Sobey one day. My guess is that he shares my views, and that he needed the extra stimulation of bowling. Gary became Sir Garfield in 1975 when he was knighted by the Queen in an open-air ceremony at the Garrison Savannah racecourse in Barbados. No one could have thought of a more appropriate venue, because the only thing Gary loved as much as cricket and golf was winning money on horses. Knowing him, had he wanted to he could probably have been a champion jockey as well.

Alec Stewart

Stewie is the ultimate professional cricketer. His attention to detail, his dedication at nets and in the gym and the way he looks after himself, are lessons to any youngster making his way in the game. They are the reasons Alec was still playing for England as he approached his forties, and, even at that age, he remained near the top of the team's stamina and fitness tests.

That is not to say that Alec is a talentless or manufactured player, relying on his work ethic rather than any God-given ability. Quite the opposite. There are few better natural timers of a ball than Stewart. He can send boundaries skidding across the turf with an apparent minimum of effort. Alec's achievement in being the world's leading scorer of Test runs during the 1990s proves his ability. He is also a top-class wicket-keeper. The debate that has raged through his career over 'Should he play as a specialist batsman or a wicket-keeping all-rounder?' has sometimes obscured the fact that he is an outstanding glove man. I recall, for example, a brilliant diving catch standing back to remove Brian Lara at Lord's in 1995. As he flung himself to his left and held the ball one-handed, Alec could have been in goal for his beloved Chelsea. The catch was a turning point, and England went on to win that Test.

> 'There are few better natural timers of a ball than Stewart. He can send boundaries skidding across the turf with an apparent minimum of effort. He is also a top-class wicket-keeper.'

He is very gutsy, too. When the bouncers are flying around, Alec is prepared to wear a few in order to preserve his wicket. Remember that farcical Test match in Jamaica in early 1998? The game was abandoned after less than an hour's cricket because Courtney Walsh and Curtly Ambrose were threatening limb (and maybe even life). England's physio came on to the field half-a-dozen times as the ball kept rearing up from a pitch that resembled corrugated iron. Stewart, opening the batting for England, finished nine not out. It must be the greatest and bravest nine not out in history.

His response to the allegations against him by an Indian bookmaker, that he accepted £5,000 for providing information on the England 1993 tour was, typically, to soldier on with a stiff upper lip. The way he continued playing in the full glare of publicity was further proof of his strength of character.

Alec spent several of his formative years playing grade cricket in Perth, Western Australia. The experience gave him a hard edge. So, if there are few verbals flying around, Stewie is happy to mix it with the best of them. He always makes sure he is involved from behind the stumps, encouraging his team-mates and putting seeds of doubt into the opposition. He is very patriotic, too, and you would probably find a Union Jack tattooed across his chest if you removed his shirt. When he scored a century against the West Indies at Old Trafford in 2000 in his 100th Test match, on the Queen Mother's 100th birthday to boot, the standing ovation lasted more than a minute and was a magical and very proud moment for him.

Stewart and Mike Atherton reached the 100-Test milestone in the same match, and their careers have run parallel. For years, their records have been almost identical in terms of average, total runs and centuries scored. I enjoy their rivalry which, even though both insist does not exist, is healthily bubbling in the background. Nothing wrong with that.

BEEFY ON STEWART

Born: 8 April 1963, Merton, Surrey
Country: England
Tests: 115
Hundreds: 14
Average: 39.31
Caught: 220
Stumped: 11
Beefy analysis: The ultimate professional. Whether opening the batting or shoring up the middle order, whether keeping wicket or captaining England, he has never let his country down. England's best all-rounder since…
Beefy moment: A brilliant diving catch standing back to Brian Lara, England v West Indies, Lord's 1995.
Do mention: England v South Africa, Old Trafford, 1998 (his 164 is a Test record for a captain/wicket-keeper).
Don't mention: John.

For many years, Alec shifted between opening the batting and the middle-order, sometimes with the 'keeper's gloves, sometimes without. Towards the end of his career, he has settled in the middle-order and become a genuine all-rounder. That is right because, in his late thirties, it would be asking too much of him to open the batting as well.

Like me, Alec is another player who is immaculate in his appearance. Two of his most important accessories when traveling overseas are a hairdryer and a trouser press. While most people look totally disheveled after a 24-hour flight to Australia, Stewie strides into the arrivals lounge with not a hair out of place. He could wear his England blazer and slacks in bed and they would not be creased. Alec looks the part on the field, too, with every item of kit numbered and his collar standing firmly to attention. That's why his team-mates call him 'Peter Perfect' or 'Squeaky Clean'.

'Alec loves to be involved in every facet of every match in which he plays – he would make the sandwiches and do some umpiring if he could.'

A lot of people also refer to him as 'the Gaffer'. Allegedly, it comes from when he was appointed Surrey captain, and one of his players asked:

'What shall we call you now Alec – skipper, or what?'

'Just call me the Gaffer,' came Alec's reply.

The nickname certainly sums him up. Alec loves to be involved in every facet of every match in which he plays – he would make the sandwiches and do some umpiring if he could.

Again, following my example Alec has always looked after himself physically. You will not find him propping up the bar at 2 am after ten pints and 20 fags. He also watches his diet. During the 1996 World Cup in India and Pakistan, Alec ate grilled chicken on 42 consecutive days and he was proud of the fact, too. If he is feeling really adventurous, he might risk some Pot Noodles.

He is a private man. When, a few years ago, both his mother and his wife suffered serious health problems, he kept his feelings to himself. It was obviously a worrying time, but nobody would have known the emotions spinning round inside his head.

Micky Stewart

I had some great times with Micky Stewart on the tour of Australia in 1986–87, the last occasion that England won the Ashes in the twentieth century. Micky had been appointed England's first full-time coach/manager and he was brilliant on that trip.

He and the captain, Mike Gatting, helped to create a buoyant team spirit and a relaxed but purposeful attitude towards training, gave us a certain amount of leeway in the build-up to the series, and even held their nerve when, after we started so badly that one cricket correspondent famously wrote: 'There are only three things wrong with this England team. They can't bat, can't bowl and can't field.'

That shrewd judge was not alone in having to eat his words. England ended up winning the Test series 2–1, as well as two one-day competitions in which the then mighty West Indies team also took part. There is no question that Micky Stewart was an important factor in England's success.

Micky and Gatt were very close, with similar ideas about practice. Despite his sergeant-major demeanour, in those days Micky was a great believer in allowing players to rest. Just because someone had been dismissed for nought the previous day – or the team had lost – did not automatically mean another gruelling session in the nets was necessary. Micky understood that players needed to stay mentally and physically fresh on a long tour. Days off were just as important as hard training. This, of course, was a theory with which I fully concurred!

'In his playing days, Micky was a good enough batsman to win eight Test caps, and appeared in that famous match against West Indies at Lord's in 1963 when Colin Cowdrey came out to bat with a broken arm.'

So, if David Gower fancied only a few throw-downs, or Chris Broad would rather relax in his room, that was fine by Micky. Everyone was treated as an individual. When we did practice, Micky ensured the drills were fun, which helped to make the 1986–87 tour to Australia one of the happiest I went on. There was a rapport and unity among the party. We were all pulling for each other and the results showed the success of that approach.

That is why I was surprised that, later on during his time as manager, Micky introduced a more regimented and robotic approach. Perhaps it was because Graham Gooch, who became captain for the 1990 West Indies tour, was almost obsessive about his physical fitness and practice. I think it was a mistake to be so inflexible, especially as Micky had seen how well the more laid-back approach worked in

1986–87. Perhaps it was the influence of Gooch, or maybe it was because England had started losing. Micky and Goochie also started to analyze in great detail the strengths and weaknesses of the opposition, again something that Micky had not done previously. My attitude has always been to forget about the opposition and just make sure we got our own game right. I must also say I felt let down by Micky in 1989, when he pleaded with me not to sign up for the rebel tour of South Africa. The money was good and I was approaching the end of my career, but he virtually guaranteed me a place on the

'Micky was a fine all-round sportsman who had played soccer at inside-right for Charlton Athletic, Wimbledon, Hendon and Corinthian Casuals.'

plane to West Indies that winter if I said no to Ali Bacher's rands. So you can imagine my fury when, the night before the squad was announced, Ted Dexter rang to say I was not included in the team going to the West Indies.

In the second half of his time as manager, one of his charges was his own son, Alec. This was a potentially difficult situation but, as anybody who knows Micky and Alec would expect, they kept their relationship on a strictly professional footing, in public, at least, which led to some hilarious episodes, particularly during my final World Cup campaign of 1992. In press conferences Micky would refer to Alec as 'our No 6' or 'the wicket-keeper', never by name or relationship, while Alec called his dad 'manager' or even 'ger'. And the father–son thing certainly didn't stop either of them from cursing and swearing out loud at each other in practice. Micky, in fact, voted for Alec to succeed Gooch as captain in 1993. But Mike Atherton got the job instead, and I know Micky was upset that Dexter, chairman of England's selectors at the time, made Micky's preference known.

In his playing days, Micky was a good enough batsman to win eight Test caps, and appeared in that famous match against West Indies at Lord's in 1963 when Colin Cowdrey came out to bat with a broken arm.

He was a regular member of the Surrey team which won the County

Championship an unprecedented seven years in succession, and he later captained them to the title in 1971. He was a brilliant fielder who once held seven catches in an innings and 77 in a season, mostly at short leg. In 1979, Micky returned to the Oval as one of county cricket's first full-time managers, and it was his success in that role that earned him the England job.

Micky was a fine all-round sportsman who had played soccer at inside-right for Charlton Athletic, Wimbledon, Hendon and Corinthian Casuals. Later, on cricket tours, he liked to show off his skills with the big ball, but soon changed his tack when he found he wasn't quite quick enough any more to avoid the many late tackles that came his way. On the football field, any respect for his authority as team manager quickly disappeared. He became more and more reluctant to play soccer with us as time went on!

Micky, looking as immaculate as ever, is still a regular on the cricket circuit. He was President of Surrey for two years before being succeeded by some chap called John Major, and flies overseas each winter as leader of a supporters' group, and to watch Alec, of course. One day he might even call him 'son'.

Chris Tavare

Chris Tavare batted for England in a way I could never have imagined, let alone managed, and he had my utmost respect for it. Tav was patient, disciplined and stubborn, and had unbreakable concentration. Such qualities – and the contrast between us – were never illustrated more graphically than at Old Trafford in 1981.

I scored 118 in the fifth Test of that memorable series against Australia, with my final 90 runs coming from 49 balls. To me, it was a better innings than the 149 not out I scored at Headingley earlier in the series. But I could not have done it without Tav.

He was at the other end throughout and contributed 28 runs to our partnership of 149 for the sixth wicket. Tav was blocking when I came in and he was still blocking when I was out. In the first innings he had positively sprinted in Michael Slater fashion, racing to 69 in just four-and-three-quarter hours. This time, in our second dig, his innings of 78 occupied seven hours and included the slowest half-century in Test history, taking 304 minutes. He actually broke his own record the following summer when he took 350 minutes to reach his 50 against Pakistan at Lord's. Tav became the only man in the recorded history of the game to have two runless period of more than an hour in the same innings.

> 'His powers of concentration were fantastic and he was able to remove all thoughts about the previous delivery. Whatever had happened – whether he'd played and missed, or been slow-handclapped for another forward block – simply did not matter. The only thing he cared about was the next ball.'

During a Tavare innings, spectators could commit to memory each of the 92 Football League clubs (as there were then), in alphabetical order! Or perhaps go shopping, have a couple of pints and return to the ground sure in the knowledge that Tav would have added only a couple of runs. In fact he was so slow that once in a Test match a spectator came onto the field with a chair for him. But I thought he was brilliant. When I reached my century in that Old Trafford match, Tav walked up to me and said: 'Jeez, Beefy, I don't half make you look good.' As far as I was concerned, Tavare's innings was an epic.

His powers of concentration were fantastic and he was able to remove all thoughts about the previous delivery. Whatever had happened – whether he'd played and missed, or been slow-handclapped for another forward block – simply did not matter. The only thing he cared about was the next ball.

Tavare received some fearful criticism from the press and public, and it's true that some of his knocks were only marginally more interesting than watching grass grow. But he was doing a specific job and following instructions to the letter. From his position at No. 3 his orders were to stay in at all costs, so the others could bat around him and, with people like myself, David Gower and Mike Gatting, there were plenty of strokemakers attempting to do the necessary damage at the other end. No matter what others might have said, you never heard any complaints from inside the dressing-room about Tav's tactics.

It probably wasn't much fun for him, either, because his natural game was to play strokes. Believe me, in one-day cricket for Kent, and later Somerset, he was one of the most exciting, attacking batsmen in England. He would have no qualms about dancing down the track and whacking the ball over the top, and he was bloody good at it, too.

In the same way that Tavare was wrongly pigeon-holed as a boring blocker, most people assumed this was reflected in his personality as well. But the perception was that he was a dull man because he batted for England in such a dull fashion was way off the mark. In fact, Tav possessed a very dry sense of humour.

A meticulous man, he was as tidy with his words as he was with his immaculate flannels and shirts, hence his nickname 'Rowdy'. When he did rouse himself to direct speech, what he came up with was invariably either amusing or intelligent and often both. After another Tavare classic, a sprightly 35 in 332 minutes in Madras in 1981–82, he commented, 'I don't actually enjoy batting that much.'

One of his greatest moments was in Melbourne in 1982–83 – although it was nearly a disaster. At the climax of a thrilling Test match, one of the best I played in, Jeff Thomson was helping Allan

> 'A meticulous man, he was as tidy with his words as he was with his immaculate flannels and shirts, hence his nickname 'Rowdy'. When he did rouse himself to direct speech, what he came up with was invariably either amusing or intelligent and often both.'

Border to edge Australia towards victory with an amazing last-wicket stand. Australia needed just four for an unlikely victory when I managed to nick the edge of Thommo's bat and the ball flew to Tav in the slips.

To everyone's horror, he succeeded only in parrying the ball and, for a split second, we all thought the catch had gone to ground. But Geoff Miller leapt behind Tav and clung on to the rebound.

In all the excitement it is sometimes forgotten that in Tav's first innings 89 in that match he struck Aussie spinner Bruce Yardley over the top on several occasions. He could do it, you know.

Bob Taylor

Bob Taylor was a born wicket-keeper. He lived almost his entire life with the gloves on, and he will probably have a pair alongside him in the hereafter. Which is why, when the emergency call came that July day in 1986, two years after he'd retired from professional cricket and two weeks after celebrating his 45th birthday, Bob was ready, willing and more than able.

The occasion was the first Cornhill Test between England and New Zealand at Lord's. I mention the name of the sponsors because that was who he was working for at the time, in his role as meeter and greeter, public relations officer and general good egg. He was just sitting down to an early lunch in the hospitality area with some of the sponsors' guests and preparing to hand out the raffle tickets for the first prize of a bat autographed by an England player, when a message from the dressing room altered his immediate plans.

England's wicket-keeper Bruce French, groggy from a blow on the back of the head from a Richard Hadlee bouncer, was pronounced unfit to take the field. Bob was needed out in the middle. Not later. Now. Although Bob hadn't played international cricket for three years and had quit the game altogether a year before, because he also worked for a sports goods manufacturer, he happened to have some kit in the boot of his car. And after he answered the SOS he proceeded to prove he had lost little of his form and fitness. It was a marvellous cameo. And I tell you what ... I reckon Bob could wander out today and keep wicket in a Test match perfectly well, even though he has now passed his 60th birthday. He was a master craftsman.

Bob's role with Cornhill, which continued until they withdrew their sponsorship of English Test cricket after the 2000 season, was certainly not a case of jobs for the boys. He was one of the most personable blokes you could ever hope to meet, the perfect choice to make Cornhill's clients feel relaxed during their day at the Test. Indeed, his willingness to pass the time of day with cricket enthusiasts earned Bob his nickname of 'Chat'. On tour, there are always plenty of official functions to attend: cocktails at the Deputy High Commissioner's; canapés with the Chairman of the Cricket Board; local food with the Director of Tourism; that sort of thing. What most players dread is being ambushed by some chap in a blazer who wants to bend your ear for an hour and a half about the day he saw you score 33 at Weston-super-Mare. It might sound ill-mannered, but the natural instinct of cricketers when under such threat is to circle the wagons. Bob was different. He was more than happy to be dispatched to small-talk with the local dignitaries.

Bobby Taylor was very unlucky to be around at the same time as Alan Knott. There was nothing to choose between their actual keeping, but Alan got the nod because of his superior batting. It meant that, after making his debut in New Zealand in 1970–71, Bob did not play another Test match for seven years, by which time Knotty had signed up with Kerry Packer. He did then enjoy a decent run in the side and ended up appearing in 57 Tests, still playing for England at the age of 42. If he hadn't overlapped with Knotty, however, Bob would have played a hundred and plenty Tests.

They say wicket-keepers are mad, but Bob was the exception that proved the rule, especially compared with the likes of Alan Knott and Jack Russell! He was as fastidious in his preparation as those two nut-cases, and he did once tell me that he used pieces of raw meat in his gloves as cushions, but that was as far as he allowed himself to be eccentric. The consummate professional, he summed up his disillusionment with how English cricket was going when he said on his retirement: 'England won't improve in world terms until the younger players rediscover some professional pride.'

'Chat was a determined batsman, and to his great delight – and everyone else's – he finally managed to make his maiden first-class century in his 21st season, against Yorkshire in 1981.'

As a keeper he was simply brilliant. On countless occasions I stood at second slip while Bob was 'keeping and could barely hear the sound of the ball entering his gloves, so soft were his hands. He was a perfectionist, and when he felt the Derbyshire captaincy was affecting his keeping, he immediately gave up the job. Not that anyone else had noticed any evidence of decline, of course.

In the Jubilee Test against India in Bombay in 1979–80, Bob set a world record of ten dismissals in a Test match, a figure that was subsequently exceeded by Russell and equalled by Adam Gilchrist of Australia. In that match, Bob and I also compiled a partnership of 171 for the sixth wicket. We shared many stands, in fact, because I normally batted at No 6, and Bob tended to come in at eight – and on two occasions at least, Bob probably wished we hadn't. The first time I ran him out, I'd scored 99 and was on the brink of my maiden Test century. In my nervous state, I called him for a suicidal single and he perished for 45 after five hours' solid support. The next time I did him like a kipper was against Australia at Adelaide in 1978–79. It wouldn't have been so bad, but we were actually going for a fourth run! But, in the second innings of that match, he registered his highest Test score of 97 and put on 135 with his Derbyshire team-mate Geoff Miller.

'During my Leukaemia Walk from John O'Groats to Land's End in 1985, we went through Stone, in Derbyshire, where a familiar figure was waiting on a street corner in his tracksuit. It was Bob Taylor, who joined the march. Typical of the man – wanting to do his bit but with the minimum of fuss.'

Chat was a determined batsman, and to his great delight – and everyone else's – he finally managed to make his maiden first-class century in his 21st season, against Yorkshire in 1981.

Bob overtook John Murray's world records for first-class catches and dismissals. He finished his career with 1,649 dismissals and 1,473 catches. Because of the reduction in the amount of first-class cricket, it seems unlikely that those records will ever be broken. Russell might get close but, at his current rate of progress, he will have to play at least until his mid-40s.

During my Leukaemia Walk from John O'Groats to Land's End in 1985, all kinds of people turned up unannounced. As we went through Stone, in Derbyshire, a familiar figure was waiting on a street corner in his tracksuit. It was Bob Taylor, who joined the march. Typical of the man – wanting to do his bit, but with the minimum of fuss.

And finally ... most people know that Dennis Lillee and Rod Marsh had a bet on England at 500–1 during the Headingley Test of 1981. Not many are aware, however, that Bob Taylor was the only England player to have a flutter at those amazing odds. Trouble is, he did not tell us about his win for another three years.

Les Taylor

Few professional cricketers have the opportunity, if that is the right word, to see life from the outside. Most have their careers mapped out for them from an early age. Spotted at club or school level, they graduate through the junior ranks to a county contract. The very best make it all the way to the top. And the blinkers need to be on throughout the process. For those guys it can be difficult to appreciate how fortunate they are to make a career out of their chosen sport, because they simply have no 'real' life experiences to compare with their privileged existence.

Les Taylor was one of the few men in my time in cricket who can say with total authority: 'Believe me, playing cricket is a lot better than being down the pit,' because before Les joined Leicestershire that was exactly how he earned his living. Indeed, I believe his early experiences as a coal miner prior to making his first-class debut for Leicestershire at the grand old age of 23 allowed him to put, and keep, the game in its proper perspective.

'Les was a great trier with a heart as big as a mountain. But he knew that cricket was always only a game.'

Les was a great trier with a heart as big as a mountain. But he knew that cricket was always only a game. When, in 1988, Les's team-mate, Jonathan Agnew, threatened that he would take up a career in broadcasting if England didn't pick him again, Les commented: 'I'm going to threaten them with going back to coalmining.'

There was an old maxim that you had only to whistle down a mine and up would pop a fast bowler. That might have applied in the days of Harold Larwood, but there have been very few seamers in recent years who have worked at the coal face. After Les, David Millns, also of Leicestershire and later Nottinghamshire, is the only other professional cricketer I can name who made the same journey.

Les was a brilliant bloke who had two never-to-be-forgotten characteristics: he called everyone 'me dook' and he was stone deaf in one ear. I really got to know Les on England's tour of the West Indies in 1985–86, when we often shared a room, and I quickly discovered he was great fun with a dry sense of humour. Les would always sleep with his good ear pressed against the pillow, which meant that, if the phone rang in the room, or I called out, he wouldn't be disturbed. He couldn't hear a thing, so the only way to wake him was with a good shake.

For some reason, Les refused to wear his hearing aid on the field, and this sometimes led to chaos and confusion, notably on the occasion when Leicestershire took the field on the first day of a county championship match in 1985. Les had taken his hearing aid off as usual, and he marched out on to the field, as usual; the only problem was that he hadn't heard his skipper David Gower telling him he'd been dropped. Aggers stretched himself and prepared to send down the first delivery of the match and conferred with David over the field he wanted. 'The usual, please, David. Three slips, a gully, short leg, cover, mid-off, mid-on, square leg and fine leg ... and a ... third ...man ...?' It was only when the fielders added up to eleven, plus the keeper, that they realized the numbers didn't add up.

Les wasn't the greatest fielder, as another incident involving Aggers in a county match against Worcestershire at Kidderminster in 1989 underlined. I was away at a Test match against Australia, but when I got back to the county I was told about Les's part in a cunning plot to dismiss Graeme Hick that went sadly awry. The plan was that Aggers would bend his back and dig in a short ball to Hicky to test his prowess with the hook shot. Aggers told Les that, on his signal, he should move wider from mid-on towards mid-wicket while he was running up to be in position for a possible catch. When the moment came, Aggers and Les exchanged winks and thumbs-ups and the plan worked like a dream, Hick attempted the hook and the ball ballooned gently towards Les ... Les ... LES!!! Sadly for Aggers, Les had been distracted momentarily and started too late. The result was that, instead of collecting the catch like one you would throw to your granny on the beach, the unfortunate Les ended up collapsing in a heap some two yards short of where the ball hit the deck. Hick went on to make millions, of course, and it was a good job Les didn't have his hearing aid in for the remainder of that day.

Les never ever let anyone down with the ball, though. In the 1981 season he took 75 wickets at 21 apiece and narrowly missed selection for the tour of India and Sri Lanka that winter. Instead, he signed up for the first England rebel tour to South Africa and, but for the three-year ban from Test cricket which followed, he would surely have won more than two caps. He was the English team's best bowler on that trip and was quick enough to strike even the great Graeme Pollock on the head with a bouncer.

He was eventually picked for the final two Tests of the 1985 series against Australia, at Edgbaston and the Oval. And while he took only four wickets, the last of them, when he caught and bowled Australian tail-ender Murray Bennett, was the wicket that actually clinched the Ashes for England.

Les was chosen for the tour of the Caribbean the following winter, but made only occasional appearances. Indeed, because of his dark hair, moustache, somewhat gloomy-looking appearance and the fact that he was spotted so rarely, we dubbed him Lord Lucan.

'What can they know of cricket who only cricket know?' goes the saying. Les, if you can hear me, you made the saying make perfect sense.'

As I said, I got to know Les well in the Windies. Les, myself, and Gerry Waller, my father-in-law who came out to watch the cricket, spent a lot of time playing dominoes with local fishermen in quiet bars away from the spotlight. Les even managed to break the bed in our room when, confined to barracks because of a virus, he flopped down to try to get some sleep.

Away from cricket, Les loved life in rural Leicestershire, and he had a passion for horses. Not the sort that deliberately conspire with bookmakers to steal my cash and yours, but hunters. I remember once how terribly upset he was after one of his beloved four legged-friends had suffered a brain haemorrhage, and had died with his head cradled in Les's arms.

'What can they know of cricket who only cricket know?' goes the saying. Les, if you can hear me, you made the saying make perfect sense.

Sachin Tendulkar

Sachin Ramesh Tendulkar should count himself lucky that he wasn't born in England. Given our atrocious record of handing young players a chance to show they can perform at international level, he would have been forced to wait until he was 26, not 16, for his debut. Luckily, India had the foresight to give him a taste of Test cricket at an age when my contemporaries were still waiting to sit their 'O' Levels – and what a star they unearthed.

There are very few players I will pay money to go and watch, but the Little Master is a batsman for whom I would happily part with my cash at the turnstiles. When Tendulkar is in full flow, it is a privilege to see him play – and if he stays fit, I don't think he will just go past Allan Border's world record of 11,174 Test runs: I'm convinced he'll blow it out of the water.

'There are very few players I will pay money to go and watch, but the Little Master is a batsman for whom I would happily part with my cash at the turnstiles. When Tendulkar is in full flow, it is a privilege to see him play.'

India have an enviable tradition of producing batsmen with talent, temperament and technique of the highest class. After the likes of Gavaskar and Viswanath, this fellow is a worthy successor. One of my biggest regrets in the game is that I never got the chance to pit my wits against him in Test matches, although I did manage to find a useful leg-cutter for him in the 1992 World Cup tournament in Australia, where England's route march to the final began with a tense win against India in the opening group qualifier at the WACA. Although you don't put a price on every batsman's head, there are certain players you are always glad to see the back of, and we regarded Tendulkar's wicket as the key to winning the game. For opposition sides, little has changed since then.

He is also still the same, humble character who came to be regarded as a schoolboy superstar by his own people. More than once, I've had to tick him off for calling me 'Mr Botham', and when he played county cricket for Yorkshire he could often be found in the dressing-room, passing on tips or advice he had acquired from 'Mr Gavaskar'. It's an extraordinary attitude for someone who is regarded as a sporting god in his home town, Bombay, where his house is under 24-hour siege by fans and well-wishers. Just as Brian Lara has had to cope with hero-worship bordering on obsession,

'One of my biggest regrets in the game is that I never got the chance to pit my wits against him in Test matches.'

Tendulkar has never allowed the fame game to compromise his genius. In this country, we enjoyed an early taste of his inspiration in the 1990 Test series, which England won 1–0. He produced a sensational one-handed, running catch in front of the Nursery End sightscreen at the Lord's Test to dismiss Allan Lamb – and it took something special to stand out in the memory from a match in which Graham Gooch scored 333 in the first innings and 123 in the second. Then, even more stunningly, he made a fabulous maiden Test century at Old Trafford, 119 not out, to save the game from an apparently hopeless position.

> 'The world has not been allowed to see as much of Sachin Tendulkar as it would like – but perhaps the best is yet to come.'

By then, he had already demonstrated he wouldn't be cowed by opponents with loftier reputations. Bishen Bedi, India's great left-arm spinner from the 1970s, once told me the story of Pakistan's attempts to intimidate sixteen-year-old Tendulkar at a one-day tournament in 1989–90. Abdul Qadir, who could spin a cricket ball round corners with his leg-breaks, tried to goad Tendulkar into playing a loose shot, saying, 'Come on, you're supposed to hit me out of the ground.' Tendulkar's reply went something along the lines of, 'How am I supposed to hit you out of the ground when you are a great bowler and I'm just a young boy?' Then he proceeded to take 14 off Qadir's next over. Ouch!

BEEFY ON TENDULKAR

Born: 24 April 1973, Bombay
Country: India
Tests: 89
Hundreds: 27
Average: 57.96
Beefy analysis: The greatest batsman in the world today, the Little Master is set to break all batting records if he continues to flourish with the bat. When he is on song, there is no more majestic sight in cricket.
Beefy moment: As a sixteen-year-old, taking 14 runs in an over off Abdul Qadir, a spinning magician in his prime.
Do mention: His brilliant batting against Shane Warne in India, 1998.
Don't mention: Respect for your elders.

Since then, Tendulkar's record has spoken for itself. You've got to put him in the same bracket as Viv Richards, Border, Gavaskar, Lara and Steve Waugh. He entered the new millennium knowing that, if he stayed injury-free and his appetite for the game remained undiminished, he could spend another 10 years at the top and break records left, right and centre.

One area in which he has never been found wanting is his ability to concentrate on the basics of the job in hand whatever the distractions. As his fame spread, so the pressure increased on Tendulkar to perform every time he went out to bat for India. But he seemed to thrive on this expectation, and relish the burden he carried. That's what sets him apart from almost every other batsman of his day, and ultimately it will prove to be the difference between genius and greatness.

It's just a shame that, for the first 10 years of his career, India seemed content to maintain only a passing acquaintance with Test cricket. The world has not been allowed to see as much of Sachin Tendulkar as it would like – but perhaps the best is yet to come.

Jeff
Thomson

Thommo was the fastest bowler of my lifetime. He was mind-bogglingly, earth-scorchingly quick. I am sure that, if speedguns had been around in the 1970s, there would be no debate now about who will be the first bowler to break the 100mph barrier. Jeff Thomson would have achieved the speedster's version of Mach I a quarter-century before the likes of Shoaib Akhtar and Brett Lee were attempting to crack three figures.

In fact he himself is convinced he bowled faster than 100 mph on several occasions. The secret of Thommo's speed was his athleticism. His approach to the stumps was little more than a leisurely lope, but he was so supple that he was able to coil his body and release the ball at a vicious velocity. He gained extreme bounce, too, which made the prospect of facing him even more daunting. Viv Richards says Thommo was the quickest bowler he ever faced, which will do for me. I heard about a famous occasion when Thommo hit Viv on the cap with a bouncer – no helmet for Viv, of course – only for Viv to hook the next ball for six. As fast bowlers the world over understand, such a response from the masterblaster represented the ultimate mark of respect.

I wouldn't recommend that anyone attempts to bowl like Thommo – they would probably snap in half unless they were blessed with his athleticism, suppleness and strong shoulders. But, when one analyzed his method in slow motion, it was in many ways the perfect action for bowling quick.

Most bowlers allow the batsman to view the ball in the hands all the way, from the start of the run-up to the moment of release. Someone like Michael Holding, with his textbook delivery, allowed batsmen to have an unimpeded sight of the ball at all times. But one of Thommo's greatest weapons was the element of surprise. His slinging style meant that the ball was hidden behind his back until just before he let it go, so the first time a batsman saw it was when it was already on its way down the track at speeds of 90 mph-plus.

I never faced Thommo in his pomp. My encounters with him came after he tore his shoulder muscles in a collision with team-mate Alan Turner during a Test match against Pakistan in Adelaide in December 1976, as they both went for a catch. He was never quite as fast again.

During the 1974–75 Ashes series, Thomson and Dennis Lillee terrorized many of England's batsmen. It was a rude shock, because Lillee, following a back operation, was not expected to be as fast as he had been on Australia's tour of England in 1972, and Thomson's only previous Test appearance two years earlier had been distinctly unmemorable. Thomson took 33 wickets in the first five Tests, before injury kept him out of the sixth and final match of the series. England were left battered, bruised and beaten. Thommo, hurling the ball with his action like a javelin thrower, speared them good and proper.

As a teenager, I watched the highlights of that series on TV at home. The speed and bounce generated by Lillee and Thomson was incredible. I decided in the end it was safer to sit behind the settee – in case any of their bouncers came flying through the screen!

David Lloyd now jokingly tells the story of how Thomson hit him in the meat and two veg – and actually turned his plastic box inside out. Once, when Keith Fletcher was hit on the cap, the ball bounced off his head to be caught at cover point, on the full.

Colin Cowdrey, aged 42, was flown as a replacement and introduced himself to Thomson. 'Hello, my name's Colin Cowdrey. Jolly nice to meet you.' Thommo's reply was less charitable – and less printable. Indeed, he has never been afraid to speak his mind in colourful language. I think TV and radio producers are on tenterhooks when Thommo is commentating, in case a swear word slips out. When the grey-haired David Steele walked out for his Test debut against Australia in 1975, Thommo observed, 'Who's this, then, Father Bloody Christmas?'

'Thommo has always been a colourful, happy-go-lucky character, and was once probably the fastest bowler who ever lived.'

He's always revelled in gory talk about how he enjoyed hitting batsmen more than he enjoyed getting them out. He used to claim he liked nothing more than seeing blood on the pitch. A lot of it was bravado, of course, and I think Thommo usually said such things for a lark, or to give the press lads a decent headline. It's the same with his ritual Pommie-bashing: 'We could beat you lot even if we were pissed,' is a typical Thommo line. At the outset of his short-lived career as a columnist for the *Daily Star* his first comment to the ghost writer whose job it was to put his thoughts into a form suitable for a family paper was nothing if not direct: 'These poms,' said Thommo, 'are on a rollercoaster ride to the shitheap.' Thomson was left out of

Australia's side for their 1981 tour of England. Instead, he played for Middlesex and produced some very quick spells. In the match against the tourists, Thommo was determined to prove a point and put opener Graeme Wood in hospital.

He recaptured much of his former pace when he was recalled against England in 1982–83, and topped the Aussie averages with 22 wickets at 18 apiece in four Tests. In the Melbourne Test that winter, Thommo and Allan Border put on 70 for the last wicket to take Australia to within three runs of an amazing victory. But then Thommo drove at a wide delivery from me and edged the ball to Chris Tavare in the slips. Tavare dropped the catch and, with everything seeming to happen in slow motion, Geoff Miller clung on to the ricochet.

Typically, Thommo marched into our dressing-room afterwards and warned us he'd be out for revenge in the next match. He wasn't wrong, either, and took five for 50 in the first innings at Sydney. These days, I see Thommo socially whenever we are in each other's country. We get on very well and he is one of my favourite Aussies. We play golf and go fishing – we've caught quite a few trout together now. Thommo has always been a colourful, happy-go-lucky character, and was once probably the fastest bowler who ever lived.

Sam
Torrance

It was the perfect end to a vintage summer for British sport. England had regained the Ashes, Barry McGuigan had won the world featherweight title – and then, in September 1985, Sam Torrance sent them bats at The Belfry. Torrance sank the putt which ended the United States' post-war domination of the Ryder Cup, and I've been fortunate to count him among my closest friends in sport ever since. Even now I can still picture Sam in his red sweater, watching his 25-footer drop and then raising his regulation-length putter – the telescopic long handle came later in his career – when the significance of the moment dawned on him.

I could not have been happier for him when he was named Europe's Ryder Cup captain 16 years later – and they couldn't have chosen a better skipper. Torrance is a great motivator, a man genuinely in love with his sport, and a terrific advertisement for the European tour.

'As for my own experiences out on the course with Sam, all I can say is that he's an expert at picking your pocket. He gets you to relax, lulls you into a false sense of security, and then takes your money. I can't think of a single continent on which he's not made my wallet lighter over 18 holes. For all that, he is a great friend, and our families are the best of mates, too.'

Anyone lucky enough to have played a round with him, either socially or in a pro-am tournament, will testify that he's fantastic company: always jovial and a master at keeping his playing partners relaxed to maximize their enjoyment. I can remember one pro-am event at The Belfry when his playing partner was a rather nervous corporate guest who was carving divots the size of pot-holes, and hitting everything into sand, water, woodland, heavy rough ... every which way but straight. Sam had the patience of a saint and the silver tongue of a spin doctor. He encouraged this guy to relax, not to worry about the lost balls, and to make sure he just enjoyed the day. And when the round was finished, Sam was the life and soul of the 19th hole; his guest went home that night beaming like a Cheshire cat after the greatest day of his golfing life.

That's Sam for you. Whether he's playing with Johnny Hacker or Gary Player, he treats his own profession with enviable respect. And that's why he was a popular choice as Ryder Cup captain – because he cares so much about the game. Even when he doesn't swing the club himself, he's tootling around in his buggy living every shot. Like everyone else with golf's fundamental etiquette at heart, I know he was appalled by the scenes in 1999 at Brookline, when half of Boston invaded the 17th green after Justin Leonard sank the monster putt that virtually clinched the Cup for America.

Some of the abuse aimed at the likes of Colin Montgomerie, not to mention the players' wives, was beyond the pale. Mark James, who was Torrance's predecessor as European captain and is a big mate of Sam's, was particularly distressed, and everyone felt for 'Jessie' in that situation. Emotions were running high and, frankly, some of the hangers-on became a bit tribal. It's an episode that all golfers, and golf-lovers, want to forget, and the appointment of Sam was an ideal choice to restore a bit of decorum to the proceedings.

As for my own experiences out on the course with Sam, all I can say is that he's an expert at picking your pocket. He gets you to relax, lulls you into a false sense of security, and then takes your money. I can't think of a single continent on which he's not made my wallet lighter over 18 holes. For all that, he is a great friend, and our families are the best of mates, too. Torrance is wonderful company at the dinner table – he has an inexhaustible supply of good humour and is always a genial host. When he went on the wagon for a couple of years, he would plonk a bottle of the finest red wine from his cellar unselfishly on the table, and spend all night sipping, without a trace of envy, from his glass of water.

Sam also joined me in the closing stages of my last walk from John O'Groats to Lands End. We were stomping across the fringes of Dartmoor, crossing the last county boundary between Devon and Cornwall, and for 18 miles or so he kept up with the front line admirably. Then, not long after we'd passed a pub, I suddenly realized Sam was no longer with us. Slightly concerned that he'd taken a wrong turning and was now lost in the fog on Dartmoor itself, I'd barely finished asking the support team if anyone had seen him when the back-up truck rattled past. No prizes for guessing who was in the back, with his feet up on a crate, a large glass of Guinness in one hand and a roll-up in the other!

Nobody was going to tell Torrance that he hadn't earned his light refreshment that afternoon because, like any proud Scotsman, he is always prepared to stand his corner. When England beat the Scots 2–0 at Hampden Park in the play-off for a place at soccer's Euro 2000 tournament, Sam flew up to Glasgow for the day with his son – and could be heard on the plane home that night, warning any Englishman within earshot that Scotland would win the return at Wembley. Anyone who ventured to disagree was invited to step outside – at 30,000ft!

Phil Tufnell

If Phil Tufnell believed in himself as much as that other loony leftie, Phil Edmonds, he could have been a world-beater. Tuffers' problem has always been a lack of self-confidence, which will sound surprising to those people who believe the image of him as being a cocky, Artful Dodger character.

One moment, Tuffers' emotions are as high as a kite, the next his behaviour is that of a manic depressive. The only other player I can recall who endured similar mood swings was Derek Randall,

who could go from the clouds to the deepest ocean in a matter of minutes. At practice sessions or during matches, Tuffers would often wander over and ask me: 'Is the ball coming out all right? Am I bowling okay?' He sought reassurance constantly and even when you gave it never seemed to be able to bring himself to believe it.

I have always rated Tuffers highly. He has flight, can turn the ball and possesses excellent control. There is certainly no lack of talent, and when he's bowling well, his description of bowling as though he has the ball on a piece of string is entirely apt. He's enjoyed some excellent days for England, notably his six for 25 against the West Indies at the Oval in 1991, seven for 47 versus New Zealand in Christchurch the following winter, and seven for 66 against Australia at the Oval in 1997. All three performances helped England to victory.

Yet Tuffers has never established a regular place in the England team. I think this is partly because his lack of confidence makes him his own worst enemy, but I'm also convinced he has been badly handled at times. Tuffers is an emotionally fragile character who has suffered from all kinds of personal problems and crippling self-doubt. Often, he needed nothing more than a sympathetic arm wrapped around his shoulder. But, instead, too many England regimes brandished the big stick.

'I have always rated Tuffers highly. He has flight, can turn the ball and possesses excellent control. There is certainly no lack of talent, and when he's bowling well, his description of bowling as though he has the ball on a piece of string is entirely apt.'

Sure, he has certainly never conformed to the traditional idea of a professional sportsman. Booze and fags, a shuffling gait, feet splayed at ten-to-two and, to borrow a phrase, a face like an unmade bed, the Middlesex man has a natural aversion to such things as bleep tests: give him 20 Bensons, a couple of large ones and forty winks any day. His disregard for authority and conformity is probably matched only by his hatred of flying. At times, especially when the going gets a bit choppy up in the sky, Tuffers is pinned to his seat and clearly crapping himself.

Over the years he's found himself in more scrapes than are usually experienced by a hundred cricketers. These have ranged from spending a night in the psychiatric wing of a hospital in Perth, Australia, after he threw a wobbly – the team management barely succeeded in keeping that particular escapade quiet – to boring old motoring offences. Not to mention fines for tantrums on the field, like the incident when he kicked his England cap all over the field at Vishakaptnam when teammate Richard Blakey missed a stumping to dismiss Sachin Tendular on the 1993 tour to India. He has been through the ordeal of a divorce and a public break-up with the mother of his first child. I'm sure that would have upset the strongest of people, and doubtless contributed to his occasionally erratic behaviour. I would tell Tuffers to try to ignore the lurid newspaper headlines, but his problems clearly ate away at his confidence and equilibrium.

BEEFY ON TUFNELL

Born: 29 April 1966, Barnet, Hertfordshire
Country: England
Tests: 42
Wickets: 121
Average: 37.68
Beefy analysis: Left-arm orthodox spinner with plenty of guile in the flight. When he needed a sympathetic arm round the shoulder from the England selectors, he rarely got it.
Beefy moment: The on-field spat with captain Graham Gooch in Australia in 1990–91.
Do mention: England v Australia, The Oval 1997 (his seven for 66 won the match for England).
Don't mention: England v Australia, The Oval 2001 (after which he was left out of the winter tour to India).

On his first tour, to Australia in 1990–91, he had a bit of an on-field spat with captain Graham Gooch, and the Aussie spectators were relentless in the way they took the mickey out of his fielding. It was pretty poor, admittedly, but I think such ridicule also helped to erode his self-belief.

Tuffers says in his autobiography that, when we first played together for England in 1991, I announced my arrival in the dressing-room with a belch 'like the horn of an ocean-going liner'. And he apparently saw a kindred spirit in my reluctance to lap the outfield! I saw a good bloke riddled with doubts, while he liked the way I refused to take things too seriously. He says I lifted the mood and stopped players being frightened of their own shadows. We hit it off immediately. I always treat people as I find them, and I found Tuffers to be friendly, witty and entertaining company.

Tuffers is still finding it difficult to get away from his reputation, but started the twenty-first century bowling as well as ever. England have struggled for many years in the spin bowling department. Many slow men have been tried as an alternative to Tufnell, whether they be off-spinners, wrist-spinners or left-arm spinners, but I don't reckon any of them have his natural talent. So who is to say that he can't come back into the England reckoning? Tuffers was 36 in April 2002, so should not be written out of Test contention just yet.

Derek Underwood

'Deadly' Derek Underwood was a remarkable bowler. On most pitches he was accurate and awkward; on damp or drying surfaces, he was virtually unplayable.

Although he was a left-arm spinner who could flight the ball if necessary, Deadly usually bowled at something approaching medium-pace, which made it difficult for batsmen to use their feet to attack him. If the pitch offered the slightest assistance, Deadly could make the ball turn, lift and spit ... at pace. He was land-it-on-a-sixpence accurate, too. Play that!

In the days before covered pitches, Deadly would normally find a couple of wet wickets for Kent each season and produce figures such as nine for 28 (against Sussex in 1964), nine for 37 (against Essex in 1966) or nine for 32 (against Surrey in 1978). There was an art to bowling in those conditions; too many spinners would get carried away and lose focus. But Deadly's patience, pace and precision were the perfect combination. There was nobody in the world to touch him.

"Deadly' Derek Underwood was a remarkable bowler. On most pitches he was accurate and awkward; on damp or drying surfaces, he was virtually unplayable.'

The only time I can recall any batsman getting after him was at the Oval in 1976, when Viv Richards scored 291 and the West Indies made 687 for eight declared. Deadly's figures in that innings were three for 165, and it was one of the few occasions when he came off second best. Mind you, it was a boiling hot summer, the pitch was a shirtfront and he still conceded runs at fewer than three an over. Viv was not a bad player, either, and there was no disgrace in taking some tap from him. Deadly became a little less effective after the decision was made to cover pitches during breaks for rain. It meant that the days of drying pitches were over.

One can only imagine what Deadly's wicket haul would have been had he played in the 1920s or 1930s, when 'sticky dogs' were commonplace. But, even on covered pitches, Deadly was always a handful.

On tour, I roomed with Deadly on several occasions. Once, during the Jubilee Test in Bombay in 1979–80, he actually ran and hid from me, which was a little odd. His excuse was that he fancied a quiet night, and he kipped down on the settee in a friend's room. Another night, he put a pair of my smart blue leather shoes outside the door to be cleaned. We never saw them again. If anyone spots them being worn about town in Mumbai, by the way, there is a significant cash reward on offer.

At the time, Deadly was collaborating on a book with a great journalist friend of ours, the late Chris Lander. It was supposed to be

an account of Derek's experiences on tour in Australia and was due
to be called 'Deadly Down Under'. They didn't get very far. Lander
would come to our room with the intention of conducting
searching interviews with his co-author. Instead, the three of us
would chat all evening and half the night, with the result that little
or no work was done. They would try to escape me by going to
Lander's room and taking the phone off the hook. But I'd soon
become bored on my own and join them. One evening, I dragged
Deadly and Lander up to the restaurant at the top of the hotel.
Deadly became so intoxicated that he started dancing and gyrating
on a table where a couple were trying to eat their meal. Then
Lander joined in with catastrophic consequences, slipping and
landing head first in the lap of one of the diners. Next morning, I

'He ended up with 297 wickets from 86 Tests, despite missing some of his best years and, as the statistics indicate, he was without question England's leading spinner for two decades.'

asked the hotel manager if he knew
whose evening we had disturbed. I
arranged for them to be sent a
couple of tickets for the Test match
by way of apology.

As punishment, I set Deadly and
Lander the challenge of standing on
a table, drinking a glass of brandy,
eating a plate of tandoori chicken

and reading a passage from the Gideon Bible, all at the same time.
I can report that Deadly was not up to the task.

Deadly didn't look much like a professional sportsman. Like
Phil Tufnell, one of his successors in the left-arm spin department, his feet were splayed at ten-to-two, but there was nothing
Chaplinesque about his bowling. He was a teenage phenomenon who
played for Kent at seventeen and became the youngest player to take
100 wickets in his first season. His partnership with wicket-keeper
Alan Knott flourished from the very beginning. For Kent and
England, they were one of the great double-acts of all time. So well
could they read each other's game that no signals were necessary; if
they spotted a batsman overbalancing at the crease, for instance, the

message that Deadly would be firing one in behind his pads for Knotty to try a leg-side stumping was transferred by thought and instinct alone. It was mesmerizing to watch.

By the age of 25, Deadly had captured 1,000 first-class wickets, and only two men in history reached that milestone at a younger age. A lot of those wickets also had Knotty's name against them, figuratively as well as literally.

Perhaps Derek's most memorable performance was against Australia at the Oval in 1968 when, after a thunderstorm, spectators helped to dry the outfield. Underwood took seven for 50 and a famous photograph records the moment of victory when, with the entire England team circled round the bat as last man John Inverarity was out with just a few minutes remaining.

Against Australia at Headingley in 1972, when a fungus called Fuserium damaged the pitch, Underwood wrought havoc with ten for 82 in the match. On a different occasion, when overnight rain leaked under the covers, Deadly had eight for 51 against Pakistan at Lord's in 1974.

Derek made himself into an effective, if ungainly, tail-end batsman, who lacked nothing in courage which explains another famous picture which shows him airborne, arching his head out of the line of a high-velocity bouncer from Michael Holding, but with his eyes still fixed on the ball as it whistled past his nose.

He enjoyed the role of nightwatchman and usually managed to do his job by surviving until close of play. And one of his proudest achievements was scoring his maiden first-class century at Hastings in 1984 at the age of 39, for Kent against Sussex.

If he had not joined Kerry Packer's World Series Cricket in 1977 and then signed up for the rebel tour of South Africa in 1982, Deadly might well have become England's greatest Test wicket-taker, exceeding my total of 383. As it was, he ended up with 297 from 86 Tests, despite missing some of his best years and, as the statistics indicate, he was without question England's leading spinner for two decades.

Courtney Walsh

Courtney Walsh is the all-time greatest wicket-taker in Test cricket. He finished with the amazing total of 519. I say finished, but nobody can be certain with Courtney, of course. Walsh's tally is testimony to his remarkable consistency, stamina, skill and dedication.

Walsh is neither the fastest bowler of all time, nor was he the best, but nobody can match his longevity. Walsh has been able to put together his remarkable record only by staying largely injury-free – he hardly

ever pulls up with a niggle. When I first saw him playing for the West Indies, I thought he would never last, because he was as thin as a garden rake. He's tall and slim, certainly, but he has a natural suppleness, and that has allowed him to keep going brilliantly.

In his early days, Walsh was the support act to the likes of Michael Holding, Malcolm Marshall and Joel Garner. In fact, on his Test debut in 1984 at the WACA in Perth, he didn't even get a bowl in the first innings because the other three bowled out Australia for just 76. When he was finally thrown the ball in the second innings, left-handed opener Graeme Wood became the first of his 519 victims. I'll say that again – *five hundred and nineteen.*

In those days, as the rookie, he was usually asked to bowl into the wind or uphill, or both. But, as the others retired one-by-one, Walsh gradually became the senior strike bowler. Or at least the joint No. 1 with Curtly Ambrose. The partnership of Walsh and Ambrose has to be rated among the great fast-bowling duos of history. Without them, West Indies would have been in an even greater mess than they found themselves in recent years. They are close friends, and Courtney says, 'Curtly is like a silent assassin. He has this expression which appears to say 'don't get close to me', but he is a very close friend and a very good team man.'

BEEFY ON WALSH

Born: 30 October 1962, Kingston, Jamaica
Country: West Indies
Tests: 132
Wickets: 519
Average: 24.44
Beefy analysis: Capable of bowling very fast, especially in his younger days, but Walsh's greatness was in the ability to vary his delivery, with subtle changes in pace, line, and length combined with movement in the air and off the seam. Add to that the stamina for long spells unchanged, and you had the ideal bowler.
Beefy moment: His bowling against Mike Atherton, Jamaica, 1994.
Do mention: West Indies v South Africa, Port of Spain, 2001 (Walsh becomes first bowler to claim 500 Test wickets).
Don't mention: Uphill into the wind.

Walsh always loved bowling. I'll bet he never said 'no' when his captain asked him to turn his arm over. He is a great technician who worked out his strengths and formulated a game plan to keep batsmen under pressure. He has taken wickets consistently in every country around the world, which tells you he's very good.

Walsh has basically been a seam bowler, not a swing bowler, who brings down the ball from a great height (he's 6ft 5ins tall) with a snap of his wrist. Although not express, he was capable of extremely hostile spells. I remember one epic battle with Mike Atherton in Jamaica in 1994, when he bowled for two hours non-stop, and had Athers ducking and diving away from a string of bouncers. Athers rates it as perhaps the most aggressive sustained spell he's ever faced. His bravery and defensive skill received a thorough examination and, in the end, Walsh got his man. In the same match, Walsh also showed a streak of utter ruthlessness as he unleashed a string of bouncers at England's No. 11 and renowned rabbit, Devon Malcolm.

'Courtney Walsh is the all-time greatest wicket-taker in Test cricket. He finished with the amazing total of 519. I say finished, but nobody can be certain with Courtney, of course. Walsh's tally is testimony to his remarkable consistency, stamina, skill and dedication.'

Walsh might be fast, but he can also be very slow. Towards the end of his career, he developed a devastating slower delivery which dropped like a doodlebug from the heavens. Graham Thorpe was bamboozled by it twice during the summer of 2000, proving that Courtney is also a cunning, thinking bowler.

Courtney is one of the nicest guys in the world of cricket, very much taking over that mantle from his fellow Jamaican, Michael Holding. Everybody has time for Courtney, and everybody enjoys his company. He is just a thoroughly nice guy. And, throughout his career, Walsh has also shown great personal dignity and pride about the region he represents. When Courtney was captain, he asked for the West Indies team badge to be moved to the left-hand side of team's shirt, so that it was placed over the heart. That showed how much leading the Windies meant to him. Later, when he was sacked as skipper and replaced by Brian Lara, many thought he had been treated shabbily and would retire. But, typically, Walsh gave Lara his total loyalty, and even made a public gesture of support by shaking Lara's hand in front of the main stand at Sabina Park.

They love him at Sabina Park, of course, and it was entirely appropriate that he should break Kapil Dev's world record of 434 Test wickets at that ground. It was a very emotional moment. I suppose it brought to mind the moment when Geoff Boycott scored his 100th first-class century in a Test match on his home ground at Headingley in 1977. Being such a popular and proud man, it's perhaps not surprising that the Jamaican government has given Walsh ambassadorial status.

Courtney grew up playing at the Melbourne Cricket Club in Kingston, Jamaica – where Holding also played – and, like Mikey, Courtney pops in to Melbourne for a relaxing game of dominoes with his mates. His mother still serves a mean goat curry, stewed peas and rice.

Courtney's classy character, as well as his brilliant bowling and professional approach, made him a hugely popular figure with Gloucestershire. In 14 seasons, he collected 859 wickets in the county championship, which is a remarkable tally. It meant he was bowling virtually 12 months a year. His swansong was memorable – he took 106 wickets in 1998. Sadly, his split with the county was a touch acrimonious, but I'm sure Courtney has been delighted to see the amazing success Gloucestershire have enjoyed in one-day cricket in recent years.

Walsh should enjoy putting his feet up after his retirement – he will have deserved it. And, whatever happens in the future, he was the first man to take 500 Test wickets. That achievement is written in history for ever.

Waqar Younis

For a decade, Waqar Younis was one of the most compelling sights in world cricket. The way he charged to the stumps as though running the final of the Olympic 100 metres before launching his high-velocity deliveries was always magnificent to behold. And, even though his pace and powers declined a touch in later years, he still had the lowest balls-per-wicket strike-rate of any bowler of the modern era.

Waqar patented a delivery all of his own – the fast, inswinging yorker. Released with a slightly round-arm action, he has dismissed dozens of batsmen either bowled or lbw with the ball that became his trademark. If it was tough for high-quality players to resist, it was virtually impossible for tail-enders to stop. To have a ball swerving in towards the toes at around 90 mph is very alarming, I can tell you. Many bowlers tried to copy Waqar, and it's a tribute to Darren Gough that he came closer than most to perfecting his own inswinging yorker.

'For a decade, Waqar Younis was one of the most compelling sights in world cricket. The way he charged to the stumps as though running the final of the Olympic 100 metres before launching his high-velocity deliveries was always magnificent to behold.'

When he burst on the scene in the late 1980s, Waqar was something of a phenomenon because he broke many of the traditional rules for fast bowlers. Most quickies down the years preferred the hard, new ball and used bouncers to soften up batsmen. By contrast, Waqar was at his most effective when the ball was old and scuffed, allowing him to impart reverse swing. Leaving aside exactly how that was achieved, and I have made my position on the subject clear elsewhere in this book, you still need to be able to make the most of exploiting it. At this, Waqar had no equal in world cricket – for my money, not even Wasim Akram. Waqar could also take wickets with conventional weaponry, of course, and, although he was not averse to a touch of the short stuff, his main danger came from bowling fast and straight to a full length. I used to love watching contests between Robin Smith and Waqar, which were great entertainment. The Judge, never one to shirk a challenge, used to take on Waqar and it led to some compulsive viewing.

'Vicky', as his Surrey team-mates called him, might not have retained the same extreme speed as when he was in his pomp, but he was still quick enough at the start of the twenty-first century, something Nasser Hussain's England team found to their cost when he ran through them in the second Test of the 2001 series at Old Trafford. What is more, he compensated for a slight dip in pace with experience and cunning.

Waqar and Wasim Akram – Pakistan's two W's – will always be linked together, even though they didn't often see eye-to-eye. Halfway though the England 2000 tour to Pakistan, several newspapers reported Waqar claiming that Wasim was trying to destroy his career. And, according to the people in the know over there, the new captain Waqar only agreed to include Wasim in the squad for the England tour in the 59th minute of the eleventh hour, when persuaded by the chairman of the Pakistan Cricket Board to bury the hatchet. Even though their relationship has been strained at times, however, they never allowed that to undermine their partnership. In fact, their rivalry probably brought out the best in them as bowlers.

Somebody did some research recently which revealed that Waqar and Wasim have averaged more than nine wickets per Test between them when they've played together. The animosity between Waqar and Wasim is typical of the Pakistan team. On paper, they should have been one of the great forces in world cricket for more than 20 years, but they always seem to be blighted by squabbling.

Over the years, the Pakistan dressing-room has often resembled a war zone, full of divisions, jealousies and power struggles. In fact, it's been like that for as long as I can remember, which is a great shame

BEEFY ON WAQAR

Born: 16 November 1971, Vehari
Country: Pakistan
Tests: 78
Wickets: 352
Average: 22.65
Beefy analysis: At his peak, one of the most awesome sights in world cricket. His speciality is the toe-crushing, in-swinging yorker, bowled at express pace, which had many an unsuspecting batsman doing a soft-shoe shuffle. Proved a capable captain during the tour to England in 2001.
Beefy moment: Battles between Robin Smith and Waqar were tremendous entertainment, with neither giving an inch.
Do mention: New Zealand v Pakistan series 1990–91 (his haul of 29 wickets in three Tests is a record by a Pakistan bowler).
Don't mention: His age; injuries.

because, with their mix of all the talents, devastating quicks, finger and wrist-spinners, and wonderfully-gifted stroke-playing batsmen, if they were ever able to sort out their internal rows for good, they could challenge for the title of best side in the world.

One reason for the 'ticking time tomb' atmosphere in Pakistan's dressing-room might be the amazing pressure the players are under. Nobody can fully appreciate the passion for cricket in Pakistan and India until they visit those countries. The players are treated like demi-gods, mobbed and fêted wherever they go, but also blamed when things turn pear-shaped. Can you imagine people in England burning effigies of Nasser Hussain in the street if England lost a Test match?

The popular perception that Waqar was plucked from total obscurity and thrust into the Test team is a bit of a myth. He had actually been playing first-class cricket for a couple of years before he sprinted on to the international stage. But his impact was still sensational. Even though Waqar was a teenager, it was obvious that a remarkable fast-bowler had emerged. Some of the world's best batsmen were staggered by his pace and movement, and he started taking wickets at an amazing rate. His early hero was Imran Khan, but Waqar was soon a big name in his own right.

Waqar signed for Surrey in 1990 (Sussex had rejected him), and cut a swathe through county batting line-ups. In 1991, he finished with 113 wickets at fourteen apiece. He was simply too good and too quick for most batsmen. The story goes that he broke five toes that summer with his inswinging yorker. In Test cricket, his strike-rate continued to rise and, by his 35th match, he'd completed 200 wickets. At that stage, he was taking a wicket approximately every six overs. But the strain of bowling so fast took its toll. He suffered severe back problems, and a stress fracture kept him out of the 1992 World Cup. But, because of his determination and rigorous fitness regime, he kept coming back. I've seen him training harder than any of the other Pakistan players, even when he's not in the side.

Glamorgan signed him in 1997 and it proved to be an inspired choice, because they won the County Championship that summer, with Waqar taking another sackful of wickets. He was appointed captain of Pakistan's tour of England in 2001, just months after it looked as though he was drifting out of the side for good. As I say, cricket in Pakistan is nothing if not unpredictable.

Waqar's age has been the cause of much debate over the years. When he captained Pakistan in England in 2001, most of the record books reckoned he was 31. Others had him as low as 29. But some followers of the Pakistan team thought Waqar was in his mid or even late thirties. I'm 35, by the way.

Shane Warne

S hane Warne's influence as a cricketer extends
way beyond his extraordinary number of wickets
for Australia. Shane is the man who, in the early
1990s, probably saved leg-spin bowling from
extinction. For years, international cricket had been
dominated by fast-bowling nuclear warheads. Spin
bowling – and particularly wrist-spin – seemed to be
something that would forever be associated with
sepia images from another age. About as likely to
reappear as the dodo.

But Warne changed all that. After his emergence, spin became – how can I put this? – sexy... it's now no longer something bowled by people who were too short, feeble, lazy or nice to bowl fast.

Warne is a brilliant craftsman, with a bag of tricks and a sharp cricketing brain. But, crucially for the marketing men who sought to lure the new generation of young Australian sports enthusiasts back to the oldest game, he was also a bleach-haired former beach bum, who smoked, drank, ate pizza, wore an earring and usually courted a fair amount of controversy.

Like a Pied Piper of leg-spin, Warne brought kids into the game who wanted to emulate him, from London to Lahore, Madras to Melbourne. And the impact on the world game soon became obvious. By the end of the twentieth century, most Test teams had at least one world-class spinner – whether it be Saqlain Mushtaq, Muttiah Muralitharan or Anil Kumble – and some had a couple. For that reason, Warne's impact on cricket will continue to be felt long after he's sent down his last flipper. No wonder he was voted one of the five Cricketers of the Century when *Wisden*, the 'bible' of the game, conducted a poll among 100 luminaries.

BEEFY ON WARNE

Born: 13 September 1969, Ferntree Gully, Victoria
Country: Australia
Tests: 98
Wickets: 430
Average: 26.72
Beefy analysis: The man who saved leg-spin bowling from extinction. Leg-spinner, googly, top-spinner, flipper – you name it and Warne has got it.
Beefy moment: Mike Gatting bamboozled by Warne's first delivery in Ashes conflict – England v Australia, Old Trafford, 1993.
Do mention: His record 356 victims in Test cricket, thanks to the English batsmen in the summer of 2001.
Don't mention: Weight, Indian bookmakers.

The moment when Warne announced himself to a worldwide audience came at Old Trafford in June 1993. People in England had heard all about him – he'd had a fair measure of success for Australia in the preceding months – and there was a genuine sense of anticipation as he prepared to send down his first delivery in Ashes conflict. Warne had not been particularly successful in the warm-up matches, but he claimed he was holding back his best stuff until the Test series.

What would he do? It wouldn't be easy for him, surely, because he was about to bowl to Mike Gatting, an outstanding player of spin. His first ball was bound to be a loosener, wasn't it? What happened has become one of the most frequently replayed TV clips of cricket action. Warne's opening delivery, the supposed loosener, swerved in the air and landed outside the line of leg stump. If it had continued on the same course, it would have missed the timbers by at least two feet. But the ball gripped, turned and lifted, and struck the top of off stump.

Gatting, the English master of spin, was totally bamboozled – and I'll never forget the look of sheer bewilderment on his face as he began his walk back to the pavilion. Phil Tufnell, watching the game intently on the dressing-room TV set, memorably described the event like this: 'The last time I saw that look on Gatt's face, someone had nicked his lunch.'

While that delivery became known as the 'Ball of the Century', and guaranteed Warne everlasting fame, there have been plenty more great moments; if not always Ball of the Century, then certainly Ball of the

'Shane Warne's influence as a cricketer extends way beyond his extraordinary number of wickets for Australia. Shane is the man who, in the early 1990s, probably saved leg-spin bowling from extinction.'

Week, Month or Year and it didn't take long for him to record his first Ashes hat-trick in the second Test in Melbourne the following year, when Phil DeFreitas, Darren Gough and Devon Malcolm became the victims of only the seventh 'three-in-a-row' in Ashes history, and the first for 90 years.

Warney realized very early on in his career that, if he concentrated on bowling tight, grinding down the opposition and then offering the occasional ball to tempt the most patient batsman he could be a more than useful Test performer. But he wasn't prepared to be merely more-than-useful. On top of the accuracy with which he builds suffocating pressure, he wanted to attack, attack and attack again, and he armed himself with the weapons to do just that.

He mastered all the conventional wrist-spinner's variations – leg-spinner, googly, top-spinner and flipper – without too much trouble. And then he really set to work. The first delivery he claimed to have invented was the 'zooter', and thereafter he always seemed to be working on some new 'super ball' which turns in some amazing fashion.

'Warne is a brilliant craftsman, with a mass of tricks and a sharp cricketing brain. He was also a bleach-haired former beach bum, who smoked, drank, ate pizza, wore an earring and usually courted a fair amount of controversy.'

He's not averse to a bit of kidology. In truth, though, every ball is a variation because he changes the amount of rip he applies to each one, as well as mixing up his pace. No wonder he captured wickets at such a tremendous rate, and passed Dennis Lillee's Australian record of 355 victims in Test cricket. He is no less effective in one-day cricket, either.

Wrist-spinning places great strain on the body – especially the shoulder – and Warne has endured his fair share of injuries and operations over the years. Speaking from a fair bit of personal experience, shoulder injuries are the worst. The shoulder is a flexible, moving joint which is fundamental to everything a bowler does. This means that Shane has to have constant massage and physiotherapy to keep the joint loose.

But, for me, Shane is by far the best leg-spinner who has ever lived, and I'm convinced he still has a lot to offer. In fact, my money is on him to become the second bowler after Courtney Walsh to take 500 Test wickets.

Shane has rarely been out of the headlines since his 1993 sensation at Old Trafford. He has always been a magnet for the newspapers, whatever the chosen subject of the moment – whether it was his weight, some alleged late-night escapade, his admission that he received money from an Indian bookmaker for what he called 'banal' information, smoking cigarettes, or sledging an opponent – as he did so successfully when getting Nasser Hussain out in a one-day international Down Under on the 1998–99 tour. England needed around 50 from 10 overs with six wickets left when Warney decided the only way Australia could win was to goad Nasser into losing his cool. When Nass hit him back over his head for four Warney stood and applauded the shot sarcastically. Then he started to remind Nasser of what might happen if he missed next time. 'This is where it's crucial not to get out,' he told him. 'Don't let your team down now.' Hey presto, Nass allowed himself to get sucked in, charged down the track only to be stumped by yards, and Australia ran out winners. Although the England man claimed he merely got out attempting a legitimate attacking shot, the Aussies were convinced that Warney had tricked him into losing his rag and his wicket.

Such intense media interest creates its own problems, as I discovered to my cost. And I was glad to be able to pass on some advice to him from time to time. When will people ever learn that players like Warne must be allowed to live their own lives like every other player? I know he's not proud of the events during his time in England as Hampshire's overseas player in 2000 that led to his losing the vice-captaincy of Australia, but he was honest enough to confront them and deal with them, and he and his family are now stronger as a result. Beneath it all, I think most people who have met Shane will agree he's actually a terrific bloke.

Shane and I have become good friends over the years, and we stay in touch 12 months a year. The big difference between us is that I occasionally ring him back!! And he's easy money on the golf course, too. As for cricket, although I never faced him in a competitive match, we've messed around a little with a bat and ball, and my experiences tell me that I would obviously have smashed him all around the park, given the chance.

Shane Warne remains one of the great characters of the game, a crowd pleaser who has done so much for Australian and world cricket alike.

Wasim Akram

Wherever Wasim Akram travelled throughout his magnificent career, controversy was never more than a couple of steps behind.

Whether it was claims of ball-tampering, allegations of match-fixing or barely-concealed rows between him and his swing partner Waqar Younis, someone, somewhere always had a bad word to say about Wasim.

In some ways, that is part of what you get for being a superstar in Pakistan, or anywhere else for that matter.

You are there to be shot at by people who, in terms of sporting achievement, are not fit to screw in your studs. And in Wasim's case I find all that unutterably sad because the images of him that will remain with me are of a fantastic cricketer with bat and ball and in the field; a true, free, instinctive all-rounder of world-class stature – in short everything a great player should be.

'Wherever Wasim Akram travelled throughout his magnificent career, controversy was never more than a couple of steps behind.'

I have to say I believe that Allan Lamb and I were right to alert the cricketing world to what we saw then as deliberate ball-tampering during the second one-day international between England and Pakistan at Lord's in 1992.

Ever since the late 1980s rumours of deliberate roughing up of the ball to achieve reverse-swing had surfaced from time to time, but for the most part no-one really took them too seriously. Such stories were easily absorbed into the library of cricketing tall tales and, in general, were regarded as such. That was why Imran Khan's admission that he had used a bottle-top to scratch one side of the ball in a county match as far back as 1983 came as such a shock because it suggested that such practices had been in common use for far longer than any of us imagined.

By the time England reached the 1992 World Cup Final against Pakistan at the Melbourne Cricket Ground, however, most international cricketers were aware that certain bowlers had mastered the arts. Although at the time we didn't fully understand the practices and techniques of achieving the phenomenon of reverse swing, nor that they had been handed down to Wasim and others by guys like Sarfraz Nawaz and Imran Khan, we did believe that what was happening was against the laws of the game.

And when Wasim removed Lamb and Chris Lewis in successive deliveries to end any realistic hopes we had of taking the prize, that was the moment a few of us within the England dressing room decided something had to be done about it. Throughout the summer series of '92 that followed the World Cup we were on the lookout for clues to support our case and the moment the umpires changed the ball during that fateful one-day international at Lord's was the moment our detective work finally bore fruit.

With the passing of the years, and as people's knowledge of reverse swing grew, my attitude has softened somewhat. In some ways I understand that Wasim and others may have thought what they were doing was accepted practice. In their eyes, giving the surface of the ball the odd scratch here and there to speed up the process of roughing up one side that creates reverse swing might have been just the way things were done to equalize the struggle in what has always been a batsman's game.

In favourable conditions Wasim's bowling with the old ball in certain circumstances was more or less unplayable. He could make the ball do almost anything he wanted. With his accuracy and control the slightest unforeseen or unforeseeable movement left you dangling on his hook. But even with the new ball he could also move the ball considerably off the pitch and at pace. And his bouncer was as hard to cope with as any that I faced, on a par with Malcolm Marshall. What made it so dangerous was that when he got it right he managed to disguise the delivery so well that you never saw it coming until it was too late to do anything about it. When he added the slower ball to his

BEEFY ON WASIM

Born: 3 June 1966, Lahore
Country: Pakistan
Tests: 104
Wickets: 414
Average: 23.62
Beefy analysis: One of the all-time great left-arm pace bowlers, lightning fast in his early years, then reverting to guile and control in his later career. A dangerous lower-order batsman who never quite fulfilled his potential.
Beefy moment: Caught behind off Wasim for nought, England v Pakistan, World Cup Final 1992. I was hacked off because the ball brushed my shirt. Wasim was delirious.
Do mention: Sri Lanka v Pakistan, Colombo, 2000 (becoming only the fourth bowler in history to take 400 wickets).
Don't mention: The Qayyum Report.

armoury he had everything he needed to keep the best batsman guessing all the time.

For a bloke who spent his teenage years dreaming of making a living from playing table-tennis, he wasn't too shabby with the bat in his hand either. And his achievements in all departments of the game are all the more impressive when you consider that he suffers from diabetes and has to inject himself every day.

'It is amazing to think, however, that Wasim might never have become a cricketer. He told me his early ambition was to make a living playing table tennis, and he used to practise for two or three hours each afternoon. He wanted to be a professional but, thankfully, he chose cricket bats and balls instead!'

As for allegations against Wasim of match-fixing, which he has always strenuously denied, all I can say is that the laws of natural justice must apply. Like everyone else Wasim has the right to be considered innocent until proven guilty.

All I know for certain is that Wasim was one of the toughest competitors I ever came across. As 'Waz' on the Test stage, or Wally Akroyd as they named him affectionately when they made him one of their own at Lancashire, my impressions of him at his peak are of an all-rounder without peer in the modern game – to my mind, probably the greatest since Sir Garfield Sobers, who was unquestionably the greatest of all-time.

That is how Wasim should be remembered by history. That is how I will remember him.

Steve Waugh

Steve Waugh is a cricketer who has squeezed every drop out of his ability. He is highly-skilled, sure he is, but the elder of the Waugh twins has made himself into an all-time great as much through determination and judgement as through God-given talent.

There have been few more flinty characters in the game's history than Steve Waugh. He's been a pivotal figure in Australia's success since the late 1980s. Waugh has exerted huge influence on the international stage – first as a dashing batsman and seam-bowling all-rounder, then as a prolific scorer in the middle-order, and, finally, as captain.

Indeed, after he succeeded Mark Taylor as skipper, Waugh helped to make Australia indisputably the best side in world cricket. He was the man in charge when they completed their record-breaking sequence of 16 consecutive Test victories, the captain of the good ship 'Invincible'.

Under Waugh, Australia have been an ultra-competitive and successful outfit. They are disciplined, confident, talented and aggressive. They have taken the ideals of attacking – and counter-attacking cricket to another level, and they've been fuelled in their endeavours by a great sense of pride for the baggy green cap; all in all, a team in Steve's image.

Steve has introduced certain things which highlight the Aussies' sense of patriotism. I understand it was his idea for the whole team to wear their baggy greens in the morning session on the first day that Australia are in the field. He also suggested presenting debutants with their new caps on the outfield before the start of the match and for each player to have his personalized number – identifying what number player he is to be selected for Australia – embroidered on his cap. These are all ideas that England have copied subsequently. Waugh also has a feel for history, too. When Australia played the Millennium Test, he came up with the idea of the players wearing caps dating back to the turn of the previous century. They were almost like skull caps, with short little peaks.

Interestingly, for a man so tough and ruthless on the field, he has also been responsible for encouraging his players to express the more artistic sides of their nature, particularly as poets, would you believe. Now there was a time when the nearest you would find poetry and Aussie cricketers colliding was along the lines of 'Ashes to ashes, dust to dust – if Thomson don't get ya, Lillee must,' or 'There was a young sheila from Stoke, etc'. Frankly, the thought of hairy-arm-pitted Foster's-swilling ockers like Merv Hughes, Allan Border, David Boon or even the legendary Terror Tomkins, grappling with iambic pentameter and the like is just too mind-boggling for words! But Steve introduced the tradition within the Aussie dressing-room and encourages his players to pen something appropriate to be read out aloud before the start of a day's play, in the manner of their famous 'bush' poets like Henry Lawson, and the players responded.

'I'm not only interested in watching my players grow as cricketers, but as people as well,' he explained. 'One thing you will find with this team is that when you give people opportunities and responsibility, you will get a lot of surprises. Whether on the field or off, players like challenges. The whole experience is about what the day is offering, and adding something to that. That's what this side is all about.'

Steve never claimed that his own work should be compared to Dylan Thomas or W. B. Yeats, for instance, but there is no mistaking that it comes straight from the ticker, like this offering he wrote and read out on the eve of Australia's World Cup Final victory over Pakistan at Lord's in 1999:

> 'Well, here we are, at the home of W. G. Grace.
> It has taken something special to arrive at this place
> So let's make a pact to fight as only we can
> To show the ANZAC spirit where it all began.
> It'll be a time we never forget
> And one where we can all say I have no regret.
> I can't wait to get the goosebumps
> From shoulder to hand
> As Punter sings
> 'Under the Southern Cross I Stand.'

On the field, the Australians are a different matter altogether. They play utterly without compromise, and Waugh leads by example. He is the sort of man who would be first out of the trenches, and that makes it hard for anyone else in the team not to jump out with him.

As for the controversy over sledging, there is no doubt that, under Steve, the Aussies became the best in the business. Their take on the issue is that putting a batsman under psychological pressure with a word or two passed between them, as in 'If he carries on like this, he's going to have a long hard summer,' or 'Do you think that bat is too small for him?', making an opponent think about something other than the bowling he is facing, this is a valid part of the battle. One thing is certain, though. Steve and his players never complained if it was done to them.

I think Steve's approach was borne of his early experiences in Test cricket, when Australia struggled so badly. Those memories stuck and, ever since, Waugh has vowed to himself never to be involved with such failure again.

When Steve first came on the scene, we were convinced he was suspect against bowling that was short or directed at his ribcage. So we peppered him regularly with bouncers in an attempt to unnerve him. Over the years, Waugh has disproved the theory in spectacular style. He sorted out his own game by assessing his strengths and weaknesses, learned to eliminate the hook shot almost completely, and instead chose to duck or play defensively. He removed risks from his batting, and scored runs with a few favourite shots – the square cut, the punch through the covers and working the legside.

In fact, Waugh almost reinvented himself – with staggering results. He hoisted his average from the high-30s to 50-plus, where it has remained for most of the latter part of his international career. Anybody who averages above 50 is an exceptional player. Waugh was rated the world's No. 1 Test batsman for several years, and has been

BEEFY ON WAUGH

Born: 2 June 1965, Canterbury, Sydney
Country: Australia
Tests: 145
Hundreds: 27
Average: 50.82
Beefy analysis: One of the all-time great batsmen, his unflinching competitiveness and brilliantly aggressive captaincy were the key factors behind the greatest Australian Test side ever.
Beefy moment: His century against England, The Oval, 2001, in which despite injury he set an indelible example to his team after their unexpected defeat at Headingley.
Do mention: Australia's record-breaking sequence of 16 consecutive Test wins.
Don't mention: Poms.

consistently in the top three. He has certainly been the best and most prolific No 5 or No 6 batsman in world cricket for around a decade, and it is doubtful whether there has ever been a better player at shepherding the tail. And as a captain in the field, he is more than a motivator. It must help when you have bowlers like Glenn McGrath and Shane Warne at your disposal, but he has the ability to make things happen when the game looks like drifting – which, to me, is the hallmark of any great skipper.

Waugh has also been an influential player in one-day cricket. When Australia won the World Cup in 1987 – a triumph which many have identified as the turning point in their fortunes – he scored 167 runs and took 11 wickets. His exploits in the Aussies' victory in 1999 included an incredible knock of 120 not out against South Africa at Headingley, which saved his team from certain defeat and elimination.

'An outstanding cricketer, a fearless, uncompromising captain, and an extremely impressive man.'

But the extraordinary thing about Steve is that he has never once looked anything but at the top of his game. Most players who have been around as long as he are bound to get the wobblies at one time or another. The pressure on you to perform in the middle is one thing, and the good players thrive on it. But the life of an international cricketer – with all the travelling, living in and out of suitcases, and missing your family for long periods on tour, can become a grind if you let it.

Steve never let it, not just because he adored the game with every atom of his being, but also because he made a point of looking beyond it. As he travelled the world, he looked beyond the confines of the dressing-room, the practice ground and the hotel, taking photographs and putting his thoughts down on paper in seven published tour diaries that make fascinating reading. And as if that was not enough to convince people of his status as cricket's renaissance man, he also went out of his way to give financial support to an orphanage in Calcutta.

An outstanding cricketer, a fearless, uncompromising captain, and an extremely impressive man.

Bob Willis

There should have been two awards for the 'Man of the Match' at Headingley in 1981: the other one should have gone to Bob Willis.

Of course, what Bob calls my 'slog' (and I'm not arguing, by the way) changed the course of the third Test of that amazing Ashes series. But until the time Bob began one of the most memorable bowling stints in the history of Test cricket, my 149 not out was still only a gesture of defiance. When he ended the best spell of sustained, aggressive fast-bowling I had ever seen, his eight for 43 meant we had won a match that couldn't be won. And the rest became the stuff of legend.

What Bob achieved was to transform a team heading for Ashes defeat into an unstoppable winning machine, to rekindle national interest in a sport that was struggling for its commercial life, and to remove a few question marks against the international future of a clutch of England cricketers, including Bob himself. Not bad for an afternoon's work.

Had it not been for an eleventh-hour reprieve, Bob would never have even been given the chance to turn the tide of history. Bob had been struggling with injury prior to the match, and had failed to convince Alec Bedser and his co-selectors that

'Bob was an outstanding bowler, who combined pace, skill and hostility with a big heart. What I admired most about him was the way he came back time and again from so many injuries.'

he was fit enough for selection. Indeed the invitation to Derbyshire's Mike Hendrick to replace him had already been sent out. When the selectors rang Bob to tell him the news, he convinced them to give him a final chance to prove his fitness by playing for Warwickshire 2nd XI. It worked, and the administrative staff at Derby managed to tear up the letter to Hendo just in time to avoid embarrassment.

The turning point of the match, the moment that altered my life and Bob's too, came with Australia comfortably placed at 56 for one, chasing their final innings target of 130. Reckoning that my performance with the bat meant that he should let me have my head, Mike Brearley had started with me running down the slope and Bob coming in from the football stand end. Nothing was really happening; then Bob made a heartfelt plea to the skipper that changed everything: 'I'm too old and too knackered to be running uphill into the wind. Give me the slope and I'll see what I can do.'

The effects were dramatic and instantaneous. Bob simply bowled like a man possessed. His face was so focused as to be almost glazed – he was experiencing total tunnel vision. Charging down that hill like Hagar The Horrible on benzedrine, he blew the Aussies away before they knew what had hit them. So intense had been the experience, that after he battered Ray Bright's stumps to bring the match to its incredible conclusion, he sprinted from the field before any of us could lay a hand on him. 'I just had to get off the field,' he told me later, 'because I couldn't stand the tension of being out there any longer.'

After he'd calmed down a bit and we were able to discuss the events in greater detail, he insisted that the match would have been over even more quickly if he'd been given choice of ends from the start. Come on, Bob. Where's your sense of drama?

Bob was an outstanding bowler, who combined pace, skill and hostility with a big heart. What I admired most about him was the way he came back time and again from so many injuries. I suffered serious injury myself, and therefore know all about the mental uncertainties as well as the physical reconditioning required to play at the highest level again. Bob had a series of knee operations – the long scars are still clearly visible

'For a man whose game was based on raw aggression, Bob's character has always been remarkably laid-back.'

– and once suffered a thrombosis on the operating table that almost proved fatal. He ended up playing 90 Test matches, which was a tribute to his determination as much as to the wonders of medicine and surgery.

When you watched him bowl, though, it was no wonder he had so many problems. With his long, gangling body, Bob's mad run-up earned him the nickname of 'Goose', and that could not have been more apt. And his explosive action was like a windmill set on the wrong speed. He was remarkably effective, though, and probably the best out-and-out fast-bowler at England's disposal for at least 25 years. His tally of 325 Test wickets proves that, and, for a time, he was England's all-time leading wicket-taker. With his height, mop of curly hair, open-chested action and liberal use of the bouncer, when he was in the 'zone' of total concentration, some batsmen found him quite terrifying.

He inflicted some nasty blows over the years. The Australian opener, Rick McCosker, came out to bat in the Centenary Test of 1977 with his head swathed in bandages after Bob had broken his jaw with a bouncer. More seriously still, Aussie Rick Darling almost died after being struck on the heart by Bob – his chewing gum became lodged in his throat, and he was struggling to breathe. No blame could be attached to Bob in either case, of course. Batsmen expect a bit of a battering when playing against top-quality fast bowlers.

'His dry, laconic sense of humour kept me amused throughout our careers on the field and subsequently in the commentary box.'

For a man whose game was based on raw aggression, Bob's character has always been remarkably laid-back. Indeed, sometimes you could be engaged in a conversation with him and suddenly realize he hadn't heard a word you'd said. After he took over the captaincy from Brearley, critics would sometimes point out that he appeared to let things drift on the field because he seemed to be in a world of his own.

Nevertheless, his dry, laconic sense of humour kept me amused throughout our careers on the field and subsequently in the commentary box. His famously low-key delivery style is not everyone's cup of tea, hence the song penned by the Barmy Army he loves to hear: 'Bob, Bob, Boring Bob, Boring Bobby Willis', but the content is invariably spot on. He's not afraid of airing a controversial opinion, no matter who might be upset.

There has always been a bit of the rebel in Bob, hence his obsession with the great American protest singer/songwriter Bob Dylan, so intense that many years ago, he changed his name to Robert George Dylan Willis.

I'm not sure that Dylan would have approved of Bob's other choice of hobby, as in recent years, he's become a keen golfer, although anybody who saw him wielding a bat might not be surprised to learn that he's hardly threatening a single-figure handicap. Sometimes, I'm amazed he ever makes contact with the ball! At least he normally remembers to bring his clubs – unlike that famous occasion when he walked halfway to the middle in the Test match before realizing he'd left his bat back in the dressing-room.

Andy
Withers

To millions of television viewers, minders are for the likes of Arthur Daley. But for eight years, Andy Withers was much more than just my bodyguard. He was, at various times, my personal assistant, chauffeur and confidant. Through good times and bad, Andy stayed solid as a rock, and he is one of the worthiest, and nicest, guys with whom I have ever had the privilege of working.

Since he opted for the quiet life, got married and settled in East Yorkshire, I haven't seen as much of him as I would like. But when I say Andy was a big part of my life, I mean BIG. He is a great, lovely, cuddly teddy-bear of a man – built like a prop forward, but a gentle giant by nature – and I owe him a lot for being my shadow through more scrapes than I would care to remember.

We got to know each other during my playing career with Somerset, when it soon became clear we had much in common. Like me, Andy loved his rugby and he's taken nearly as much pleasure from my son Liam's progress into the England squad as old man Botham himself. Down at Taunton, we hit it off immediately and when he joined the payroll, so to speak, nothing was too much trouble for him.

'He was, at various times, my personal assistant, chauffeur and confidant. Through good times and bad, Andy stayed solid as a rock.'

Andy enjoyed doing the good jobs, like driving me through the gates of a Test match venue to collect another England cap, and undertook the menial chores – like carting kit-bags across car parks, taking messages and generally restoring some order to my life – without a murmur of complaint. He was so loyal, and so attentive, that he became synonymous with me. Andy Withers was the unsung hero of our double act.

One of his first jobs as my 'minder' was to lift me off the floor of a car park after some lunatic had decided to spike my pint of beer. Andy had recently succeeded a great friend, Peter 'Jock' McCombe, who died suddenly from a heart attack, as a 'liaison officer' at Somerset – appointed to keep hangers-on at arm's length from me and Viv Richards. After hosting a day's shooting as part of my benefit season, the hunting party had retreated to a country pub for dinner, and I had only just started slaking my considerable thirst when everything went dizzy.

Before the last of my senses had been scrambled, I managed to grab Andy's arm and told him to get me out of there. All I can remember, before keeling over face-down outside, was this feeling of sheer terror, and I remember nothing of getting home that evening. What

I do know is that Andy stayed awake all night to make sure this comedian's prank didn't become a full-blown medical emergency, and amazingly I was well enough to appear as a guest on Terry Wogan's TV chat show the next day.

That was by no means the only occasion when I was grateful for Andy's alertness and quick thinking. Several times he's been a useful deterrent when the odd loudmouth in a pub – some of them, I'm convinced, egged on or even planted by the press – has tried to make a name for himself by having a pop at yours truly. And in 1989, just before the Old Trafford Ashes Test against Australia, I was grateful to have him around after receiving some threatening letters which Special Branch recommended me to take seriously. One morning they even gave Andy and me a briefing about the procedures for checking suspicious packages. It's a strange feeling when you climb into your car outside a Manchester hotel, and prepare to face Terry Alderman, Geoff Lawson and Merv Hughes, after your bodyguard has been advised to check under the chassis and screen the vehicle for explosive devices first.

Happily, my friendship with Andy has mainly been played out against a backdrop of happier times – and a barrel of laughs. Like me, he knows a nice drop of red wine when he tastes one and, after I'd moved to Worcestershire, there was one priceless episode involving half-a-dozen cases of the stuff. After 'discovering' some rather nice Burgundies, we ordered a few bottles of the best ones and, at breakfast one morning, our somewhat substantial mail order arrived.

Kath and the family had joined us for the weekend, and her face was a picture when the invoice arrived with the Burgundy ... for nearly £6,000. That's another occasion when I was grateful for the presence of a minder! What became of the Burgundy? I'm sure Andy helped me with the tasting – it's the least he deserved for his loyalty. He was as good as gold.

Ian Woosnam

Many people get the impression that a career in golf is the ultimate gravy train. Private jets, apartments in Monte Carlo, stately homes in Ireland – and that's just for the caddies. I've known Ian Woosnam from the days when he and fellow golfer, David Russell, travelled round the circuit in a camper van in which they used to sleep to save cash.

One morning, the thing collapsed. It just gave way. One wheel was here, another over there. And the engine expired in a puff of smoke. It may be the life of Riley for Woosie now, but he's worked damned hard to make it so. As far as anyone can who chooses to make a living out of the greatest of all individual sports, he came up the hard way.

Woosie is a real pocket battleship, only 5ft 4ins tall but as tough and determined as they come. He grew up on a farm and boxed at school. It helped him to develop a strong physique, which means he can drive the ball further than most players are able – as well as having the confidence not to worry about his small stature.

I've played golf with Woosie dozens, probably hundreds, of times, especially when we both lived in the Channel Islands. Woosie, myself and a couple of mates had a regular game together at the La Moy Club in Jersey. The normal arrangement was

'Woosie is a real pocket battleship, only 5ft 4ins tall but as tough and determined as they come.'

that the three of us would each put 50 quid in the hat and Woosie would match it. None of us received any shots, so it was the best gross score of the three of us against Woosie's.

One morning at La Moy, we were playing really well and thought we had a chance of beating him. We shot four under par between us. But Woosie went round in 61 without even breaking sweat. As Woosie had cleaned up, he agreed to buy lunch at a little restaurant called Zanzibar, where we often ate. Nice gesture, especially as the meal ended up costing £100 a head.

That's typical Woosie. Away from the great tournaments, he loves nothing better than to play a social round of golf with friends, with a little wager involved. He's a pint-and-fag type of golfer, which makes him one of the most popular men on the tour. But what a talent. I cannot think of many more naturally gifted players – and it's hard to believe that anyone hits middle and long irons more sweetly. His swing seems almost effortless. Woosie has won around 40 tournaments worldwide, although not so many recently, mainly because of his inconsistent putting. But the early days were pretty desperate.

Woosie turned pro in 1976 after enjoying some success as an amateur in regional competitions such as the Shropshire and

Herefordshire Amateur. But he needed three attempts to qualify for the tour and, even after earning his card, won only £6,000 in his first five years. It was a tough time for Woosie in his camper van. His perseverance paid off, however, and now all those dreams have come true.

Woosie's first big breakthrough came in 1982, with victory in the Swiss Open. Then, by finishing third in the 1986 Open, he proved his ability to compete with the best in the world. The following year, 1987, Woosie won eight tournaments and topped the European money list. In 1989, he was second in the US Open.

Then in 1991, the year he topped the world rankings, he triumphed in dramatic fashion at the US Masters. After a par 72 in the first round, Woosie shot 66 and 67 to set up a three-way battle for the title with Jose Maria Olazabal and Tom Watson. The American tailed off, but Ollie fought Woosie to the finish. On the final green, Woosie needed to sink a putt of around six feet to take the title. I'll always remember the picture of elation on his face as the ball rolled in and he received his green jacket from Nick Faldo, winner the previous year. Of course, Woosie has also been a vital member of Europe's Ryder Cup team for many years.

Woosie was also the man who led Darren Gough astray the night before England's victory over South Africa at Centurion in January 2000. The England cricketers were convinced the game would be abandoned, because there had not been any play for the previous three days, so Goughie felt a bit demob happy as he wandered into the bar at the team's hotel.

'What a talent. I cannot think of many more naturally gifted players – and it's hard to believe that anyone hits middle and long irons more sweetly. His swing seems almost effortless.'

Woosie and several others golfers, who were competing in the Johannesburg Open, happened to be there, and Woosie asked Goughie what sort of wine he would like. When the Yorkie told him, Woosie promptly ordered a bottle for him and that's how the evening progressed, until 3.30 am when Woosie decided the time had come to give England's opening bowler a putting lesson.

Suitably illuminated, Goughie staggered off to bed, sure he wouldn't be required to play cricket the next day. But that was the match when captains Hansie Cronje and Nasser Hussain each forfeited an innings to contrive a finish. First, Gough was forced to bowl ten overs off the reel – Hussain knew he'd been out late – but redeemed himself by hitting the winning runs as England swept to a thrilling two-wicket victory. It was only later, of course, that we discovered Cronje's motives for ensuring a result.

And Woosie? He went out next day, played one of the worst rounds of his life and missed the cut.

He needed his much-loved sense of humour that day, as he did in the 2001 Open at Royal Lytham & St Anne's when an error by his caddy left one too many clubs in his bag and resulted in penalty shots that cost him dear. When asked if he had any special method for making sure he had the correct number of clubs out on the course he replied, 'Yes. I start counting at one and stop when I get to fourteen.'